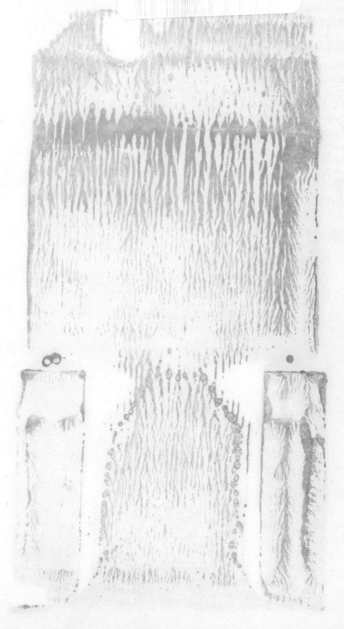

DRYDEN'S POETIC KINGDOMS

DRYDEN'S POETIC KINGDOMS

---

by

ALAN ROPER

NEW YORK

BARNES & NOBLE, INC.

Printed in Great Britain

TO MY MOTHER
AND IN MEMORY OF MY FATHER

Contents

PREFACE   *page* ix

PROLOGUE   1

ANALOGIES FOR POETRY   15

RHETORIC FOR POETRY   35

THE KINGDOM OF ENGLAND   50
   Heroic Stanzas   51
   Restoration Panegyrics   62
   Annus Mirabilis   74
   The Medal   87

THE KINGDOM OF ADAM   104
   To The Duchess of Ormonde   113
   To Driden of Chesterton   124

THE KINGDOM OF LETTERS   136
   To Dr. Charleton   141
   To Sir Robert Howard   148
   To Lady Castlemaine   158
   To Mr. Congreve   165

EPILOGUE   185

NOTES   199

INDEX   205

Preface

THIS study is based upon a doctoral dissertation submitted to
The Johns Hopkins University in 1961. Although it was of
course necessary to revise whatever was retained from it, I
have followed in most cases the main interpretative line of the
analyses included in the dissertation. This book therefore
reflects my debt to Professor Earl R. Wasserman of The Johns
Hopkins University, who directed my dissertation and from
whom I have learned most of what I value in my approach to
literature. In my attempt to bring theoretic coherence to the
separate explications I have benefited greatly from conversa-
tions and correspondence with Professor Earl R. Miner of the
University of California at Los Angeles and from the advice of
Dr. John Holloway of Queens' College, Cambridge, who read
and commented upon the second and third chapters and part
of the fourth. I have tried to record in the notes all specific
debts to previous commentators on Dryden, but I have no
doubt taken unintentionally from them many things I have
thought my own. In partial atonement for such lapses and in
acknowledgment of my large general debt to those who have
studied Dryden before, I can only repeat Dryden's remark in a
different context: *facile est inventis addere*. The reading of *The
Medal* in the fourth chapter first appeared in a slightly different
form in *ELH*, and I am grateful to the editors for permission to
re-use this material. I am grateful also to the President and
Fellows of Queens' College, Cambridge, for a research fellow-
ship that has enabled me to complete the study more quickly
than would otherwise have been possible.

In quoting from Dryden's poems I have throughout used the
text of James Kinsley's four-volume edition in the O.E.T.
series, although I have reversed the italics when quoting prose

ix

from this edition. Most quotations from the prose follow the text of George Watson's two-volume Everyman edition, *Of Dramatic Poesy and other Critical Essays*, supplemented where necessary by Scott and Saintsbury's edition of the works. When quoting from early editions I have altered u and v to conform with modern practice.

A. R.

Prologue

FEW things in literary history are less accountable than the way in which some works come down to later generations more or less freed from the social and intellectual contexts in which they were originally produced and to which they originally referred, while others survive to their posterity equipped with some at least of their contemporary reference. Largely by the efforts of Dryden's editors, the key to the characters of *Absalom and Achitophel* is part of the general experience of the poem, whereas— despite the efforts of editors and scholarly commentators—the religious and constitutional history of the sixteenth century and the foreign policy of George and Anne are to a much smaller extent part of the general experience of the first and fifth books of the *Faerie Queene* and of Gulliver's voyage to Lilliput.

A circumstance that is properly seen as an historical accident has frequently prompted some dubious critical corollaries. The first is that *Absalom and Achitophel* is a work so fixed in a specific historical context that it is unable to transcend its own topicality, and must consequently be valued below works that do. The second is that the way to read the poem is to make a series of mental substitutions rather like correction slips in a book: for Absalom read Monmouth throughout, for Achitophel read Shaftesbury, for David, Charles II. The third corollary has a more ambiguous status, for it consists in an assumption that *Absalom and Achitophel* occupies a special position in the Dryden canon, because it appears to employ a poetic mode markedly different from that of other works, with the exception of the obviously topical fables in the third part of *The Hind and the Panther*. The biblical fable of the poem is accepted as a slightly indirect method of reflecting upon topical events: we know this

I

to be the case because we have evidence (ultimately the 1716 key to the characters) that its first audience read the poem in these terms. Because there is no such evidence for most of the other poems, it seems that they do not possess such continuous reference, however much they make isolated topical allusions.

Each of these corollaries contributes to misrepresentations of Dryden's practical poetic. Since the experience of Dryden often begins with an isolated reading of *Absalom and Achitophel*, which is followed after an interval by a wider sampling, the misunderstanding that can result from the earlier experience is of special significance. Attempts to correct this misunderstanding have taken the form of scholarly articles, editorial annotations, and specific observations in more general works. Until recently, there has been no systematic attempt to bring together these detailed corrections and elaborate them into a general discussion of Dryden's poetic, illustrated by the analysis of particular works. Professor Hoffman's discussion in *John Dryden's Imagery* constitutes, although not explicitly, such an attempt, and no subsequent reading of Dryden can safely ignore his account.

The particular approach adopted by a critic to the works before him inevitably implies, if not a theory of literature in general, at least a theory appropriate to those works. It further implies a theory about the nature of criticism: the kind of work it can and should do. An exposition of both theories, the literary and the critical, can at least serve to articulate the fallacies and dangerous assumptions incident to the approach. Whatever form it takes, practical criticism entails an unavoidable distortion of the literary work, because it is an attempt to find conceptual equivalents for matters and relationships which are not at all or not entirely conceptual. Most obviously, by making the implicit explicit, criticism unduly simplifies or unduly complicates the verbal composition it analyses.

The common danger of exhausting a reader's patience and his interest in the literary work is most assiduously courted in explicatory analysis, an approach which will be adopted throughout the greater part of this study. Because explication commonly proposes as its end the unfolding of as much of a work's meaning, suggestion, and referential allusiveness as a critic can accomplish, it is especially vulnerable to a charge of

ingenious overreading on the one hand and a charge of re-
iterating the obvious on the other.

Explication characteristically attempts a demonstration of
the principles of coherence in a work, and in non-narrative
works these principles are most likely to obtain in the development of a subject in the unifying implications contained in (or,
rather, between) the repetition with differences of key terms
and images. The explicator must both postulate coherence in a
general statement of subject and demonstrate coherence
through an analysis of its detailed manifestations. If he fails to
provide adequate demonstration, he has failed to provide the
grounds for his generalization, the specific application of which
is likely to be by no means apparent. If he provides a demonstration, it is difficult to avoid implying that his represents the
only correct reading of the work, whereas it is more properly
seen as but one of several available applications of his general
statement. Whether or not this last suggestion is present, the
exhaustive explication is unavoidably jealous of insights. It does
not require a reader to experience the work in the light of its
analysis and discover for himself suggestions and implications
that it ignored or overlooked. Instead it requires him to understand the analysis and thereby to experience the work. The
value of a general statement of subject is that it affords a
mnemonic epitome of the detailed discussion which a reader
can then apply or reapply to the work for himself.

The dilemma is pointed when explication becomes historical,
as it usually does when applied to preromantic works. The attitudes, ideas, conventions, allusions and images which together
comprise a literary work have reference both to exterior intellectual and social contexts and to a system of relationships
within the work itself. In varying degrees for different readers
and in different works there is a tension between the centrifugal
pull toward the exterior contexts and the centripetal pull
exerted by the interior relationships. Most readers are, indeed,
more conscious in preromantic works of the centrifugal pull.
Because the exterior contexts were widely known to the original
readers, the work's reference to them could be elliptic or allusive, and a modern reader, aware that reference is being made
to something with which he is not immediately familiar, is in-

evitably more conscious of the reference because he cannot take it for granted. When, for various reasons, the exterior contexts were not widely known, or when, to be more accurate, the matter of poetry no longer consistently referred to those contexts which were widely known, the exterior had to be more fully internalized for a work to contain within itself the terms by which it was to be read. *Lamia* and the *Ode to Psyche* do not refer to Burton and Apuleius in the way that *Absalom and Architophel* refers to Milton.

The critical problem with an earlier work is, then, a question of to what extent it is appropriate or justified to supply the original contexts. It is very easy to lose *Absalom and Achitophel* as poem in the labyrinthine passages of the Exclusion crisis and Tory propaganda. On the other hand, it is not possible to separate the 'poetic qualities' of *Absalom and Achitopel*—its wit, its internal relationships and use of couplets—from its referential qualities. In an obvious way the internal relationships are often assisted, perhaps even fully effected by an existing exterior relationship between, for example, commonplace images for political activities.

The danger of thoughtlessly supplying an historically excavated exterior context is that it is likely to blur the criteria for a value judgment on the work that is served in this way. Whether or not an explicator decides to proceed himself to a final evaluative assessment, it may be confidently urged that he has a responsibility to present as clearly as he can the grounds for such an assessment. The explicator can demonstrate the presence or absence of coherence, but coherence obtains in a work when it makes some sort of selection among its manifold referential possibilities. To fabricate a modern example, no one would suggest that an invitation to eat a mushroom omelette should set the recipient's mind running on atom bombs (it can only do so at the level of free association). If it were observed, however, that the audience's growing discontent with the speaker's argument suddenly mushroomed into a cloud of open disapproval which threatened to destroy the order of the meeting, then it is apparent that the metaphoric association with nuclear explosions is established by fully applying to the subject of discontent a comparison (destructive mushroom clouds) popularly consecrated to the subject of nuclear explosions. The

4

barely possible referential association of the first example has been rendered probable in the second because the terms in which it is conveyed direct the attention toward the required interpretation.

The investigation of contexts can easily take the form of supplying possibilities, of glossing mushroom omelettes with Hiroshima. If it remains at this level; if, that is, it fails to show to what extent the work chooses among possibilities and converts them into probabilities, the contextual investigation can endow the work with a spurious referential richness which it may have done nothing to deserve. It may be argued, with obvious justice, that the results of such an investigation often have independent value as a contribution to the history of ideas; but conceived critically, in their application to the work nominally under consideration, they represent a scholarly version of Jungian theories. Such a version inevitably tends to value the work on the basis of its associational possibilities for a reader who has patiently investigated, say, treatises of mythological and biblical exegesis, or, more pertinently, the political and religious tracts contemporary with the work. The work is hailed as richly and perhaps learnedly allusive; it may well be, but it is the explicator's responsibility to demonstrate that the allusiveness is demanded by the work itself rather than by his understandable reluctance to sacrifice the fruits of his own research. It is necessary to demonstrate probability, not possibility. It is necessary to demonstrate, indeed, that *Absalom and Achitophel* will make reference to the people and events of the Exclusion crisis without the artificial assistance of the key to the characters.

It might seem, then, that the solution lies in an explication which argues out the evidence for a reading in terms of the work itself and concludes by presenting the historical context as a species of proof which bears out the conclusions of the explication proper but which is not essential to it. Such a solution has the apparent merit of distinguishing between those works which depend entirely upon the associations of an existing context for their allusive richness and those works which more or less successfully and however allusively re-create the context within themselves. It is a distinction which ought surely to assist a final evaluation. Unfortunately, it is not always a meaningful distinction. The destructively mushrooming disapproval of the audience certainly suggests nuclear explosions to someone familiar with the prior association, but it would be difficult, to say the least, for someone unfamiliar with the association to intuit nuclear explosions from the observation. If the nuclear reference were fully internalized for the benefit of this second person, the observation would almost certainly have to be expanded into a simile, and—even at this level—such an expansion would surely constitute a less imaginative use of language, a less witty use in the seventeenth-century sense.

We unavoidably have recourse to external aid whenever we read an earlier work, if only to determine the original meaning of a word—whether we use a dictionary or can supply the information from our existing knowledge. What we are looking up or supplying is the historical reference of a word, and it is arbitrary to permit this activity but deny its logical extension in supplying the historical reference of an idea formed by a group of words. Moreover, our often unconscious application of existing knowledge to the reading of an early work is likely to place too great an evaluative emphasis upon the merely accidental survival into our own age of some allusions rather than others. We can readily respond to an analogy between the human and political bodies, because the analogy is still part of our common figurative awareness (even though it now lies farther from the surface of awareness than it did in earlier centuries). On the other hand, an analogy between the economy of Eden and the economy of a kingdom is no longer part of that shared figurative consciousness, and, lacking a knowledge of the historical context, we can only appreciate the significant operation of the analogy in an early work when it is fully internalized by means of an expanded simile. Even then we are likely to be chiefly conscious of the tenuousness of the association. If we prefer a work employing the analogy of bodies to one employing the analogy of Eden, we are really evaluating by the dubious criterion of the author's relative skill in prophesying which figures and allusions will survive more or less unimpaired into the etiolated figurative awareness of the twentieth century.

The presentation of a large historical context without a detailed analysis of the way the work selectively refers to that context represents an investigation of possibilities. A detailed discussion of a work's reference without the presentation of historical contexts represents a similar investigation of possibilities. Referential probability obtains in an interchange between an existing exterior context and the specific terms of the work. The extent to which we can first intuit the possible reference and then confirm it by the application of historical data will vary from work to work. It may be postulated that many of Dryden's poems which possess a non-political subject (the grounds of literary excellence, for example) establish within themselves a general political relevance (the grounds of princely excellence, for example) by qualifying that subject with a politically charged comparison. The probability of a specific political reference (to the restoration of Charles II or the deposition of James II) can usually be established only by the application of the topical context. It may be further postulated that the establishment of political relevance in superficially non-political works is of crucial evaluative significance, since it presents at least some of the evidence for a properly witty use of language to effect a parallelism between dissimilar matters. In much the same way, a poem which is explicitly political may achieve additional range and suggestiveness by means of comparisons which refer to further political or non-political matters of general or topical import. There can be, in fact, no fixed rule. Once it is decided to analyse a work in terms of its probable reference, the only continuously valid criterion is the operation of critical tact in determining the merits of each case.

In the late poem addressed to Driden of Chesterton the poet's cousin is congratulated for having inherited an estate that descended to him from his mother's family, while, as a second son, he could not inherit the paternal estate: 'The First-begotten had his Father's Share; / But you, like *Jacob*, are *Rebecca*'s Heir.' As soon as we attempt to invoke the biblical context to which these lines superficially refer, we realize its irrelevance. Jacob, the second son, was his mother's favourite, but he inherited nothing from Rebecca (in fact, of course, he inherited the paternal estate by a trick). Genesis has supplied the poet with a hint which he adapts in a way that leaves the nominal source far behind. On the other hand, *The Medal* makes obvious external and topical reference to the issuing of a medal by Shaftesbury's supporters to commemorate his release from the

Tower. The external context is modified and reinterpreted within the poem, but it remains of referential relevance in a way that the allusion to Jacob does not. It is between these extremes of nominal and significant reference that Dryden's poems characteristically operate: the explicator's task is to determine the tendency of each occurrence toward one or other of the extremes.

One of the most tempting and most dangerous of aids is the context established for any given work by the author's other works. In an obvious way a writer is relevant to himself. Images, allusions, themes, and attitudes recur more or less clearly to suggest the validity of elucidating an obscure image or allusion by reference to its more readily comprehensible occurrence in another work by the same author. The danger of elucidating in this way is that it may either blur or falsify the criteria for evaluation. It will blur the criteria by hurrying over the fact that the second context does not properly establish the value for itself; it will falsify by distracting the attention of a reader, aware of the 'failure,' away from the different value that it does establish. The way an author uses images and themes in one work contributes to their contextual possibilities in a second work, which may or may not establish their probability by a choice of phrasing. Their value for the second work is similar to that afforded by a more general historical context, and if their possible relevance is greater there is all the more reason to adduce their evidence with caution.

In the lines to his cousin Dryden described William III's defeat of Louis XIV by allusion to Alexander the Great's victory over Darius:

> When once the *Persian* King was put to Flight,
> The weary *Macedons* refus'd to fight:
> Themselves their own Mortality confess'd;
> And left the Son of *Jove*, to quarrel for the rest.

The context of these lines establishes the probability—indeed the certainty—of topical reference, and it is tempting to transfer their values to *Alexander's Feast*, written two years earlier and closer to the time of William's victory over Louis. Transfer is especially attractive when Timotheus sings of '*Darius* Great and

Good . . . Fallen from his high Estate.' But in these terms the fate of Darius at the hands of Alexander could even more pertinently recall the fate of James II. Since *Alexander's Feast* presents a king recently victorious in battle, its possible reference to the battles and triumphs of the reigning king of England is obvious. For probability to obtain some modification of the historical data is essential, but the ode pointedly avoids modification when it proceeds to lament the death of Darius in battle, for which there was no topical equivalent. In the lines to Driden the allusion ceases with the flight of Darius, and thus permits full topical application.

It would be disingenuous to pretend that a critical study of one author can (or should even try to) avoid all the consequences of the intentional fallacy. The unity of such a study depends largely upon the fact that the different works it considers are referable to one man, a reference which unavoidably introduces the problematic relationship between author and work. A critic may properly concern himself with the technical development of a writer, his increasing ability in versification, the handling of imagery, or the shaping of a poem. Less defensible is a concern with a writer's intellectual development, the changes in his religious or philosophic views as they are expressed in his works. For one thing, these views will be modified to suit the demands of particular subjects; the praise of a king and the praise of a minister will require different constitutional emphases which, when juxtaposed, might suggest their author's political inconsistency. The fact of Dryden's conversion has obvious relevance to the religious position adopted in *The Hind and the Panther*, but the (presumably) Anglican position which helped to prompt *Religio Laici* has relevance only to the later conversion and not to *The Hind and the Panther*. A critic may reasonably adduce biographical information to confirm his interpretation of an intellectual position adopted in a poem, but, except occasionally and in general terms, that biographical information should not be derived from the position adopted in earlier poems. A critic may argue from man to work (although with great caution), but the only defensible argument from work to man is usually too general to be of value. All we can learn about the political position of the man Dryden from his poems is that he was a royalist and apparently a believer in the divine right of the Stuart succession. The detailed implications of his royalism are all referable to the subjects and occasions of his poems. A man is more complicated than the things he writes; at the very least, he is complicated in a different way.

For critical purposes, then, an admittedly artificial hypothesis may be adopted. The works constitute a body of material evidence which the critic can survey. Similarities in the use of image, vocabulary, theme or rhetorical device provide the grounds for generalizations about the nature of their practical poetic. These generalizations can then be applied to works not included in the preliminary survey, with a view to determining their practical relevance. Their relevance is all the more likely because there is a connection, however extracritical, between an author and his works. The relevance is not absolute, for each work will modify the generalization in some way by the operation of its own internal relationships. In fact, the critical study of a single author manifestly entails a heightened version of the empirical dilemma over the precise point at which inductive survey may properly yield a deductive generalization. An awareness of the dilemma does not invalidate generalization; it is, rather, a check against unduly dogmatic assertion.

Generalizations about the nature of interior relationships are, on the whole, more valid and critically more valuable than generalizations about similar exterior references. Despite this, the possible, I have suggested, can be shown as probable only when both exterior and interior references are considered. A further advantage of this double consideration derives from the fact that exterior reference is principally (but not entirely) effected by the parts of the work as parts, while interior reference is effected by the parts as contributions to the whole. When we consistently remember that the parts have significance in themselves as well as in their relationship with other parts, we will be critically conscious of the successive quality of literature, of our experience of the work in time. This consciousness may be used to call in question the theory that some or all works of literature possess spatial rather than temporal existence, that like paintings they present themselves all at once to a reader's scrutiny. The analogy is obviously inexact. Because we move from part to part, from detail to detail, we experience a work of literature first temporally and successively, and attempt a total or spatial view only at the end of the initial reading. A painting is usually experienced first totally and then, in a special sense, temporally, as the eye follows line, mass, and colour. The 'temporal' experience of a painting will confirm or (more usually) modify the spatial experience. In literature the spatial experience confirms or modifies the initial temporal experience. For the painting analogy to hold it is necessary to ignore the first reading, and, as it were, to intuit the spatial experience, which is then confirmed or modified by what is, strictly, a second reading. This critical sleight-of-hand is all the more deceptive because a satisfactory analysis of a work is commonly the result of not one or two but many readings.

The point is best illustrated by recalling that a work of literature characteristically functions through the development of subject, attitude, tone, or situation. To the extent that it contributes towards this development, each of the parts (if the work is fully integrated) potentially contains the final values of the developing subject, while some parts will more or less fully realize that potential. If the work and our response to it are functioning properly, the development will appear inevitable but not necessarily predictable: each part will effect a number of possible references to exterior contexts the nature and extent of which will be successively modified until the total interaction of the parts converts possibility into probability and requires that the work be read in terms of some contexts rather than others. In the light of such total awareness a second reading will be more alert to the kind of potential possessed by each part and will (usually) notice confirmatory details whose import was not apparent at the first reading.

To take a simple (and therefore weighted) example, Arnold's *Dover Beach* may be described as a poem which generates its own symbol. The sea of its opening line has a fixed reference (supplied by the title) to the English Channel, but it also has possible reference to those seas of love, death, or life established by literary convention. As the speaker meditates upon the significance of the sea, implicit use is made of the last possibility (and perhaps the first), but they are not permitted to become explicit because it is a different possibility, the sea of faith, which is to be finally preferred. On a second reading, the English

Channel of the first line is in no sense invested with the values of the sea of faith, although the possibilities of the opening description will now be seen in terms of their potential relevance to the description of the symbolic sea. The twin coasts and the secluded bay viewed through a window suggest security and protection, a protection which is to be undermined when the sound of the waves breaks in upon the silent contemplation of the sea. On a first reading, such a suggestion of security is a possibility equivalent to the possibly significant confrontation of England and France across the Channel. An awareness of the way the poem develops the suggestions of illusory security and discharges them in the symbolic sea of faith produces in the second reading a concentration upon the relevant possibility undistracted by the sea of death or a confrontation of England and France. Omitting the wide canvassing of possibilities, a critic may properly analyse the work before him in terms of this 'second' reading.

The prior existence of the values to be established in earlier works produces a slightly rather than a radically different effect. It means that the potential references are more clearly definable and, to a point, more predictable than in Romantic works. Products of the public mode reflect, after all, a common experience, while products of the private mode present an individual experience. The disjunction is more apparent than significant, however. When the public mode is unsuccessfully used, it will merely reflect the common experience and values; when used successfully, it will reinterpret or re-create those values and thus afford a significantly individual emphasis. When the private mode is used unsuccessfully, it will fail to objectify and thus fail to communicate the individual experience; when used successfully, it will establish a meaningful reference to common experience, however individual it remains.

The task of successfully re-creating and reinterpreting public assumptions can only be achieved through a developing subject, attitude, or situation, and the prior existence of the values will both hinder and assist this development. A work like *Absalom and Achitophel* can and obviously does draw upon connections already established in the social and intellectual context. For this reason, if the context is known or supplied, each of the parts can more fully realize in itself its potential relevance for the final values of the poem than can the comparable parts in a work like *Dover Beach*. But, because the possible references of each part are much more precise (even, indeed, more probable) than those of *Dover Beach*, the task of selecting those references which will support an internal relevance is much greater, and the fact that *Alexander's Feast* might refer to William, James, and Louis can hinder a comprehension of the actual principles of coherence in the ode.

The title of *Absalom and Achitophel* makes fixed reference to the Bible and possible reference to conventional seventeenth-century typology: Achitophel the false politician and Absalom the deluded prince. The first six lines of the poem establish a potential for topical import through an emphatically historical viewpoint marked by the accumulation of temporal prepositions and conjunctions. The force of 'in pious times, ere . . . before . . . when . . . ere . . . when' is to imply the relevance of *after*, *now*, and *later*. It is the intention of the poem to realize the potential of the general and topical reference. David has possible reference to Charles II at his first introduction because both were kings and because David had served as type for Charles since the days of his exile. The realization of the potential can only be effected through the development and accumulation of suggestion. It is not true that David stands for Charles in line 7 of the poem; he can only do so in the mind of a reader who confuses the deductive evidence of the key to the characters with the possibilities of seventeenth-century political typology.

The consequences of this confusion account in part for the uneasy status of *Absalom and Achitophel* in literary history. It is accorded respectful admiration for its pungent characters and the forceful rhetoric of its couplets. It is a short epic with a broken-backed and inconclusive narrative. It is journalistic in its topicality and 'original' only in its versification; a piece of *ad hoc* propaganda ludicrously prejudiced in its account of Shaftesbury and his supporters. We have notes on the referential identity of minor figures and on the psalm which would have remained unwritten if David had been moved to poetic praise of Achitophel. We have the suggested source for David's concluding speech, some annotation against Milton's epics, and considerable information about seventeenth-century views on melancholy and enthusiasm. We have, in fact, a mixture of accurate analysis, referential possibilities, and critical improbabilities. Perhaps the most convincing testimony to the poem's stature is the multiplicity and variety of the approaches it has prompted and will doubtless continue to prompt.

One thing which may emerge from past treatments is that *Absalom and Achitophel* is not a poem which benefits from exhaustive analysis. So much of its art lies close to the surface that a critic's function is most usefully discharged by pointing to its operation as a poem in which statement, image, and attitude are simultaneously developed. Because *Absalom and Achitophel* reflects a practical poetic observable in different forms in its author's other works, a fuller analysis of some of those works may serve as critical context for a brief account of *Absalom and Achitophel* that endeavours to increase rather than distract from a reader's enjoyment of Dryden's most considerable poem.

Analogies for Poetry

Drilled as we are in poetic ambiguity and ambivalence, we are usually ready to applaud a writer's ability to synthesize the two halves of a comparison. I. A. Richards's distinction between tenor and vehicle, between the object, quality, or situation to be described by comparison with something else and the something else with which it is compared, has prompted critics to enquire into the way in which poetry frequently seems to break down the distinction.

In the figures used to illustrate normal discourse the vehicle or means of comparison remains subordinate to the tenor, the object or end of comparison. The simile, 'her hair's as black as coal,' is accepted as a slightly more vivid superlative than 'her hair is very black.' The point to be conveyed is the degree of blackness possessed by her hair, rather than a degree of blackness shared by coal and her hair. For this reason we are not arrested by the introduction of coal, which simply serves a local purpose in describing or defining the blackness of her hair.

If the simile is extended into 'her hair's as black as coal dug from the darkest mine,' the relationship between tenor and vehicle is altered. The extension of the vehicle intensifies the impression of blackness, but it does not do so by mere accumulation of detail, as it would if a totally different object were used as a second simile: 'her hair's as black as coal or a raven's wing.' Logically, the darkness of the mine makes no difference to the blackness of the coal dug from it. The second part of the vehicle does not intensify the suggestions of the first and thereby intensify its suggestions for the tenor. What happens is initially similar to the effect of the double comparison with coal and a raven's wing. The blackness of the coal and the darkness of the mine separately describe the colour of her hair, but because there is a prior relationship between coal and mine as product and source and because their separate qualities of blackness and darkness are combined in the woman's hair, there is a fusion of relationships and the darkness of the mine seems to be, in defiance of logic, the source of the coal's blackness. Separately, then, coal and mine are vehicles for her hair; together, her hair serves as vehicle to their tenor. As a result, the nominal tenor and vehicle are syntactically interchangeable and are therefore of equal significance.

We have, properly speaking, a creative use of language in the sense that, instead of using words simply for referential communication, the example also exploits the syntactic possibilities of word combinations both for their own sake and in order to intensify the reference value. Verse has greater opportunities for this kind of exploitation than has prose because, apart from anything else, the demands of metre and (where appropriate) of rhyme make acceptable an elliptic syntax with its contingent juxtapositions, combinations, and creative ambiguities. In predominantly assertive or descriptive writing, whether verse or prose, such creative uses of language will be local, and the overall success will be determined by how clearly and accurately the referential meaning is conveyed. In poems the language will often be predominantly creative in this sense, and the local creative uses will, commonly, be connected with each other, either creatively or discursively, to form a creative whole in which the values of the nominal vehicles will be of equal significance with the nominal tenor or tenors.

Because Dryden's poems are characteristic of the public mode, their effect derives from the way in which they reaffirm or re-create the shared assumptions of the age. Reaffirmation can be simply argued or stated, as it is in *Religio Laici*, the second part of *The Hind and the Panther*, or a prose essay like the Postscript to *The History of the League*. Re-creation fully exploits the potential similarity of apparent dissimilars by placing the particular value to be affirmed either in the tenor or the vehicle of a comparison. The poem, that is, may talk about the nature of the constitution and illustrate it by reference to a building, or it may talk about a building and illustrate it by reference to the constitution. If it is true that a creative use of comparison effects an interchange of syntactic roles between the two halves, so that tenor illustrates vehicle in addition to vehicle illustrating tenor, then it follows that in the poetry of the public mode a creative comparison will confer the status of public value upon the superficially non-public element, whether it be found in the tenor or the vehicle: the building as well as the constitution will be of public significance. The building will not simply illustrate some aspect of the constitution, it will be interchangeable with the constitution; metaphorically it will be the constitution.

In his richly illustrated study of *Absalom and Achitophel* Professor Schilling draws attention to the architectural metaphor in lines 801–8:

> If ancient Fabricks nod, and threat to fall,
> To Patch the Flaws, and Buttress up the Wall,
> Thus far 'tis Duty; but here fix the Mark:
> For all beyond it is to touch our Ark.
> To change Foundations, cast the Frame anew,
> Is work for Rebels who base Ends pursue:
> At once Divine and Humane Laws controul;
> And mend the Parts by ruine of the Whole.

Professor Schilling points out that 'the control of change, even when necessary, is here carried by the figure of an ancient fabric, strengthened by the religious note of sacrilege from the Old Testament ark.'[1] But Dryden's image operates more wittily and creatively than Professor Schilling indicates. Superficial amendment of the constitution is likened to minor repair of a long-established building; radical alteration of the constitution is likened to a desecration of the ark. So stated, there appear to be two distinct vehicles illustrating two aspects of a single tenor. The ark, of course, contained the God-given covenant of the Jews, their law; to lay hands on the ark accordingly represents an attempt to control divine and human laws. Indeed, the man who touched the ark died for his sacrilege, just as an attempt to overthrow the constitution is an act of high treason punishable by death. Moreover, the final resting place of the ark was within the temple. The effect of the ark reference is, then, to convert the anonymous building of the preceding couplet into the temple and consequently to realize the full spatial potential of *beyond*. Amendment should cease with repair of the temple's outer walls; to penetrate beyond the walls to the Holy of Holies is sacrilegious rebellion and high treason. The superficially distinct vehicles are thus two aspects of the same vehicle corresponding to the two aspects of the tenor.

One convention supplies the figure of constitution as building; history supplies the conventional identity of ark and law (and hence, by extension, of the constitution); history further supplies the topographical relationship of ark and temple (itself a building). Separately, the three pairs are highly conventional; it is in their creative combination that the poetic originality resides. Once again the tenor has illustrated the vehicle as well as the vehicle the tenor, for the particular and implicit temple achieves constitutional status by attraction from the tenor in its conventional relationship with the generic and explicit building. By this means the conventional building image has been made appropriate to the episode of Jewish history which affords the poem's fable, and the relationship of part to whole is thereby emphasized.

What the ark contains is the fundamental law of the land: the constitutional relationship of king and people and the disposition of sovereignty. The walls of the temple represent the incidental manifestations of the fundamental law (the precise method of collecting taxes or electing representatives, for example). Just as the ark is within the temple, so the constitutional relationship informs the detailed workings of the law, much as the soul informs the body. In the late address to the Duchess of Ormonde, Dryden in fact used the temple and ark to convey the relationship of body and soul (ll. 122–26). For this reason, the act of moving beyond the outer walls to the Holy of Holies is equivalent to a total reconstruction of the temple. The different physical reactions to the temple illustrate the same political action. Logically, the desecration of the ark and the reconstruction of the temple are not equivalent, but by uniting them in the nominal tenor they are given a metaphoric truth similar to that of black coal and dark mines.

Dryden in this passage uses metaphor as analogy: the equivalence of tenor and vehicle is confirmed by arguing that point for point correspondence between two objects or qualities which is the special property of analogy. Professor Wimsatt has suggested that analogy is found in a comparison between objects of the same species, metaphor in a comparison between objects of different species:[2] Charles II is analogous to King David and metaphorically a lion. It is true that the equivalence of the two halves and the logical working out of correspondence will most readily obtain in the circumstances described by Professor Wimsatt. But Dryden's characteristic poetic is most successful when his comparisons achieve the status of analogy as I have described it. Whatever their superficial differences, in Dryden's works the same poetic effect is achieved by likening Charles to David or a lion and by likening the English constitution to the Roman or a building. The function of the biblical fable in *Absalom and Achitophel* is similar to the function of the beast fable in *The Hind and the Panther*: both the kingdom of Jews and the kingdom of beasts will serve to illustrate the kingdom of England.

One way of defining specifically creative analogy is to find it in comparisons where an established or agreed likeness between two objects is shown to be of greater extent and significance than was initially realized. The prior agreement will then derive from the fact that the objects are of the same species or from the fact that objects of different species are already linked in the common figurative awareness of the age, as were constitutions with buildings and as are nuclear explosions with mushrooms. The long inventory of commonplace analogies drawn up by Professor Schilling thus has value in making available to twentieth-century readers the source material of much of Dryden's poetry. It simplifies the task of appreciating the poetry by permitting a concentration upon the way in which the commonplaces are extended and re-created rather than merely reflected.

To achieve a working out of correspondence that maintains the equivalent public significance of the two halves of a comparison, Dryden often modifies the referential terms of the tenor or the vehicle (as is the case with the Jacob allusion in the lines to his cousin). When this equivalence is not maintained, when the vehicle merely illustrates a proposition or description instead of conveying and enlarging upon it, Dryden's poetry is usually unsuccessful. It is in these terms that the general failure (if partial success) of *Annus Mirabilis* should be considered.

All critics of Dryden have drawn attention to his skill in verse argument. Like many good arguers, Dryden operates most effectively when working from and exploring the implications of an agreed basic premise, whether logical or figurative. He is less successful in establishing a new basic premise and then arguing from that. He is less successful, in fact, when handling images which lack the force of established analogy.

Both Dryden and Donne were skilled in verse argument; both drew much of their material from conventional, if different sources. At his best Donne modifies his material into a new first premise from which to work out his argument. At his best Dryden restates an existing first premise from which to work out the analogous correspondences. In seventeenth-century terms, Dryden's invention, his finding of ideas and images, is usually less exciting than Donne's because it is, in twentieth-century terms, less inventive. Donne is a master of the private, Dryden of the public mode. With Donne we are aware of a new individual experience suggesting general relevance; with Dryden we respond to an original reworking or re-creation of matters of established general relevance. When, in some of his early poems, Dryden attempts a Donnean new first premise, the result is often unconvincing because he fails to establish as equivalent the two halves of his comparison. Because he apparently lacked the individual perception of similarity between dissimilars, Dryden's so-called metaphysical mode in the early work usually produces a subordination of vehicle to tenor in which a reader is chiefly conscious of an unsuccessful and over-ingenious attempt to unite the disparate. Donne's individual perception has general relevance to other individuals as individuals; Dryden's public perception has general relevance to other individuals as members of the public.

This distinction may be briefly illustrated. When in *The Sun Rising* Donne celebrates the relationship between himself and his mistress by proclaiming that 'She'is all States, and all Princes, I,/ Nothing else is,' his assertion has, despite the source of the metaphor, no political reverberations. The neoplatonic idealism of *The Sun Rising* permits the poet to subsume all external values into the wholly private relationship with his mistress. In this ironic aubade the man and woman have responsibilities only to each other, and none to the inhabitants of the expanding landscape outside the window: the city prentices, the court huntsmen riding on the outskirts of the metropolis, the labourers deep in the country, the East and West Indies. The view from this room, which the lovers do not in any case take, expands only to contract again. The poem's situation, the coherent attitude it expresses, has significance for the individual solely as individual. But when David begets Absalom with 'diviner Lust' and 'a greater Gust,' the private pleasure he experiences is overshadowed by the public consequences of his careless promiscuity: the threat to the royal succession from the bastard prince. Similarly, Achitophel's demonstration of virility results in a son 'Got, while his Soul did hudled Notions try;/ And born a shapeless Lump, like Anarchy.' Achitophel's fatherhood is but one more evidence of his dangerous public character: the anarchically shapeless body of his son is symbolic of the consequence of Achitophel's plots against the body politic of Israel. Even in their more intimate moments, then, the characters in Dryden's poem are seen in terms of their public status, and the poem's attitudes accordingly have significance for individuals as members of the public.

A similar emphasis in Dryden's heroic plays may account for their general failure to achieve tragic status. Tragedy draws its strength from the dichotomy between the significance of an action for an individual and its significance for the public. Successful tragedy is a synthesis of the private and public modes in which each is of approximately equivalent weight. Dryden, who could present the public case with such clarity and energy, could not convey, except occasionally in plays like *All for Love* and *Don Sebastian*, the contrary force of the individual lot.

The clearest indication of the heroic plays' failure as tragedies is provided by a discussion of the analogy they most consistently employ. Although it is customary to find Dryden's plays deficient in the kind of metaphoric unity achieved by the best Jacobean drama, it is more accurate to seek their metaphoric 'failure' in a repetitious application of the same analogy to their enduring concern with the conflict between love and honour. Professor Winterbottom has convincingly argued that the love-honour conflict is consistently presented in terms of the opposition between a Hobbist voluntarism and a more orthodox rationalism.[3] The Hobbist position is that man is controlled by his passions and wills himself to attain the object of his desires, which is for him synonymous with the good. In this system the reason has the comparatively minor task of aiding the passions to select which objects they most wish to attain. Opposed to this selfish ethic is the (ultimately Greek) position that it is the function of the reason to control the passions, which have an unruly tendency to desire things that are far from good in a scale of rational values. Although many characters in Dryden's plays are caught in the Hobbist snare, there are foils to them who exhibit a control of passion by a reason which has formulated a viable and honourable ethic. The persistent analogical expression of this persistent ethical conflict is that love is a tyrant passion usurping or attempting to usurp the right rule of reason, which is in turn trying to maintain its public and political obligations. There is, in fact, a constant warfare between love's empire and the king's.

The ramifications of this warfare involve multiple variations upon the question of obligation as it affects friend, lover, son, and subject. Finally, the rationalists are triumphantly vindicated and the voluntarists either converted or defeated. An individual is permitted just so much right as an individual as is compatible with his role in a public system. It would not matter that it is in some sense ethically wrong to submit to the tyrant passion rather than the sovereign reason—in these terms Phèdre is obviously culpable. The tragic failure results from an inability or unwillingness to present such a submission as inescapable. The whole emphasis of the plays (except for *All for Love* and *Don Sebastian*) is on a conviction that a passion-driven lover, tyrant, or rebel is avoidably wrong; they are selfish and if they suffer it is their own fault, for unselfishness is readily attainable.

The failure in tragic consciousness is, then, most clearly evidenced by the frequency with which the analogy between love's empire and the king's is used. Not only is the moral and political issue simplified by such a charged opposition as that between tyrannous passion and sovereign reason, but the very use of the political terminology removes love from the sphere of the private and individual to that of wholly public significance. Instead of maintaining an equivalence between the demands of love on the individual as individual and the individual as member of the public, the analogy effects an entirely public equivalence between the demands of love and the demands of the state. Love's empire and the king's, in fact, operate in Dryden's heroic plays as a completely successful example of analogy as I have described it: the non-public element in a comparison is accorded public status by attraction from the other half of the comparison. The trouble is that analogy of this kind is inappropriate to tragedy, and the characteristic matter of the heroic play renders it, as the Restoration realized, a variety of tragedy.[4]

The empire of love is but one of the conventional human analogies in which man or some aspect of man serves as microcosm for the state. The most common of the human analogies is, of course, that underlying the idea of a body politic, a public corporation. Professor Schilling has recorded many of the variations upon this analogy, with its paraphernalia of health and sickness, disease, plague, good doctors and false mountebanks, royal, parliamentary and satiric physicians. The ingenius fertility of the analogy is apparent in such exhortations as that to 'apply fresh leeches to the posteriours of the kingdom,'[5] while its hackneyed overuse is evidenced by the breakdown in correspondence implicit in solemn debates between Whig and Tory over the comparative ability of the state to renew its royal head or its popular body without loss of political strength. So thorough was the journalistic investigation of the analogy's resources for comparison that the poets of the public mode had little scope for further exploitation, and Dryden only achieved a compellingly original turn a year before his death in the lines to his cousin and, rather less effectively, in the address to the Duchess of Ormonde. Such was its popularity and adaptability that it is perhaps not surprising that Dryden's announcement of himself as a poet of the public mode comes in his first published work with the aid of this analogy.

The unfortunate elegy on the death of Hastings (1649) has frequently attracted the good-humoured attention of Dryden's admirers as an example of the decadent metaphysical style

C

against which he early rebelled. It is certainly true that in later poems Dryden rarely produced such lines of thick, clogged, stumbling diction as are found abundantly in his first work, but its other great fault of over-ingenious images often in bad taste is something which occurs even in the work of the 1680's. Hastings's smallpox blisters, 'which th'row's flesh did sprout / Like Rose-buds, stuck i' th' Lily-skin about,' are in no worse taste than the remarkably unfunny couplet which blemishes the rollicking description of Og: 'A Monstrous mass of foul corrupted matter, / As all the Devils had spew'd to make the batter.' Apart from sounding this warning, the Hastings elegy is chiefly interesting for its attempt to give public status to an essentially private event and then draw out the implications of that status.

The first sixty-two lines of the poem function in one sense as an answer to the question of line 7: 'Is *Death* (Sin's wages) Grace's now?' The grace for which Hastings has died consists in the beauty, learning and virtue for which he is praised in the opening lines and which are compendiously restated in lines 31–2. The first forty-six lines progress through a series of amplifications (frequently of tenuous relevance) whose point is to convert the human grace of beauty and learning into a divinely appointed grace until Hastings's 'whole Frame render'd was Celestial' (l. 38). It is this divine grace which is to be awarded the death normally earned by sin, as Dryden moves into the notorious description of the young man's smallpox by recalling the question of line 7:

> Replenish'd then with such rare Gifts as these,
> Where was room left for such a Foul Disease?
> The Nations sin hath drawn that Veil, which shrouds
> Our Day-spring in so sad benighting Clouds.
> Heaven would no longer trust its Pledge; but thus
> Recall'd it; rapt its *Ganymede* from us.
> Was there no milder way but the Small Pox,
> The very Filth'ness of *Pandora*'s Box?
> So many Spots, like *nœves*, our *Venus* soil?
> One Jewel set off with so many a Foil?
> Blisters with pride swell'd; which th'row's flesh did sprout
> Like Rose-buds, stuck i' th' Lily-skin about.
> Each little Pimple had a Tear in it,

To wail the fault its rising did commit:
Who, Rebel-like, with their own Lord at strife,
Thus made an Insurrection 'gainst his Life.

(ll. 47–62)

No attempt at historical imagination can ever render acceptable Dryden's description of the pustules, but it is worth recalling the evidence collected by Professor Wallerstein and the
editors of the Clark Dryden.[6] Not only did the elegiac genre
entail an elaboration of the cause of death, but the smallpox
was itself a fascinating subject to poets, who vied with each
other in the figurative beautification of the disease's unattractive symptoms. The elegy frequently contained a lament for the
state of the world, and the Clark editors have noted the connection between Hastings's death and Charles I's execution established by the reference to the nation's sin, although they feel
that Dryden did not elaborate the connection beyond an
implicit disapproval of rebellion in the last couplet.

What we have in this passage is an early example of Dryden's
characteristic use of public analogy to effect an equivalence between the two halves of a comparison. The nominal tenor is the
fact and cause of Hastings's death; its vehicle is the fact and
cause of Charles I's execution. The nation's sinful rebellion has
divorced England from the sun-like divine approval because the
execution of Charles was a sacrilegious murder of God's deputy.
The funereal clouds that shroud and veil the sun are a reminder
that the wages of sin is death—for someone—while the metaphoric death of the sun brings into play the conventional analogy between king and sun with rebellion as a dark night in
which the sun's beneficent influence is lost. It was an analogy
which proved popular at the restoration, when the process was
reversed and the night of rebellion retreated before the sunshine
of Charles II's return. Because the tenor of the second couplet
is the death of Charles I, the recalling of heaven's pledge in the
next couplet is equally appropriate to the fate of the king and
the fate of Hastings, and the equivalence is rendered complete
by asserting the metaphoric origin of smallpox in Pandora's
box, the actual contents of which were sins. If disease is a metaphoric sin, it is also true that sin is a metaphoric disease by way
of a reversal in the last two couplets of the analogy between the
human and political bodies. Rebellion is a disease of the body

politic; disease, therefore, is a rebellion against the human body. The question of line 7 is answered: Hastings's divinely infused grace of beauty and learning must inevitably be rewarded with the death normally earned by sin because he could not escape the sinful disease of smallpox in a country where the divinely infused grace of heaven's royal deputy had been desecrated by the diseased sin of rebellion a bare six months before. The final equivalence of the two deaths is asserted by the penitential weeping of Hastings's tumescent blisters, an action figuratively true of smallpox and literally true of the nation's proper response to rebellion and execution. The vehicle of Charles I's death confirms the public significance of Hastings's death, while the tenor illustrates the vehicle by establishing that rebellion is both a disease and an action which can only be expiated by a flow of penitential tears. Charles II was later assured in *Astraea Redux* that 'tears of joy for your returning spilt, / Work out and expiate our former guilt' (ll. 274–75).

Dryden was later to improve upon the kind of creative analogy he achieved in his first poem, in part by taking more attractive subjects than smallpox for political elaboration and in part by holding more closely to the terms of his developing analogy. There is perhaps no clearer sign of the poet's immaturity in the Hastings elegy than the way in which he delays the resolution of his analogy for the sake of an anagrammatic pun on *Venus* and *næves* (with the Latin singular, *nævus*) and the infelicitous 'beautification' of smallpox in terms of lily flesh and sprouting rosebuds. In a sense, however, such improvements were incidental; their nature and the means to their achievement were obvious enough and certainly involved less difficulty than the improvement of rhetoric and versification. The essential fact of a creative use of language through public analogy was something to which Dryden always returned. Thus early in his career and in perhaps the most frequently abused lines that he ever wrote Dryden hit upon the poetic mode which so largely contributes to his special eminence.

It is clear that the human analogy of the smallpox passage is accorded divine extension by the recalling of heaven's pledge, and it is tempting to seek further divine reference in the tumescent rebellion of the blisters against the life of Hastings. Such a reference would be to Satan's revolt against God or its classical counterpart in the revolt of the Giants against the Olympians; both served as frequent analogies for mortal insurrections. In fact, the separation of heaven's pledge from the rebellious blisters by the Venereal and floral conceits militates against the elaboration of the divine reference, although, like Satan, the blisters swell with pride. The half-realized possibility may serve as a reminder that in other poems Dryden often made use of permutations upon the divine analogy. The most interesting, if not necessarily the fullest exploitation of the analogy occurs in *The Medal*, and a discussion of its ramifications may properly be given in a reading of that poem.

The possibility is a further reminder that in the public mode of Dryden a creative and witty use of analogy often consists in effecting a correspondence between analogies drawn from different sources and applied to the same object or tenor. Thus, *The Medal* not only illustrates affairs in England by reference to affairs in heaven, it also draws upon the rich stock of natural analogies in the shape of beast and monster images or allusions to the climate theory of government, while at one point the poem makes use of aesthetic analogy when rebellious disorder in the state is conveyed by the disorderly freedom of verse: 'Nor Faith nor Reason make thee at a stay, / Thou leapst o'r all eternal truths, in thy *Pindarique* way!' Characteristically, the second line both asserts the Pindaric's destruction of neo-classical restraint and illustrates it by allowing the line to spill over into a fourteener. Aesthetic analogy, of course, draws upon music, painting, poetry and architecture, each with its appropriate forms and abuses to correspond with law and disorder in the state.

I have no wish to duplicate the work of Professor Schilling in a general account of the various neo-classical analogies: human, divine, natural and aesthetic, with such subspecies as medical, scientific, astrological, geographic, or mythological. I believe, in any case, that the analogies are most properly discussed in their individual poetic contexts, for it is only there that we can determine whether the commonplaces are merely reflected or wittily re-created and extended. An exception may be made, however, in the case of the important group of analogies drawn from history.

The place and significance of historical allusion in seventeenth-century poetry is a subject of sufficient magnitude to justify a separate study, and in noting some points of relevance to Dryden's work my account will inevitably simplify the general context. Concern with a poet's relative originality suggests that the first point to be emphasized is the greater freedom of invention permitted him by the nature of historical allusion than by other available analogies. In history we have to deal with analogy as defined by Professor Wimsatt; and because the agreed initial likeness here consists in comparison between objects of the same species, variations upon historical analogy are as wide as a poet's reading and the demands of his poem will allow. History will furnish whole galleries of representative tyrants and just rulers, while nature supplies comparatively few political types from the kingdom of beasts, and these types derive most of their force from an existing conventional usage of just those examples.

It is true that certain characters and episodes from history were more frequently applied than others to similar situations in the seventeenth century. Largely because of the success of Dryden's poem, the popularity of Achitophel's intrigue is perhaps the best known example. But there were many historical precedents of equivalent popularity, and a random selection might include David's exile, Caesar's defeat of Pompey, the Catholic League of sixteenth-century France, and the succession of Edward III. The existing popularity of such allusions as illustrations of the same contemporary event frequently adds local or general complexity to Dryden's poems by calling upon the established topical application, although it must be reiterated that such pre-existent values should be applied with caution to specific poems. One reason for the possible reference of *Alexander's Feast* to William III's defeat of James II is that opponents and supporters of the revolutionary settlement occasionally sought historical authority for their arguments in, among other places, the conscientious obligations of Darius's Jewish subjects when he had been defeated by Alexander. The prior association of William and James with Alexander and Darius thus increases the topical potential of Dryden's ode, a potential which it does not realize.

Such a selection of popular precedents as that offered in the

28

previous paragraph is an indication that history indifferently concerned itself with events from the Creation through the four empires of Assyria, Persia, Greece, and Rome. Historical allusion covered references to Noah's ark, Scipio's defeat of Hannibal, and the events of the Great Rebellion. Ralegh's *History of the World* was ambitious less for its intended scope than for the detail in which he proposed to treat each empire. A similar project was entertained by William Howell, historiographer-royal during the Restoration, in his *Institution of General History*, while one of the most popular works of the period was John Sleidan's handbook on the four empires. In such a context the most frequently cited portions of the Bible were Genesis, in which the first institution of government could be observed, and the historical books of the Old Testament with the supplementary material of Josephus, for in them were observable the constitutional implications of the practical working of government.

The quantity of historical allusion in his poems would itself testify to Dryden's interest, and in his *Character of Polybius* he endorsed the high status of history in humanistic studies during the Renaissance and seventeenth century.[7] Dryden succeeded Howell as historiographer-royal in 1670, and although the duties of this office during the Restoration were as ambiguous as those of the laureateship to which he was appointed in 1668, it seems clear that it involved among other things the use of historical knowledge for royal propaganda.[8] Dryden's most considerable production as historiographer was the translation of Maimbourg's *History of the League* (1684), the chief point of which is apparently contained in the long Postscript drawing out the implications of the League for the recent Exclusion crisis and the Whig proposal for a Protestant Association to keep the royal succession from the Roman Catholic James Duke of York. Two years earlier Dryden had collaborated with Lee on *The Duke of Guise*, a dramatic version of the League with similar topical implications.

The view of history supporting these multiple allusions is the theory that history affords abundant examples of God's providential plan for the world. As Ralegh expressed it: 'the judgements of GOD are for ever unchangeable; neither is he wearied by the long process of time, and won to give his blessing in one age, to that which he hath cursed in another. Wherefore those that are wise . . . will bee able to discerne the bitter fruites of irreligious policie, as well among those examples that are found in ages removed farre from the present, as in those of latter times.' More succinctly, 'the examples of divine providence, every where found . . . have perswaded me to fetch my beginning from the beginning of all things; to wit, Creation.'[9]

Because history chiefly meant a record of such public events as the rise and fall of princes and governments, battles, treaties, and rebellions, the precedents it afforded were more often political than ethical. There is consequently a frequent and striking resemblance between treatises of government and works of history. Ralegh is for ever interrupting his chronicle to point the precept implied by some past event, while many tracts of political theory conduct their case by hopping from one historical precedent to another. The most influential work of Jean Bodin was the *République*, a vast compendium of royalist theory, but he had earlier written a Latin treatise with the engaging title of a *Method for the Easy Comprehension of History*. Predictably, the *Methodus* deduces the grounds of government from an historical survey, while the *République* is, apart from its sheer bulk, chiefly remarkable for the facility with which it supplies precedents for even the most trivial of constitutional principles.

There were, in fact, three main versions of the inevitable connection between history and governmental theory: the chronicle with digressive pointing of political precept; the political treatise with historical illustrations; the chronicle with a topical application in preface or postscript. In the first, governmental theory is a major justification for the writing of history; in the second, historical precedent affords authority for governmental theory; in the third, history and theory are mutually dependent for their value. Political poetry most often adapted the second version, although *The Duke of Guise* is more appropriate to the third and *Absalom and Achitophel* (like Dryden's projected epic on the subject of Arthur or the Black Prince[10]) is most properly seen as an adaptation of the first with elements of the third.

A characteristic example of this connection is a tract of 1661 entitled *Semper Iidem: or, a Parallel betwixt the Ancient and Modern Fanatics*, in which the age's favourite historical game is played with the aid of a conventional double column matching old and new fanatics. History is used as a species of proof: you take from the past a known fanatic, tyrant, or traitor, and, by pointing out the resemblances between his actions and those of a contemporary, 'prove' the contemporary's fanaticism, tyranny, or treason. The cogency of the argument consists in the detail with which the parallel is worked out; and *parallel* in this context is virtually synonymous with *analogy* as I have described it.

'Our Play's a Parallel,' is the confident opening of the Prologue to the *Duke of Guise*:

> The Holy League
> Begot our Cov'nant: Guisards got the Whigg:
> Whate'er our hot-brain'd Sheriffs did advance,
> Was, like our Fashions, first produc'd in *France*.

Just as an observed similarity in their grounds for insurrection inspired royalists to remark an apparently indissoluble union between old (Jesuit) priest and new (republican) presbyter, so the 1680's witnessed a similarly untiring insistence on the connection between old Guisard and new Whig, between old Catholic League and new Protestant Association. In the year that saw the production of *The Duke of Guise*, John Northleigh made use of the equally popular analogy between the Association and the Solemn League and Covenant of Civil War days in his conventionally named treatise, *The Parallel, or the New Specious Association an Old Rebellious Covenant*. When, in 1685, Northleigh followed up this work with *The Triumph of our Monarchy over the Plots and Principles of our Rebels and Republicans*, Dryden began his commendatory verses on the two pieces with the following lines:

> So *Joseph* yet a youth, expounded well
> The bodeing Dream, and did th'event foretell,
> Judg'd by the past, and drew the Parallel.
> Thus early *Solomon* the Truth explor'd,
> The Right awarded, and the Babe restor'd.

Characteristically, the implicit parallel Dryden himself fashions between the judgment of Solomon and the restoration of Charles II is only possible in the elliptic brevity of verse. Simply by using the charged word *restored* the lines permit a witty reference which is, as Sidney would say, not explicitly affirmed and therefore no lie. A conscientious historian in prose would be hard put to argue the validity of Dryden's implication, and with such resources at his disposal a poet obviously possesses greater opportunities for the witty invention (in both the old and the current senses) of historical parallels and analogies.

Equally of note is the proposition contained in the opening triplet. If, as Ralegh believed, like actions in different ages are judged alike by God, then an accurate identification of a present with a past act provides the basis for predicting the outcome of the present along the lines of the observed outcome of the past. Thus, Ralegh borrowed the Augustinian division of providence into memory of the past, knowledge of the present, and care for the future. Thus, too, Dryden's brother-in-law, Sir Robert Howard, remarked in the 1690 preface to his history of Edward II and Richard II that, having 'perceiv'd how exactly they [Charles II and James II] follow'd the steps of these two unfortunate Kings . . . I then expected to see a Revolution resembling theirs.'[11] This application of history is similar to the rhetorical figure of paradigm, Puttenham's 'resemblance by example,' through which 'we compare the past with the present, gathering probabilitie of like successe to come in things wee have presently in hand.' Interestingly, Puttenham found paradigm to consist also in 'examples of bruite beastes, aptly corresponding in qualitie or event' to some man or human activity.[12] As I mentioned, there is a similar rhetorical equivalence between Dryden's comparing Charles with a lion and with David.

Dryden's poems abound with prophecies, usually explicit, and they have no air of the visionary because they are customarily supported by a prudent consideration of the lessons of history. *Astraea Redux* ends, as its title warns, with a *pax Romana* vision of England's future greatness based upon Charles II's analogous relationship with Augustus. The contemporaneous address to Sir Robert Howard predicts the success of his volume of poems because the star of Charles II's restored fortune is fixed in its horoscope. The astrological image is converted into astronomy at the end of the panegyric on Clarendon eighteen months later with the Chancellor in orbit about a solar Charles, thus permitting the poet to prophesy, rather incautiously as it turned out, that Clarendon's career would be as enduringly successful as his royal master's. *Annus Mirabilis* borrows the apocalyptic golden age of Revelation to predict the future prosperity of a London purged by the fire of 1666. *Absalom and Achitophel* repeats the closing vision of *Astraea Redux*, while the peroration of *The Medal* commences with an assurance that 'Without a Vision Poets can fore-show / What all but Fools, by common Sense may know.' The fables of the swallows and the pigeons in the third part of *The Hind and the Panther* represent rival predictions of the outcome of James II's religious policy and the popular reaction to it.

The useful relevance of prophecy to the poetic praise of great men had been demonstrated for all time by Virgil's fourth Eclogue and the Messianic books of the Old Testament, but for the public poet of the Restoration, with his rational distrust of inspiration, the lessons of history permitted a significant modification of the tradition of the poet as vates and allowed him to predict without incurring the odium of a visionary.

Since most of Dryden's original poems were exercises in praise (or its rhetorical converse of vituperation), historical analogy functions in them most obviously as a source of rhetorical amplification, by which a man is compared with others of known worth (or infamy) and proved equal or superior to them. His poems sometimes appear to comprise little more than a series of eulogistic or denigrative parallels, meriting a loud Johnsonian snort about servile flattery. At his best, however, Dryden effects internal relevance between many of the analogies he employs, and the consistently argued historical parallel gives his work both general and local complexity. Most strikingly, *Absalom and Achitophel* turns the process inside out and ensures the consistency of the vehicle by making it, in effect, the practical tenor. In general, amplification of the king's exploits is achieved by analogy with the exploits of past kings, whereas amplification of the exploits of the less great (poets, politicians, or scholars) draws indifferently upon the example of past and present rulers.

Again and again, Dryden's complimentary addresses to his friends and fellow poets are couched in terms that shape the recipient's achievement into the image of England's current constitutional activity and situation. Sir Robert Howard's restoration of poetry to its rightful dominion over 'Morall

33

Knowledge' is analogous to the restoration of Charles to his rightful dominion over England. The witty exploitation of an analogy between affairs in the kingdom of letters and the kingdom of England does not simply afford the poem complexity and integrity. The establishment of equivalence between the two halves of the comparison both magnifies (or amplifies) the public significance of poetry and demonstrates the interconnection of all activities in the land. The stability of the monarchy assures the security of the individual, the flourishing of the arts, and the prosperity of the nation (conversely, the flourishing of the arts argues the stability of the monarchy). No matter how well such artifacts as buildings and engines may serve to illustrate the constitution, the analogy which finally underlies all other analogies is the commonplace association of the human and political bodies. Philosophically the age expressed itself in mechanistic terms, and these terms supplied it with many an incidental image, but its view of the matter which most exercised its poets, the place and obligations of man in the state, was characteristically and conventionally conveyed in terms of an organic analogy.

Rhetoric for Poetry

The first happiness of the poet's imagination is properly invention, or finding of the thought; the second is fancy, or the
variation, d[e]riving, or moulding of that thought, as the
judgment represents it proper to the subject; the third is elocution, or the art of clothing and adorning that thought, so found
and varied, in apt, significant, and sounding words.[1]

IT is the third happiness of imagination as defined by Dryden
which raises the most challenging problem for the practical
critic. Invention discovers and fancy adapts the images and
ideas by which the subject is to be conveyed. At this level, the
necessary move from a writer's view of his work to a reader's
view is both easy and instructive. There is obvious scope for
demonstrating how a particular combination of words effects
its reference to the 'invented' external source and to the system
of internal correspondences created by fancy. Elocution, however, contains an implicit invitation to consider the words individually as well as in combination. Apt significance, it is true,
can be absorbed into a consideration of the integrity of image
and allusion, but the criterion of verbal resonance forces the
attention upon matters of diction and vocabulary as (artificially)
separable from the referential value of word combinations.
Ultimately, of course, we cannot fully isolate the diction for
special consideration beyond suggesting that it permits a
slightly different critical approach to the words which make up
images and statements. Similarly, Dryden's definition is only
superficially mechanistic. There are not three tidily separate
activities, but three aspects of a single activity: the working of
imagination. Revision, the art to blot, can achieve its projected
improvement of the expression only when the imagination con-

centrates upon a more accurate representation of the subject. Dryden's lines in a different context are appropriate here: 'Thus poor *Mechanique Arts* in publique moove / Whilst the deep Secrets beyond practice goe.'

But, undeniably, the poor mechanic arts of elocution largely account for the circumstance that some poems, indeed some parts of poems, are more memorable than others. The odd lines and occasional passages, often innocent of context, which we from time to time remember are something other than fragments to shore against the ruin of total recall. They are, instead, our private contribution to the literary and critical phenomena of dictionaries of quotations, anthologies of elegant extracts, the distinction between poetry and a poem, Arnold's touchstones, Pope's criterion of the ne'er so well expressed, and an audience impatiently anticipating the great speeches in a Shakespeare play. The explicator's emphasis upon critical holism, upon determining and demonstrating the principles of integrity in a complete work, has tended at times to overlook or dismiss these phenomena as something of an aberration. 'Ripeness is all' is a sign, not that *King Lear* is a good play or good poetry, but that Shakespeare has achieved a felicitously sententious formula. Indeed, many of the touchstones have a sententious or gnomic air. Pope's large contribution to dictionaries of quotations includes many apophthegms from the *Essay on Man* and the *Essay on Criticism*. On the other hand, Spenser is represented less by the proverbs that abound in the *Faerie Queene* than by the unsententious 'sweet Thames! run softly, till I end my song.' Whatever part T. S. Eliot has played in perpetuating Spenser's line, it undeniably derives much of its mnemonic value from its ability to suggest without—or in addition to—referential precision. The sweet and flowing river has melodic implications that are appropriate to the poet's song; since these implications are relevant only until the end of the poem, the river is an objectification of the poem. The Thames becomes an English Aganippe, the poet's river muse, and thus the product of that muse, the poem. But in addition to these meanings and suggestions, the *Prothalamion* refrain makes its effect by the melodious sound of the line, which results, it seems, from its combination of liquids and sibilants.

As soon as a move is made from the criterion of verbal resonance to the problem of sound-sense equivalence, it is apparent that we face an hypothesis which is dubious and at best partial. Pope's virtuoso examples in the *Essay on Criticism* and Tennyson's onomatopoeic experiments are sufficient evidence that 'beauties of this kind' are possible in poetry. There is, however, no exact relationship between sound and sense. When swift Camilla scours the plain, the sound really does appear to reinforce the suggestion of speed and lightness; but precisely the same consonant cluster provided Chaucer with reinforcement for the suggestion of treachery: the smiler with the knife under the cloak. Sounds do not in themselves possess specific or definable meanings; were it otherwise the art of music would be very different. Sometimes, moreover, an apparent equivalence proves on examination to be false or misleading. Pope's 'and ten low words oft creep in one dull line' seems an effective illustration of a pentameter which is bad because it is monosyllabic. But the line creeps because practically every word requires a heavy stress and not merely because they are monosyllables. Pope practices a similar metrical deceit in the second half of his 'needless alexandrine,' 'that like a wounded snake, drags its slow length along.' The line drags and it is an alexandrine; it implies that it drags because it is an alexandrine, whereas it actually drags because the cesura is followed by a trochee and a spondee. Elsewhere Pope praised Dryden in the well-known lines that are an elegantly accurate pastiche of a typically Drydenian triplet with alexandrine:

> Waller was smooth; but Dryden taught to join ⎫
> The varying verse, the full resounding line, ⎬
> The long majestic march, and energy divine. ⎭

Apart from anything else, Pope's praise is an adequate demonstration that the English alexandrine need not drag like a wounded snake. Except where we have to deal with specifically onomatopoeic words, the incidental support of sense by sound is variable, largely unpredictable, and insufficiently frequent to justify the formulation of any general principle. Such support is occasionally afforded, and its effect is something more than the merely technical and nugatory that Johnson allowed. It confirms the aptness of the words and renders them the one true expression of an image or proposition; it confers inevitability.

37

Dryden thought, and Wordsworth confirmed, that he had a good ear for verse; his success with poems set to music indicates the validity of such a belief. A good ear need not be limited to the way in which sound echoes or seems to echo the sense; it has a wider and less dubious activity in detecting the way in which sound and rhythm are echoed between syllables and words. Echoes of this kind, of which rhyme is merely the most obvious, need have no connection with suggestion or meaning. Alliteration and assonance, for example, can and do indifferently assert a connection between words which are in denotative parallel and opposition. In recent years critics of neoclassical verse have devoted some consideration to effects of this kind, and have been willing to applaud the poet's wit in effecting parallels by rhyme or alliteration between words which are similar and dissimilar in referential point. Such an approach undeniably reveals unsuspected resources of subtle wit in the poet's language, but it is tempting to apply Ockham's razor to these multiple propositions and reduce them to moderate applause for the poet's use of rhyme and alliteration as devices that help bind his words and phrases. If the poet really can have it both ways, it might well be the case that there is only one way: a way similar to Ransom's distinction between essential meaning and irrelevant local texture. Dryden's frequent mention of the pleasures of rhyme is customarily in terms of its decorative irrelevance.

The distinction cannot, of course, be asserted absolutely. To recast whole lines, add or omit images will usually produce a change, more or less significant, in the total sense or suggestion of the work. The distinction is nevertheless a reminder that the alteration of an occasional word, especially in a long poem, can improve (or spoil) a local effect without perceptibly altering the general import. The alteration may convey the original sense more emphatically, more cogently, or simply more melodiously. If it is effective, the referential irrelevance of an alliterative connection (for example), will be considerably mitigated by the feeling that here is the most apt, sounding and significant expression of the thought. The opening couplet of *Absalom and Achitophel* affords an instructive example:

> In pious times, e'r Priest-craft did begin,
> Before *Polygamy* was made a sin.

Pious has an obvious connection, if not with priest*craft*, at least with something like priest*hood*, and this connection is denied by the temporal opposition, while the temporal conjunction effects a link between *pious* and *polygamy* which would not normally be accepted. The witty inversion of customary attitudes is certainly emphasized by the alliteration, but it is effected by the meaning. If *holy* is substituted for *pious* almost the same play of wit will result, although less emphatically and with a less precise shade of meaning (*devout* is closer in meaning but metrically unsuitable). The alliteration, then, reinforces but does not create the wit. In the third line of the poem, 'when man, on many, multiply'd his kind,' the pleasing rhetorical effect of the similarity between *man* and *many* is independent of the sense, which could be equally conveyed by substituting *one* for *man*. If we should be cautious in seeking subtly refined overtones in rhetorical embellishments of this kind, we certainly need not deny their part in the strange alchemy that makes a poem memorable.

In addition to the local effects of individual figures of speech, a poet's general figurative preferences may contribute to the characteristic movement of his verse. Professor Wimsatt's rhetorical analysis of Pope's work in *The Verbal Icon* has acquainted us with his frequent use of such figures as syllepsis, zeugma, antithesis, and chiasmus. It is not that every line or couplet in Pope employs one or other of these figures: rather is it a question of their occurring with sufficient frequency to suggest that they most clearly represent Pope's customary use of the couplet. Each of these figures effects the concentration of the sense; each assists the formulation of a double proposition within a single pentameter or couplet. Syllepsis and zeugma unite the propositions by making one verb or noun serve both. Antithesis and chiasmus unite the propositions by paralleling or balancing the syntax of one with the other. All work to turn the couplets in upon themselves, to pack them with meaning and suggestion. None of them is at all common in Dryden's verse, and when they do occur they are absorbed into the dominant rhythm of figures which work for expansion. Epic simile, parenthesis, and the irmus with which *Absalom and Achitophel* begins all delay the main point or its application, while the device of synonymous clauses repeats a single proposition with minor variations (most notably in the seven couplets devoted to Flecknoe's opening praise of Shadwell, each of which asserts Shadwell's stupidity). Dryden's most famous line is 'Great Wits are sure to Madness near ally'd; characteristically, the second line of the couplet is a simple repetition of the first: 'And thin Partitions do their Bounds divide' (Dryden was elsewhere capable of more interesting minor variations between synonyms). The occurrence of such figures can suggest where we should look for some at least of each poet's particular excellences; more directly, they help explain why Dryden's verse reads more quickly than Pope's, why sense and suggestion are more concentrated in Pope, in Dryden more expansive and therefore more thinly spread.

It would seem, then, that the challenge implicit in Dryden's criterion of elocution is too great for the explicator. All attempts at practical application lead to propositions that are either general (Dryden's verse reads more quickly than Pope's), superficial (the sound reinforces or appears to echo the sense), or merely assertive (this word is apt, sounding, and significant). More than most approaches to a poem, rhetorical analysis directs a harshly revealing light upon the *non sequitur* that customarily lurks between an objective explication and a final judgment of value. Despite these unsatisfactory results, it is an approach which should not be ignored, since it permits a useful check upon the misleading aspects of explicatory holism. Everyone is familiar with poems which do not seem quite to hang together and which are yet generally pleasing. There are similarly many poems which display an integrity of image, statement, and suggestion, but are none the less unpleasing or simply uninteresting. The rigorous application of critical holism has revealed hitherto unsuspected virtues in a demonstration of the integrity of many poems in this second class, but a failure to provide rhetorical analysis is likely to leave a reader uneasily conscious that he is being implicitly asked to value a poem more highly than it in fact merits. Almost by definition, critical holism seems to be saying the last word about a poem, whereas by placing a salutary emphasis upon the way part contributes to whole, it is in danger of overlooking or at least minimizing the local pleasure to be obtained from the parts as parts.

Obviously, analyses that are at once rigorously holistic and fully rhetorical will result in readings of disproportionate length.

For this reason an analysis both holistic and rhetorical of two short poems may be used to establish a critical context that can be briefly invoked in the reading of other works by the same author. This context may be established by a discussion of two poems, one early, one mature, each of which takes as its main subject praise for the work of a young poet.

Dryden's second published work, the complimentary address, to John Hoddesdon 'on his divine Epigrams,' is generically an epigrammatic epistle. It adopts a common topic of the verse epistle in arguing a meaningful relationship between writer and recipient,[2] in this case that Hoddesdon's example has moved Dryden to a similar poetic endeavour. Since Hoddesdon's example takes the form of verse epigrams, Dryden's imitation must also be epigrammatic and effect its witty point by asserting that his epigrammatic praise of Hoddesdon is inferior to Hoddesdon's own epigrams and therefore doubly accomplishes its task of compliment by setting off their superior merits. This exploitation of genre (a favourite neoclassical device) so that the poem becomes the paradigm of its own meaning is apparently undermined by the interposition of seven couplets that ignore the writer-recipient relationship and devote themselves wholly to praise of Hoddesdon's choice of subject. The praise is conveyed by the analogies of Prometheus stealing divine fire and the eaglet making its traditional ascent to gaze upon the sun: the implications of divine fire and divine sun and the prior association of Prometheus with eagles are sufficient to link the two analogies or at least to make the second follow naturally from the first. The specifically classical reference to Prometheus is supported by allusion to poetic laurels and supplemented by the Christian bias of the emblematic eagle. The two analogies are then combined in praise for Hoddesdon's ability to mingle 'Diviner streams with Helicon.' The specifically epistolary topic is, it seems, further undermined in the last two couplets, which turn from addressing Hoddesdon to addressing the reader. They do, however, maintain the relationship between the young poets or their products, and they in fact convey the epigrammatic point of relative inferiority. Similarly, the opening reference to Dryden's being inspired with (rather than by) the soul of Hoddesdon's epigrams is implicitly linked with the Prometheus reference because the stolen divine fire fills Hoddesdon's poems, just as, according to one tradition, man was created when heavenly sparks were breathed into his soul.

By holistic criteria, then, this early work, if not completely successful, has yet sufficient integrity to merit reasonable praise. The fact that it reads like poor prentice work is presumably a result of a failure to make the parts interesting and felicitous in themselves:

> Thou hast inspir'd me with thy soul, and I
> Who ne're before could ken of Poetry
> Am grown so good proficient, I can lend
> A line in commendation of my friend;
> Yet 'tis but of the second hand, if ought
> There be in this, 'tis from thy fancy brought.
> Good thief who dar'st Prometheus-like aspire,
> And fill thy poems with Celestiall fire:
> Enliven'd by these sparks divine, their rayes
> Adde a bright lustre to thy crown of bayes.
> Young Eaglet who thy nest thus soon forsook,
> So lofty and divine a course hast took
> As all admire, before the down begin
> To peep, as yet, upon thy smoother Chin;
> And, making heaven thy aim, hast had the grace
> To look the sunne of righteousness ith' face.
> What may we hope, if thou go'st on thus fast!
> Scriptures at first; Enthusiasmes at last!
> Thou has commenc'd, betimes, a saint: go on,
> Mingling Diviner streams with Helicon:
> That they who view what Epigrams here be
> May learn to make like, in just praise of thee.
> Reader, I've done, nor longer will withhold
> Thy greedy eyes; looking on this pure gold
> Thou'lt know adult'rate copper, which, like this,
> Will onely serve to be a foil to his.

It is important that neoclassical poems begin well, that—in most cases—they strike at once the note of a man of good sense speaking to his social equals or superiors. It was a principle which Dryden early mastered and which accounts for the variety and multiplicity of the poems which he began effectively. At his best, Dryden could produce something like the first line of his address to Congreve: 'Well then; the promis'd hour is come at last,' where the apocalyptic suggestions of the main proposition are checked by the casual note of 'Well then.' These first two words add nothing to the meaning or suggestion of the line, but they create its tone by providing a conversational context for a proposition remote from normal conversation. It is precisely the element they supply which is lacking from the opening line of the Hoddesdon address. The large flattering assertion is made in the epistolary context of one man speaking to another, but the tone of that context is inadequately supplied and the line is consequently abrupt and awkward.

The sense of verbal overtones is consistently lacking. Words make their referential point, but only occasionally do they pick up the sounds and suggestions of other words. 'Lend' in the third line provides the rhyme and does its work in the sense of *afford* or *provide*, but the choice of 'proficient' fails to release the potential of financial transaction or of provision from a store. The line is also pleonastic, because 'good' brings to it nothing more than a syllable to fill up the pentameter. The synonymous clauses of the third couplet are similarly pleonastic. The uninteresting assertion of the first clause effectively attenuates the linking potential of the second. The good that is 'brought' from Hoddesdon's fancy could, without this interruption, both reflect back upon the good that Dryden lends and refer forward to the divine sparks that Promethean Hoddesdon carries down to earth. The struggle to accommodate statements to the verse form renders the opening lines merely dull. The tendency of the couplet to enjamb a hanging two-syllable phrase at the end of the first line and thus to increase the emphasis on the rhyme is not exploited by putting the rhyme words in syntactic parallel or significant opposition. Each of the first three couplets contains such a hanging phrase, and in each case the syntactic relationship between the rhyme words is devoid of interest (a similar failure occurs later in the poem with the rhyme *go on* / *Helicon*).

Perhaps more striking than the lack of turns[3] exploiting verbal relationships is the collapse of the acquiline image. The image is given three couplets, the first and third of which successfully convey the tenor while maintaining the decorum of the vehicle. But the second couplet is in terms appropriate to the tenor alone. The result, of course, is the unfortunate and incongruous picture of the (pleonastically) young eaglet half-way to heaven suddenly metamorphosed into a smooth-cheeked youth. Quite simply, the vehicle is required to convey more of the tenor than it can manage: shaving is irrelevant to eagles. The collapse presumably comes about because the first hemistich of the second couplet is necessary to complete a sense that could not be contained within the first couplet. Dryden was then left with a line and a half to fill and unwisely devoted it to an elaboration of the tenor.

There are further infelicities. In the couplet, 'What may we hope, if thou go'st on thus fast! / Scriptures at first; Enthusiasmes at last,' the assertion of progress is insufficiently exemplified to save the second line from anticlimax. Scansion is virtually defied by 'May learn to make like, in just praise of thee.' Pleonasm, awkward inversion to achieve rhyme, unecessary line-fillers, failure of metaphor, metrical clumsiness, all contribute to the poem's ineffectiveness. But it is the consistent failure to release the suggestions of words by turns and fruitful juxtapositions that is chiefly responsible for the poem's insipid dullness.

Like the address to Hoddesdon the elegy on Oldham is in the form of a rhetorical epistle in which the relationship between writer and recipient gives significant shape to the work. The relationship is accorded explicit expression in the first five couplets, after which the poem concentrates upon the literary achievement of Oldham through four couplets and a triplet before discharging the valediction in two concluding couplets. Unlike the Hoddesdon address, however, the relationship is implicitly maintained throughout the lines that explicitly concentrate on Oldham. Despite the fact of Oldham's death the note of conversation frees the address from the overtones of apostrophe, and the intimate personal relationship that this note suggests (to which the poem only once gives explicit utterance) no doubt accounts for its sentimental popularity with readers accustomed to the Romantic apotheosis of the private mode. The poem is about both Dryden and Oldham; it is about the relationship established between them by their individual fame in the writing of satire: the praise of the dead young poet is reflected back upon the older living poet in a manner innocent of the disastrous note of conceit. Such a reflection establishes Dryden's qualifications to speak authoritatively about the nature and significance of Oldham's achievement.

The opening lines afford an increasingly precise definition or identification of the relationship between the two poets. The first couplet simply asserts the speaker's sympathy for the addressee; the second explains—and limits—this sympathy by arguing a community of poetic interest, which is further explained and limited in the third couplet by attaching that interest to satire; the fourth and fifth couplets mark the one significant difference between the two poets (other than Oldham's death) that is to be explored in the succeeding eleven lines. From the tentative note of 'began to think and call my own' the poem moves quickly through '*near* ally'd' to the confident assertion of identity in 'same . . . common . . . alike . . . same.' The common end is a constant, and the note of rivalry introduced with the difference in performance is, by means of the selective terms of the allusion, established as a friendly rivalry.

> Thus *Nisus* fell upon the slippery place,
> While his young Friend perform'd and won the Race.

The Virgilian reference is characteristic of Dryden's use of analogy in its careful editing of the vehicle to convey exactly the point of the tenor. Euryalus is identified, not by name, but in terms of his relationship with Nisus, a relationship, moreover, that accurately reflects the Roman note of the passionate hail and farewell at the beginning and end of the poem. In Virgil's account of the race Nisus fell upon a patch of blood where an animal had been sacrificed; when he fell, he was in the lead, and, with more regard for friendship than sportsmanship, he neatly tripped up the second runner so that Euryalus, who was lying third, was able to win. In Dryden's version the incident is transformed: there is no second runner and Nisus is in the lead when he falls because he started first—the race becoming a sort of handicap. The slippery place is innocent of blood and suggests simply the inexplicable accident that prevented Nisus from winning and Dryden from publishing a satire before Oldham. Because the failure of Nisus/Dryden was the result of an accident, the ignominy normally attached to such a failure is considerably mitigated. Thus, when edited, the allusion conveys two important points about the rivalry between the poets: it was friendly and it reflected almost equal credit on each. The succeeding evaluation of Oldham's achievement is, in part at least, directed toward establishing a more exact equivalence between the rivals.

The evaluation is dominated by the image of fruition, which follows naturally from Oldham's winning the race while a young man. The near paradox of complete maturity in youth is resolved by identifying the maturity as appropriate to satire but not necessarily to poetry in general. Both Dryden and Oldham could write successful satire, but only Dryden could succeed with the kind of poem that he writes to commemorate the death of Oldham. Once again the poem becomes the paradigm of its own meaning. The metrical harmonies that Oldham had not mastered are illustrated by a line which disorders the basic iambic rhythm without significantly interrupting the metrical flow of Dryden's poem: 'and Wít will shíne / Through the hársh cádence of a rúgged líne.' Similarly, the dull sweets of rhyme that maturity brings are exactly illustrated by a triplet, which, in a context of couplets, inevitably emphasizes the chink of the rhyme. The marking of the limits of Oldham's achievement is fully conveyed by the fruition image. At its introduction the image conveys unmitigated praise for Oldham: 'O early ripe! to thy abundant store / What could advancing Age have added more?' The formula is apparently that of a rhetorical question requiring the answer, 'nothing.' There is, accordingly, a mild surprise in Dryden's proceeding to treat it as anything but a rhetorical question and launching into a brief discourse on poetical harmony. The question, of course, is both rhetorical and not rhetorical, both eulogistic of Oldham and—by implication—eulogistic of Dryden, since the particular excellence denied to Oldham by his early death is largely (but not completely) irrelevant to his special achievement. When the image is recalled in the triplet, the suggestion of ripeness has been replaced by that of quickness in its sense of sharpness or acidity. Gathered as they are before their prime, Oldham's fruits are necessarily sour, a quality especially appropriate to satire.

With the final *ave atque vale* the relationship is dissolved, as the younger poet moves into the death where the older cannot follow him. The note of the opening 'Farewell' is thus recalled and isolated. The assessment of Oldham's achievement gives place to elegiac lament within the imperial context established by the allusion to Marcellus, the promising nephew of Augustus who died at twenty, an allusion which is fully realized by the final couplet's imitation of part of Virgil's elegy for the young man in the *Aeneid*. But the elegiac note is never completely absent. The images of race and fruition are primarily used to convey the critical estimate of Oldham's achievement, but their conventional associations with life and death are constantly suggested by the emphasis on youth, age, late and soon, time and gathering. The suggestions enforce the note of consonance, of the appropriateness of Oldham's dying when he did, with the full realization of his natural abilities and before the acquisition of the rhetorical arts (with the elliptic reference to the conventional opposition between art and nature). It is this conflation of a young man's death with the ending of a young poet's talent which places the elegy in the public mode. The significance of death for the speaker as representative individual is never permitted expression. Instead we have reflection upon the nature of the dead poet's achievement and upon the achievement that was denied him; the whole poem is an example of this second achievement.

The rhetoric of the elegy is clearly exemplified in the opening couplet by the almost tautologically balanced 'too little/too lately' and 'think/call.' Throughout, words are either repeated or slightly varied to suggest an extra shade of meaning: 'perform'd and won,' 'ripe/abundant,' 'advancing/added,' 'maturing/mellows/sweets.' The near synonyms of the opening couplets have already been pointed out, as has the series of words asserting likeness or identity. The effect is one of gradually expanding suggestion by which each addition repeats sufficient of the preceding to contain within itself the total suggestions up to that point. The retrospective echoes—from farewell to farewell, prime to ripe, or generous to abundant—establish an integrity of sense in the context of which minor but significant variations may be securely achieved. The elegy contains few verbal surprises, for the decorum of the form—and the mood —is sustained by mitigating the play of wit and concentrating instead upon allowing one word to shade naturally into another (as 'own' shades into 'allied,' 'poetic' into 'lyre,' 'goal' into

47

'race,' 'perform'd' into 'ripe,' 'rugged' into 'force' and 'error' into 'betray'd'). The rhyme is similarly carried, in most cases, by words of major significance in each couplet's image or proposition. 'Own,' for example, not only represents an important advance upon 'known,' but each word is the common term in a rhetorical zeugma. The succeeding rhyme of 'thine' with 'mine' is an obvious improvement over the Hoddesdon address in the handling of the short run-on phrase, while the final pairing of 'bound' with 'around' clearly emphasizes the syntactic parallel of the two words.

Unquestionably, the poem would still be effective if some at least of these local rhetorical effects were lacking, but they are not therefore 'irrelevant' to the meaning. The poem asserts that there are refinements of versification which are only mastered by practice; the poem is a constant revelation of those refinements.[4] If it may be doubted that Dryden would have understood the proposition that a poem must not mean but be, he would probably have agreed that a poem must both mean and be, and that, finally, being is only separable from meaning in the deliberately artificial act of critical analysis.

The elegy on Oldham exemplifies but one way in which rhetorical refinement can be fully integral with meaning while still achieving the maximum local felicity. Elsewhere the relationship is likely to be less direct. Sometimes, indeed, we seem to be faced with, for evaluative purposes, an absolute disjunction between matter and manner. The criticism of Dryden's poetry was for long dominated by an assumption that we should listen to the splendid cadences of his verse without attending too closely to what is actually said. This Wordsworthian assumption was most influentially stated by Arnold and most eloquently urged by Mark van Doren. Thereafter, the work of Professor Bredvold encouraged an increasing concentration upon the place of Dryden in the intellectual currents of his age. Dryden's religious, political, and philosophical position has received multiple definition, and will no doubt continue to be redefined. Most recently, the current interest in imagery has rather tardily caught up with Dryden studies, and we are now learning to trace the patterns of metaphor and allusion that control and integrate many of his works. It seems likely that a concern with intellectual position and its metaphoric expression will, if properly directed, effectively counter the negative aspect of the Wordsworthian assumption. But it would be unfortunate if, in making this necessary correction, we neglected to reaffirm and perhaps further explore the positive aspect.

Its cadence is neither the most nor the least important quality of Dryden's verse. But the critical status of the quality is rather different from that of the others, for its value can quite simply be asserted. Some analysis of its presence and the way in which it achieves its effects is certainly desirable, but so much of its particular contribution is apt to escape critical definition and description that a sustained attempt at analysis would rapidly lose its point and interest. The status of the thematic and meta-phorical qualities is noticeably different, for it is not sufficient to identify Dryden's politics as a version of royalism or his philosophy as a version of scepticism. It is similarly inadequate to point out that his verse contains images and that some of these recur with variations. What must be demonstrated is that a poem exhibits an imaginative approach to its subject through a creative use of language. For Dryden this activity largely en-tailed the finding, adaptation, and eloquent expression of viable analogies for poetry.

The Kingdom of England

DRYDEN'S creative poems—as opposed to his verse dis-courses—take as their subject an action, an event, an achievement, or a man. These subjects have their conceptual aspects, a theory of statecraft or the constitution. Often, too, theory takes the form of precept: the moral or lesson to be drawn. It would be difficult to present such subjects without drawing at least some inferences, but we cannot experience these inferences, these concepts, in the sense that we respond to an action that is complete and meaningful; we merely assent to, reject or ignore the proposition. What we can and do experience is the gradual revelation of an image: the projection, it may be, of an idea through the portrayal of an event or a character—or, perhaps, the portrayal of an event that suggests an idea. An in-tellectual activity is accorded physical status. A man is to be praised for his possession of the cardinal virtues: conceptually stated, it is good to be just, courageous, or prudent; poetically realized, we imaginatively see the man acting justly, coura-geously, or prudently. Once again, it is true, we are close to that analogy between poetry and painting which the seventeenth century inherited from antiquity. The analogy is as useful as ever in calling attention to the way in which a poem may realize a picture or series of pictures; it is misleading only if we permit it to obscure the fact that in our experience of a poem we are en-gaged as much and perhaps more by the process of realizing the picture than we are by a contemplation of the finished product.

The function of the conceptual element in the realization of the subject is something other than an explication of the pic-torial emblem, for the image of the poem embodies a particular response to the general proposition stated or implied by the conceptual element. To experience that response in all its implications it is important to understand at least some of the details of the proposition. As a particular theory of the nature and origin of government the divine right of kings is no longer relevant. As one version of the relationship between ruler and ruled that invokes a simultaneous irritation with and yearning for the dominance of a single personality it seems unlikely ever to outlive its relevance. The particular theory may be the alloy that fixes the soft gold of the enduring principle, and, if so, the metals are inseparable. It is the gold that we have in common with the earlier age, but it is their alloy, so different from our own, which permits an enlargement rather than a mere reflection of our experience. We value the poem not simply for its gold, but for the shape in which it is fixed by the alloy.

Just as the analogies can only be properly appreciated in the context of a poem, so it is with the theory, the conceptual element. The images and ideas, found by the invention, adapted by the fancy, and expressed by elocution, are a function of the subject. However much they help to convey the subject, it is the subject which determines the form of their expression. Since the subjects of Dryden's poems are different from as well as similar to each other, the particular expression of theory (or analogy) inevitably reveals inconsistencies between poem and poem. An interest in the journalistic or intellectual content of Dryden's poetry may refer these inconsistencies to a political cynicism or a philosophical scepticism in their author, although they can also be seen as differing emphases upon the multiple aspects of a coherent but by no means rigidly codified theory of monarchic government. The general lines of that theory may best be indicated by a discussion of a number of poems in which the subject is an event or person exemplifying the government of England. Such a discussion, while, it is hoped, of interest in itself, may then serve as context to a discussion of other poems in which the government of England functions as an idea or analogy illustrative of a different subject.

HEROIC STANZAS

All discussions of the *Heroic Stanzas* properly begin by pointing out the restraint of the praise. In the light of Dryden's subsequent allegiances, only the fact of his praising Cromwell at all could be effectively turned against him by his political opponents. The specific terms of the praise afford, with one highly questionable exception, no further grounds for reproach. Praise for the great leader who assisted his country in time of need could be as politically non-committal as the poem is sometimes taken to be, but Dryden's elegy is in fact directed toward an aspect of royalist theory concerned with what Sir Robert Filmer described as 'dangerous or doubtful times.'

The editors of the Clark Dryden have drawn attention to the series of oppositions by which the poem functions, and these oppositions are best epitomized as the rival claims of fortune and providence to be responsible for the success of Cromwell. The workings of fortune are manifested in the material vicissitudes of great men's lives; those of providence are glimpsed imperfectly at best, but ultimately represent the only acceptable sanction. The poem fluctuates between man's view of Cromwell's good fortune and God's view of his providential appointment until Cromwell is seen to contain both views within himself, although the balance in favour of providence is retained. This fluctuating progress is accompanied by polemically phrased reflections upon the theory and practice of government, for the poem is very much concerned to establish the nature of Cromwell's title, his place in the constitution.

If the major control of the poem is the rivalry between fortune and providence, its final image is further shaped by analogy with the career and obsequies of a Roman emperor. The poem begins with the emperor's pyre and the flight of his acquiline soul into deification; it ends with his ashes in an antique urn. The ashes that remain to mortal contemplation and the soul that flies above provide, in fact, a variation upon the consistent opposition between a divine sanction and the sublunary estimate of fortune. But, generalized though it is, the imperial reference establishes a Roman context that is, in the body of the poem, particularized in terms of Julius Caesar, who was among those burned on a pyre and who was further appropriate in that he shared with Cromwell great success in generalship. Both men were seemingly invincible; both owed their victories to the swift movement of their troops and their supremacy to army support; both effected a radical alteration of the constitution and ended with a marked inclination toward absolute rule. The analogy was sufficiently inevitable to be drawn at least partially by a number of Cromwell's eulogists.[1] In royalist theory Caesar's defeat of Pompey exemplified a rebellious overthrow of the forces of legitimism,[2] and, omitting the depreciative suggestion, praise of the Protector was occasionally couched in terms of a double analogy between Caesar and Cromwell and between Pompey and Charles I.[3]

In fact, the Caesar analogy enters the *Heroic Stanzas* by way of explicit allusion to Pompey alone:

> Fortune (that easie Mistresse of the young
> But to her auncient servants coy and hard)
> Him at that age her favorites rank'd among
> When she her best-lov'd *Pompey* did discard.
>
> (ll. 29–32)

It is customary for editors to explain the reference by noting that Pompey reached the height of his fame at the age of forty-five, when he was accorded a triumph; thereafter his fortunes steadily declined until his assassination at the age of fifty-eight. Cromwell first came into prominence in 1644 with the victory at Marston Moor when he was forty-five; thereafter his fortunes steadily increased until his death at the age of fifty-nine. The rise and fall of princes on fortune's wheel thus have a pleasing symmetry, but it should be noticed that the standard gloss puts too great a strain on the key word *discard*. Pompey's continued importance in Roman affairs during the decade following his triumph and the fact that he represented the chief opposition to Caesar in 49 B.C. suggest that he was not truly discarded by fortune until the crushing defeat at Pharsalia and his subsequent assassination in Alexandria. If, then, the force of *discard* directs our attention more readily to the events of 49–48 B.C. than to those of 61–48 B.C., it would appear that Dryden could as reasonably have instanced any other great man who died violently in middle age—Caesar himself would work very nicely, for he was fifty-six at his assassination. And—a fourth factor for permutation—Charles I was a bare year younger than Cromwell. External reference, then, permits a number of incompatible possibilities, and it becomes essential to enquire whether the internal context facilitates the task of selection.

It is at least questionable that Cromwell's admission to the favours of fortune is here represented by his emergence as a considerable general at Marston Moor. In itself the quatrain is not at all specific, but the quatrain in isolation does not provide the sole context for the reference. It is preceded by a quatrain comparing the nature of Cromwell's title with the hereditary rule of Charles I which he had superseded: 'No borrow'd Bay's his *Temples* did adorne, / But to our *Crown* he did fresh *Jewells* bring.' Similarly, the discarding of Pompey is followed by a quatrain arguing that Cromwell was able to benefit by observing the mistakes of 'rash *Monarch's* who their youth betray / By Acts their Age too late would wish undone.' It is true that this conventional reference to Cromwell's activities during his early obscurity is again sufficiently generalized for it to be taken as a discussion of diligent historical study, but the most likely subject of his contemplations would have been Charles I, who certainly behaved with sufficient rashness in the early years of his reign to serve as cautionary example to subsequent rulers. Whether or not an implicit Charles I is accepted, it is clear that the quatrains surrounding the dealings of fortune with Pompey are concerned with Cromwell's qualifications as a ruler, and to read the intervening quatrain in terms of generalship as well is to interrupt the development of an emerging image.

Cromwell was triply qualified to rule his country: he succeeded to the office by merit, not inheritance; he benefited from a prudent consideration of the mistake of other kings; and he was favoured by fortune, not only in his own success, but in the fortuitous removal of the major obstacle to his rule, the reigning king of England. Pompey is not the merely casual antithesis to successful Cromwell that he would be in strictly Roman terms. As the type of Charles I he maintains the focus on kingship and calls into play an existing double analogy between Cromwell and Caesar, Charles and Pompey. It is because the picture of Cromwell which thus emerges might suggest a premeditated usurpation that Dryden hastens to insist that '*Dominion* was not his Designe, / We owe that blessing not to him but Heaven.'

This fourth qualification of altruistic modesty is repeated from the quatrain describing Cromwell's accession by merit, where we are assured that his virtue was not 'poyson'd soon as born / With the too early thoughts of being King.' The repetition suggests that we should take the four quatrains (ll. 25–40) as a unit, and avoid considering them in isolation from each other. There are obvious similarities between Dryden's handling of the quatrain and his fashioning of a series of couplets into a verse paragraph, the limits of which we cannot always rely upon his printer to supply with accuracy. What he appears to say in one couplet or quatrain will often be modified in succeeding couplets or quatrains. To ignore the modifications or to treat them separately is to proceed contrary to the principles of Dryden's verse.

An awareness of the larger units can help dispose, finally, of the charge of Dryden's enemies during the Exclusion crisis that in one stanza he condones the execution of Charles I by advancing to the credit of Cromwell that 'He fought to end our fighting, and assaid / To stanch the blood by breathing of the vein' (ll. 47–48). There seems no reason to challenge the Clark editors' conclusion that the reference is to the whole body politic rather than the neck of Charles I. The syntax indicates that 'breathing of the vein' simply applies to the statement, 'He fought to end our fighting,' the figure of the quatrain's first lines: 'Warre our consumption was their gainfull trade, / We inward bled whilst they prolong'd our pain.' Disapproval is directed at those who prolonged the war, the 'former Cheifs' of the preceding quatrain who introduce a unit of seven stanzas, the coherence of which is marked by the repetition of the idea contained in 'He fought to end our fighting' by the later assertion, 'Peace was the Prize of all his toyles and care, / Which Warre had banisht and did now restore' (ll. 61–62).

The battles which explicitly involve Cromwell in 'toyles and care' are the campaigns in Ireland and Scotland in 1649–50, rather than the campaigns against Charles I, the credit for which Cromwell must in any case have shared with Fairfax and others. The Clark editors are presumably correct to understand by the 'former Cheifs' the parliamentary and presbyterian interests which sought to impose the religiously intolerant Covenant and whose power was broken by the army independents under Fairfax and Cromwell. What we have in this seven-quatrain unit is a comparison between the conduct of military affairs prior to 1649 and their conduct by Cromwell after 1649. It is a comparison which parallels that between the rule and title of Cromwell and Charles I in the immediately preceding four-quatrain unit.

The earlier comparison implied a premeditated usurpation which had to be countered by an assertion that 'Dominion was not his Designe.' Similarly, the concentration upon Cromwell's victorious campaigns might imply that he was to be praised as no more than an efficient *dux bellorum*. We are consequently assured that 'He had his calmer influence' (l. 71), a corrective reminder which also serves as transition from panegyric upon Cromwell's fortitude to panegyric upon his prudent conduct of economic and diplomatic affairs in peace.

Before exhibiting that conduct, the poem reaffirms the divine origin of Cromwell's title:

> 'Tis true, his Count'nance did imprint an awe,
> And naturally all souls to his did bow;
> As *Wands of Divination* downward draw
> And point to Beds where Sov'raign Gold doth grow.
>
> (ll. 73–76)

The minor semantic explosion of this quatrain results from the simultaneous use of a number of related images which together come close to making a mixed metaphor. There is the obvious reference to coinage (a royal prerogative) in the first and last lines, although Cromwell apparently changes from minter to minted. The practice of using divining rods to discover ore deposits not only illustrates the obeisance of Cromwell's subjects, it also permits a play upon the heavenly origin of Cromwell's title and qualifications. 'Sov'raign Gold' recalls the golden sovereign and further alludes to the king of metals and the metal of kings, while the belief that metals grow in the ground picks up the suggestions of 'naturally' in the second line.

But, for all its suggestiveness, the quatrain is a striking example of a consistent failure in the early poems to endow unexpected associations with imaginative coherence. The tenor will not hold, for the allusion to divination entails an inappropriate physical relationship: subjects bow down before their sovereign ruler, who remains above them; divining rods bow down toward the sovereign gold, which lies below them. This failure is more crucial than the fault remarked by Van Doren: the tendency of Dryden's quatrains to divide, as here, into a largely theoretic statement illustrated by a decorative allusion. In this case, the wands of divination add an association lacked by the largely theoretic second line, and the effect of redundancy is mitigated to an extent not achieved by some other quatrains in the poem:

> Peace was the Prize of all his toyles and care,
> Which Warre had banisht and did now restore;
> *Bolognia*'s Walls thus mounted in the Ayre
> To seat themselves more surely then before.
>
> (ll. 61–64)

Since it adds little to the statement of the first two lines, the allusion here invites in isolation from its context an examination which unavoidably notes its oddity. Whether or not such events are possible, they are certainly improbable. The idea to be illustrated, that war, when rightly prosecuted, can end war, is a merely syntactical paradox. To recall the extraordinary event, the miracle at Bologna, suggests that the paradox is more challenging and requires miraculous abilities for its resolution. Reasonable praise is unreasonably amplified, as the panegyrist strikes the false note of strident adulation.

This false note, which sounds so often and so disturbingly in Dryden's later panegyrics upon Charles II, is heard only occasionally in the *Heroic Stanzas* (another example occurs in the thirty-fourth quatrain). Its infrequency is properly ascribed to the poem's general restraint, to its cautious selection of detail in developing the image of its subject. Most of the detail is devoted to Cromwell's undoubted stature as a general and to the equally unquestionable success of England under his rule in diplomatic and mercantile affairs. What defines the tone and shapes the final image is the view taken of Cromwell's title, a view suggested in the opening section of four quatrains and brought into increasing prominence as the praise is developed.

The tenor of these opening quatrains is the reason for praising a Cromwell whose fame is already so well-established that the offerings of any eulogist are superfluous. But they are not irrelevant to the interest of the eulogist himself, who ministers to his own posterity by raising a verbal monument to a man whose posterity is already assured. So stated, the slight modification of the convention that poets serve the great by erecting monuments more durable than those of marble is itself conventional. It is the terms of the second quatrain which provide political extension of the established topic of encomium:

> Though our best notes are treason to his fame
> Joyn'd with the loud applause of publique voice;
> Since Heav'n, what praise we offer to his name,
> Hath render'd too authentick by its choice.

In the context of popular acclaim the otherwise blameless tributes of poets are a pretension to be responsible for the greatness of Cromwell, which had been assured, rendered 'authentick' or authoritative, by divine choice alone. The fact that this pretension is conveyed by the charged word *treason* places it firmly in the central constitutional debate of the seventeenth century, a debate over whether a monarch receives his sovereignty, his right to rule, from the hands of the people or by divine donation. The endless minor permutations upon this theoretic opposition provided the matter of countless tracts and poems in the paper war, until the problem was resolved, more or less pragmatically, by the Glorious Revolution.

No royalist ever suggested that a ruler could govern efficiently without some measure of acquiescence from his subjects, whether that acquiescence was coerced by a Hobbist exercise of power, specifically, military power, or granted in accordance with the religious obligations imposed by *jus divinum*. To this extent, then, a ruler *de facto* had need of popular consent, but this consent merely permitted his exercise of a kingship which he obtained by divine donation alone. Because the people could not make their king, they could not dictate to him nor limit his sovereignty in any way: once they submitted, their submission must be absolute. Any questioning of this assumption tended to republicanism and—in Filmer's words—'the anarchy of a limited or mixed monarchy.'

Thus, a popular pretence to be responsible for Cromwell's fame was 'treason'; his '*Grandeur*'—his majesty—was 'deriv'd from Heav'n alone' (l. 21); 'Heaven' gave him his '*Dominion*' (ll. 36–37); his regal qualities of 'Love and Majesty' were innate (l. 72); while his very features moved his people to the act of homage reserved for rulers *de jure divino* (ll. 73–76). Similarly, the section from stanzas 20 to 32 demonstrates Cromwell's success in the *arcana imperii*, the 'close *Intrigues*' of line 80. It is certainly true that even a republic would have its secrets of state, but it was the royalists who consistently argued that the exercise of government required great abilities and extensive training. It was because the outward and partial manifestations of government were likely to give an erroneous impression of the overall policy known only to the king and his ministers that royalist apologetics frequently argued the invalidity of popular judgments upon acts of state. Thus, stanza 20 asserts Cromwell's abilities as a policy maker, the succeeding eleven quatrains detail examples of his policy in action, and stanza 32 closes the unit with the conventional argument that the examples give only an imperfect idea of the superior abilities ultimately responsible for them:

> Such was our Prince; yet own'd a soul above
> The highest Acts it could produce to show:
> Thus poor *Mechanique Arts* in publique moove
> Whilst the deep Secrets beyond practice goe.

The implied analogy here is that of the state as engine, functioning by a complicated system of gears and levers, and manufacturing political and diplomatic actions at the instigation of the prince, who is a sort of superior machine-minder. It was an analogy easily associated with royalist discussions of the *arcana imperii*.

In the *Heroic Stanzas* Cromwell is consistently praised as a providentially ordained monarch rather than (as in Milton's *Second Defence*) a republican-minded dictator who was providentially to hand in his country's time of need. As the people's choice, a dictator properly credits all national triumphs to the country as a whole;[4] but a king by divine appointment is himself credited with such triumphs, for he is the source of honour and glory in the land. Thus, even when Cromwell was absent, Dryden insists that the English 'conquer'd in his right' (l. 93), because 'From this high-spring our forraign-Conquests flow' (l. 109). The terms of the praise are scarcely in accord with the principles of either the 'former Cheifs' or the sullen Commons of the twenty-seventh stanza:

> When such *Heröique Vertue* Heav'n sets out,
> The Starrs like *Commons* sullenly obey;

> Because it draines them when it comes about,
> And therefore is a taxe they seldome pay.

The tenor is a variation upon the poem's consistent opposition between fortune and providence. The direct intervention of the first cause interrupts the normal operation of second causes, the star-influenced fortunes of men. It is the vehicle which contains the public or political proposition, which, so far from merely affording a decorative illustration, develops what is virtually a separate thesis. The Commons, it appears, should grant the king's requests for extraordinary levies (in time of emergency, presumably), even though the required sum is very large. Parliament's grudging admission of this principle, the sullenness with which they obey, is a direct reflection upon the nature of their loyalty which would have easily recalled the Commons' recent attempt to control taxation in defiance of Cromwell and at the cost of speedy dissolution early in 1658.

Alone of Dryden's major political poems the *Heroic Stanzas* offers no concluding prophecy of future glory. (By contrast, *Threnodia Augustalis* commemorates the death of Charles II, but ends with a preview of prosperity under James II. Similarly, the elegy on Cromwell which Sprat published with Dryden's ends with dynastic patriarchalism, benevolently observing the change of command from Oliver/Moses to Richard/Joshua.) For Dryden the observed fact of a few months' peace after Cromwell's death prompts no prediction of its continuance, and we are left only with an assurance that Cromwell's name and example will endure:

> His Ashes in a peacefull Urne shall rest,
> His Name a great example stands to show
> How strangely high endeavours may be blest,
> Where *Piety* and *valour* joyntly goe.

It is the *strangely* which attracts attention, emphasizing as it does the touch of the extraordinary in Cromwell's career. Its possibilities were first explored in the opening flight of the eagle and ineptly forced with the aid of the miracle at Bologna. Cromwell was a divinely ordained force of nature—the confidant of nature, indeed (l. 99)—and, punningly, the protecting spirit of the land, its *genius loci* (l. 139). As such, he and his career created their own terms and their own conditions. Dryden's praise is on general monarchic grounds, clearly rejecting a republican dictatorship but without embracing a Stuart orthodoxy.

In 1652, at the low point of Stuart hopes and fortunes, with the old king dead and the young king forced into exile, Sir Robert Filmer appended to one of his tracts a few pages headed 'Directions for Obedience to Government in Dangerous or Doubtful Times.' Those times of rebellion and usurpation, times in which the hereditary succession was interrupted, occurred with sufficient frequency to ensure that, for royalists, the formulation of an appropriate political attitude and course of conduct was as necessary as it was difficult. Part of Filmer's solution lay in an affirmation that 'the title of a usurper is before, and better than the title of any other than of him that had a former right: for he hath a possession by the permissive will of God, which permission, how long it may endure, no man ordinarily knows.'[5] The monarchic terms of Dryden's praise were then, provided with such precedents as this, as well as with support in the royalist commonplace that kingly government was so natural to man that attempts to expunge it customarily ended in its actual or virtual restitution by the rebels or their descendants: the Roman republic began by ousting the monarchy, but ended in the principate and empire, while on the way it retained the forms of monarchy in the offices of consul and dictator.

The nature of an usurper's title and the obligation due to him elicited the full casuistical powers of supporters of hereditary monarchy. Their arguments were based sometimes on the hopeless dichotomy of providential authority for usurpers and the legal culpability of rebels, sometimes on an admonition to obey the usurper in order to maintain the welfare of the land, unless his commands were unjust, impious, or prejudicial to the right of the lawful heir.[6] This conscientious waiting until the king came into his own again obviously saw the period of usurpation as a *de facto* interregnum, for *nullum tempus occurrit regi*: 'no time bars a king,' as Filmer translated the royalist maxim.[7]

The *Heroic Stanzas* uses some at least of the terms of this debate, although it does not tend toward the same polemic conclusion. The poet's providence is not the transcendent dispositions of an all-wise God acting through second causes. It is a special providence, a direct and miraculous intervention of the first cause in mundane affairs, by-passing second causes, by-passing the starry influence of fortune, choosing Cromwell and permitting him to fight 'secure of fortune as of fame' (l. 53). Secure, that is, both because they are assured to him and because he could afford to be without care of them. The extent of the poem's polemic is to insist that Cromwell's dominion, his sovereignty, was by divine not popular donation. This insistence is used to support no argument about man's natural inclination toward monarchic rule, no argument about the providential authority of usurpers; there is no suggestion of a Cromwellian dynasty and none of Stuart interregnum; neither hope for the future nor regret for the past.

Unlike the panegyrics of the next few years, it is in no sense a politic poem, because its politics flatter no persuasion. If it 'proves' anything at all, it is that God will intervene to aid a strife-torn nation by providing the necessary man of strength and virtue. The poem was written during the uneasy months following the death of Cromwell, months that witnessed the experiment of Richard's protectorship, which, lacking army support, was soon ended by the restoration of the Rump and the last, brief attempt to establish a commonwealth. The times were as dangerous and doubtful as they were seven years earlier, and the restraint of Dryden's praise perhaps reflects that uncertainty. But there is no Filmerian advice to subjects. Lacking this didacticism, the poem projects and develops with clarity the image of a man acting greatly and with divinely ordained authority in a time of trouble and in a context of antique grandeur; beyond the fire and the ashes there is nothing.

RESTORATION PANEGYRICS

The cultivated growth of the *Heroic Stanzas* proliferated the following year into the luxuriant vegetation of *Astraea Redux*. To use Dryden's own terms, fancy and judgment seem to be in perpetual strife, and the reader is left doubtful where to accord the palm. Our awareness that judgment achieves some shrewd thrusts is due in large measure to an excellent brief discussion of the imagery in the notes to the Clark Dryden. The fortune-providence dichotomy of the *Heroic Stanzas* is used again, but for different ends; and its suggestiveness is much enhanced by the wealth of related ideas that Dryden's invention discovered in, among other places, the offerings of his fellow eulogists. One of the poem's major controls is that which presents the period of rebellion and royal exile as subject to the fickle sway of fortune, whose power is broken by the special providence that inspires Monck (l. 151) and guides Charles to reunion with his penitent subjects:

> Heav'n could not own a Providence and take
> The wealth three Nations ventur'd at a stake.
> The same indulgence *Charles* his Voyage bless'd
> Which in his right had Miracles confess'd.

> (ll. 238–41)

It is the nature of a special providence to manifest itself in miracles, and Virgil was authority for representing mild weather as a heavenly indulgence, a *caeli indulgentia*.[8]

In fact, the poem seems to contradict the burden of the *Heroic Stanzas*. If England was subject to fortune during the king's exile (l. 19), it could scarcely have enjoyed the simultaneous and providential benefits of Cromwell's rule. But, as everyone has noticed, *Astraea Redux* makes no specific mention of Cromwell. There are a number of general references that could be taken to include his protectorship, but greatest attention is devoted to the horrors of civil war with its culmination in regicide, while brief allusions to the period 1649–60 concentrate upon the final administration of the Rump. It would be foolish to deny the existence of a general contradiction, and equally foolish to argue confidently from the common terms of discrete poetic images to a change in their author's political persuasion. The conceptual element in one poem can contradict the same element in another poem, but the final images developed by the two poems are incapable of meaningful contradiction. Providence and divine authority in the *Heroic Stanzas* and *Astraea Redux* derive part of their value from the terms of the political debate, but they also make a large contribution to the image of each poem. In this contribution they are aided by the rival figure of fortune, which finds its principal exterior context in the traditional philosophic and literary coupling of the two powers. There is, then, no political contradiction between the different roles of fortune in the two poems; and there is no political reason why the poet should not have hailed as providential the rule of both Cromwell and Charles II.

Astraea Redux is more obviously involved in controversial matters when it considers one of the major political issues of the century: the relationship of the king to the law, the constitutionality of the crown. The *Heroic Stanzas* touched upon this issue in its consideration of the origin of sovereign power, but its neglect of Cromwellian justice as a panegyric 'place' kept the consideration free from the chief terms of the debate. Since variations upon these terms consistently provided Dryden with matter both eulogistic and controversial, it will be convenient to set the panegyrics on Clarendon and on the restoration and coronation of Charles II in the context of the debate without attempting more than a brief elaboration of the useful critical introductions to these poems in the Clark Dryden.

That the origins of the dispute were in the Middle Ages was acknowledged by frequent appeals to centuries-old precedents and the citation of fragmentary tags from Bracton. A typical discourse would move within a few pages from the nature of the Anglo-Saxon heptarchy through the deposition of Richard II to the Solemn League and Covenant. The interdependence of history and governmental theory which I mentioned in an earlier chapter was further complicated by the inclusion of constitutional law. If the seventeenth-century political debate witnessed a displacement of the Elizabethan emphasis on common law, it should none the less be remembered that Bracton and Coke, two of the most authoritative sources, were both lawyers. The interest and the confusion of seventeenth-century political theory derives from its eclectic use of formulae which had earlier been advanced independently. In the poetry especially, such rival equations as rex-deus, rex-Christus, and rex-lex lie side by side with remarkable amity.

Definitions of government were as legion as the names for it; a monarchy could be arbitrary, absolute, limited, legal, mixed, tyrannical, or despotic, to mention only the more common terms. Everyone agreed that peace, security, prosperity, and justice were desirable ends of government. Everyone agreed that as they were human, rulers were fallible and must therefore be restrained in some way. Disagreement commenced over the nature of the restraint and its implications for political obligation. A royalist in the early years of the Great Rebellion might argue the necessity or at least the existence of legal restraints upon the king's power: the king should govern according to the laws; the legislative was vested jointly in king and parliament; the king alone could not make or abrogate laws by proclamation. But if the king did transgress the limits of the law, his subjects could restrain him no further than by refusal of supply and passive non-compliance. As J. W. Allen points out, the king had in practice many ways of avoiding the full consequences of a parliamentary refusal to grant supplies: men are corruptible. Similarly, non-compliance with an unjust command, when coupled with submission to just punishment for the act of non-compliance, could only be an effective restraint when all subjects acted together, and that was improbable: men are not only corruptible, they are indolent.[9] The parliamentarians correctly saw that royalist limited monarchy was virtual absolutism. The divine right of kings, with its paraphernalia of passive obedience, non-resistance, lesè-majesty, and indivisible sovereignty, was no more than absolutism disguised. The disguise appears to have been adopted partly by a wish to pacify the opposition and partly by an understandable distaste for tyranny. But royalist hopes for good government rested ultimately on the character of the king. Their theory reduced itself to a lottery: if you wanted a father, you must take the chance of drawing a tyrant.

Peter Laslett has described Filmer as 'that extremely rare phenomenon—the codifier of conscious and unconscious prejudice.'[10] Much the same is true of Hobbes, and both men are distinguished by their honesty from the bulk of royalist thinkers. Both admitted that the sovereign power must be absolute—free from or above the laws—and arbitrary—an expression of the king's individual will: *le roy se veult*. Both agreed that no diminution of royal authority was implied by the king's normal government in accordance with the laws; such actions were no precedent for his not ignoring the laws when necessary. Practical pessimist that he was, Hobbes warned against undue compliance with the wishes of subjects in this difficult matter:

A man to obtain a kingdom, is sometimes content with less power, than to the peace, and defence of the commonwealth is necessarily required. From whence it cometh to pass, that when the exercise of the power laid by, is for the public safety to be resumed, it hath the resemblance of an unjust act; which disposeth great numbers of men, when occasion is presented, to rebel.[11]

This precept Hobbes gloomily included in his schedule of 'things that weaken, or tend to the dissolution of a commonwealth.' The king, of course, was subject to divine and natural laws, but God alone could arraign the king for breaking them. Ultimately, Filmer and Hobbes make use of all the disguises favoured by other royalists; but their uncompromising adherence to absolute and arbitrary rule marked them out for special attention in the pamphlet war.

Behind Filmer was the greater figure of Jean Bodin, the extent of whose influence on the theories of English royalists it would be impossible to estimate with any accuracy. Expounded at London and Cambridge soon after its appearance in 1575, his *République* was cited by controversialists, although not with noticeable frequency after the civil war. Filmer published a few pages of extracts from the *République*, calling his anthology *The Necessity of the Absolute Power of all Kings* (1648). The wide currency of Bodin's ideas (more accurately, of the ideas he helped to popularize) is argued by their appearance in some form in practically every royalist manifesto. But apart from an obvious case like Filmer's, it is impossible to say that any one writer is specifically indebted to Bodin; he may easily have derived his ideas from another pamphleteer who was in turn indebted to Filmer. In an age when even specific acknowledgment was likely to be derived from second-hand sources, it is reasonable to suppose that silent indebtedness does not necessarily indicate personal knowledge of the ultimate source. The frequent repetition of the same maxims from Bracton, Fortescue, or Coke is a positive indication only that somewhere along the line of transmission someone had actually read the works in which they occur. It would, then, be ridiculous to offer Bodin as the direct source of a writer's ideas, but Bodin has the charm of impressive bulk. His appears to be the most comprehensive statement of royalist propaganda: certain of his ideas could be developed, a few fresh possibilities could be raised, an overlooked contingency could be discussed. On the whole, however, he is satisfyingly thorough.

Bodin's name is primarily associated with the doctrine of indivisible sovereignty, but he was scarcely less significant for his own preferred form of government: the royal monarchy, as his English translator called it.[12] The royal monarch acknowledges the freedom and 'propriety' of his subjects, in contrast to the lordly (or despotic) monarch, whose subjects have no freedom and no property that is not held in fealty from him. The royal monarch subjects himself to the law of God and nature, but not to statute law, for that is both given and dispensed by the king, who has the further task of adjusting its inadequacy in particular cases by the exercise of equity. It was this need for the corrective virtue of equity which led many royalists to argue that the king is above the law: if he is bound to observe it in general, it is difficult for him to administer it equitably in particular cases. He can best determine where to follow the letter would be to proceed contrary to the spirit. Bodin agrees that his sovereign may promise to keep the laws of the land, and if he does, he is bound to observe that promise, because the laws of God and nature require that he deal justly by his covenants. James I regarded statute law as a codification of the king's will, which, in the early days of government, provided the sole legal standard. Just as God covenanted with Noah after the Flood, so a king covenants with his people (at the coronation) to observe his own laws. James I's monarch 'degenerates into a tyrant, as soon as he leaves off to rule according to his laws.'[13] But Bodin offers a list of occasions on which a king might justly break his promise, and if he does, his subjects, neither collectively nor individually, can impeach him. Moreover, James I ('the British Solomon') was ready in defence of the king's exercise of equity to formulate his relation to the law in terms that insist upon theoretic absolutism while recommending a practice indistinguishable from limitation:

> The King is above the law, as both the author and giver of strength thereto; yet a good king will not onely delight to rule his subjects by the lawe, but even will conforme himselfe in his owne actions thereuneto [sic], alwaies keeping that ground, that the health of the common-wealth be his chiefe lawe: And where he sees the lawe doubtsome or rigorous, hee may interpret or mitigate the same, lest otherwise *Summum ius* bee *summa iniuria.*[14]

Bodin's royal monarch is perhaps the clearest version of the ideal king described by Stuart apologists. When political controversy had stripped *arbitrary* and *absolute* of their neutrality and rendered them pejorative, royalists laboured to minimize their import by stressing the king's government in accordance with the law and his administration of equity. In normal practice the royal monarch was virtually indistinguishable from the limited, and Bodin has himself been described as a limited monarchist.[15] But as limited monarchy was described by Hunton[16] and as it is set out in a tract dubiously attributed to L'Estrange,[17] it entailed a constitutional obligation upon the king to observe the law. Such a theory requires the subordination of the king to the constitution; but because the constitution is inanimate it must be represented by some other body in the state should the king break the law in his political capacity. That body is then superior to the king, who becomes, by a favourite royalist analogy, a mere Doge of Venice. Filmer's comment epitomizes Stuart thought:

> It was not difficult to invent laws for the limiting of supreme governors; but to invent how those laws should be executed, or by whom interpreted, was almost impossible, 'Nam quis custodiet ipsos Custodes?' to place a superior above a supreme, was held unnatural.[18]

Juvenal's aphorism, here explicit and stripped of its incongruous associations, is implied in many a royalist tract. Against such a limited monarch could be set the royal, whose government by law was not determined (as Filmer put it) *ab externo*,[19] but by his own will and conscience. The practical difference, imperceptible in time of peace and domestic security, was of highest importance in time of crisis (especially constitutional crisis), when the reservations of the royal monarch theoretically permitted him to resume absolute control of the country. Royalist fears of demagogy and mob rule, so fully aroused by the execution of Charles I and its aftermath, were confirmed by the near hysteria of the Popish Plot. If the royalists were optimistic in their hopes of the king and pessimistic in their attitude towards subjects, the parliamentary or country party was precisely the reverse.

When Dryden turned in *Astraea Redux* to the matter of king and law, he expressed himself with what may now seem sufficient ambiguity to make possible an interpretation along the lines of limited monarchy as it has been described above:

> Your Pow'r to Justice doth submit your Cause,
> Your Goodness only is above the Laws;
> Whose rigid letter while pronounc'd by you
> Is softer made.
>
> (ll. 266–69)

The power in question is that of coercion:[20] when Charles compels submission it will be in accordance with the laws—he will not arbitrarily compel submission to his will when it is contrary to the common and statute law of the land. His 'Goodness,' the moral sense he derives from obedience to divine and natural law, remains above for the purpose of administering equity in his kingly character of *lex loquens*. But the subordination of Charles's coercive power to the laws of the land is a submission of his own will: he subjects his power to the laws and does not accept a necessary limitation. The reason for this is provided by the preceding reflections upon the inadequacy of Charles I. The Royal Martyr lacked the ability to coerce his subjects; he did not even have the power to uphold justice, and his execution was a direct result of that fact:

> But you, whose goodness your discent doth show,
> Your Heav'nly Parentage and earthly too;
> By that same mildness which your Fathers Crown
> Before did ravish, shall secure your own.
> Not ty'd to rules of Policy, you find
> Revenge less sweet then a forgiving mind.
>
> (ll. 256–61)

To be tied to rules of policy is to govern solely in accordance with political expediency without significant consultation of the moral principles dictated by divine and natural law. Political expediency demanded severe punishment for all important supporters of the government during the Interregnum, and the advantage of such a king as Charles is that he can override the demands of expediency in the interests of equity and mercy. Dryden's opposition between expediency and forgiveness might appear merely specious: that the Act of Oblivion was a politic decision is clear from Charles's reference to it in the Declaration of Breda:

And to the end that fear of punishment may not engage any, conscious to themselves of what is past, to a perseverance in guilt for the future . . . we do grant a free and general Pardon . . . to all our subjects . . . excepting only such persons as shall hereafter be excepted by Parliament.[21]

But against the king's words should be set the more severe demands of such stern members as the Mr. Lenthall who would have excepted all who fought against Charles I, as well as those who judged him.[22]

The related topics of equity and the law, coercive power and forgiving mercy, are elaborated in the panegyrics on Clarendon and the coronation. In the latter it is pointed out that the more militant of the Nonconformist sects could look forward to nothing but harsh punishment from the law for their late sedition. In such a case, their only recourse is to the king, who, in his exercise of equity, is the arbitrator between the law and those who break it. To this extent, again, the king is above the law, and Dryden's description of the king as arbitrator emphasizes that fact (ll. 81–88).

As poetic data this remote constitutional theory is important for the series of oppositions it provides. Again and again, the image of Dryden's panegyrics and complimentary addresses, especially in the early years, is shaped in terms of conflicting qualities or actions, often with a resolving *tertium quid*. The power-mercy conflict of the panegyrics on Charles, for example, is modified into praise for Clarendon, the king's chief minister:

> Justice that sits and frowns where publick Laws
> Exclude soft mercy from a private cause,
> In your Tribunal most her self does please;
> There only smiles because she lives at ease;
> And like young *David* finds her strength the more
> When disincumberd from those arms she wore:
> Heav'n would your Royal Master should exceed
> Most in that Vertue which we most did need,
> And his mild Father (who too late did find
> All mercy vain but what with pow'r was joyn'd,)
> His fatal goodnesse left to fitter times,
> Not to increase but to absolve our Crimes.
>
> (ll. 49–60)

It should be noticed that Charles II is the epitome of true justice because he shares an analogy with it. The conventional parallel between Charles and David, followed immediately by explicit reference to Clarendon's royal master, ensures an identification between Charles and the justice which is the manifest tenor of the David analogy. Moreover, soft mercy is balanced against the strength exhibited by Charles II's Davidic justice when it sheds the arms of military coercion. The specifically martial reference suggests the stratocracy of the Interregnum, just as the emphasis on mercy explicitly recalls the fate of Charles I. David's strength is greater than military might because it derives from true justice and is thus in accordance with divine and natural law. Bodin warned that too often 'the state of a citie or Commonweal ruinated by the too much lenitie and facilitie of one prince, is againe relieved and upholden by the austeare severitie of an other.' Ideally, for Bodin, a prince should strive 'to hold this golden meane' between severity and lenity, but, as Aristotle noted, the tendency of men to favour the extremes rather than the middle way makes this task particularly difficult.[23] Charles II's opportunity to observe the fatal goodness of undue mercy in his father and the undue power of the Interregnum will, it seems, enable him to hold to the golden mean so prized by Bodin.

The combination of law and equity provides true justice. The mercy, the fatal goodness, of Charles I is combined with the military power of the Interregnum in Charles II, the ideal ruler. Power is hard, severe, rigid; mercy is soft and sweet. With the one are associated terms of stiffness, strength, and violence; with the other, images of bees, honey, and music. From *Astraea Redux* we know that Charles II's merciful goodness comes to him as his father's heir and as God's deputy (ll. 256–7); it comes to him because he holds his title *de jure divino*. The power which upheld the government of the Interregnum, which will uphold Charles II, but which his father lacked, is the ability to rule *de facto*. These and other pairs or oppositions contribute both to the polemic end and the final image of Dryden's early panegyrics. The pattern of thought that they represent was by no means peculiar to Dryden. The age witnessed multiple variations upon the classical inheritance of an Aristotelean schematization of conflicting extremes and *via media*, or of a *concordia discors*, that fruitful harmony of opposites, mythographically represented by the union of stern Mars and soft Venus, whose issue was the graceful Harmonia. We can find the operation of this pattern in such unlikely places as Dryden's theory of translation, with paraphrase a middle way between over-free imitation and over-literal metaphrase.[24] Similarly, Dryden's *Marriage à la Mode* uses a double plot to juxtapose a libertine and an idealized view of love, with a suggested *tertium quid* in the plea of Artemis, who has a minor role in each plot, for a view of marriage at once sensible and romantic.

Professor Wasserman has pointed out the large contribution of a *concordia discors* pattern to seventeenth-century governmental theory,[25] and it is sufficient to recall the flexibility of Bodin's royal monarch to realize that the resultant harmony need not be what the age called a limited and we a constitutional monarchy. Dryden's most frequently quoted description of the English monarchy is contained in four lines from *The Medal*:

> Our Temp'rate Isle will no extremes sustain,
> Of pop'lar Sway, or Arbitrary Reign:
> But slides between them both into the best;
> Secure in freedom, in a Monarch blest.

> (ll. 248–51)

The lines are always read as Dryden's clearest account of limited monarchy. But such an interpretation is by no means inevitable. In themselves the two couplets are equally appropriate to a limited or a royal monarch. The word *temperate* associates the lines with Bodin's influential adaptation of classical geography into the climate theory of government.[26] For Bodin, governments are a reflection of prevailing weather conditions. The hardy inhabitants of the frigid zone north of the 60th parallel were disposed to republican independence; the indolent inhabitants of the torrid zone in the tropics readily submitted to a life of slavery under a despot; the temperate zone between witnessed a judicious blend of northern popular sway and southern arbitrary reign in a royal monarchy which guaranteed individual freedom by the strong indivisible sovereignty of the king. So influential was this section of the *République* that it was inevitably modified in subsequent applications, and the temperate zone could accommodate a limited as easily as a royal monarchy. In isolation, then, Dryden's description is appropriate to both theories, but *The Medal*'s preceding strictures on parliamentary attempts to restrict the royal prerogatives (ll. 228–34) suggest that, in this poem at least, limited monarchy is not the preferred form.

In the despotic (or lordly) monarchy of the torrid zone the relationship between king and subject is that of master and slave. The royal monarch of the temperate zone shares with his subjects the relationship of father and son. The familial analogy served Dryden well throughout his poetic career; but it is most consistently explicit in the work during the early years of the Restoration. In the panegyric upon the king's coronation the power-mercy opposition is developed in terms of this analogy:

> When Empire first from families did spring,
> Then every Father govern'd as a King;
> But you that are a Sovereign Prince, allay
> Imperial pow'r with your paternal sway.
>
> (ll. 93–96)

The explicit statement of the opening line makes it clear that we are offered something more than the standard analogy between state and family. For his poetic purpose Dryden has adopted one theory of the historical origin of monarchy. As it is presented in these four lines it has none of the scriptural overtones that would associate it with the patriarchalist theory of the lineal descent of all kings from Adam, who was the first monarch by virtue of his sovereignty over Eve and the beasts of the field. But the emphasis on the continuity of past and present —an emphasis which asserts by the very balance of antithetical phrases the virtual contemporaneity of the two—recalls the similar emphasis of the poem's opening lines:

> In that wild Deluge where the World was drownd,
> When life and sin one common tombe had found,
> The first small prospect of a rising hill
> With various notes of Joy the Ark did fill:
> Yet when that flood in its own depths was drownd
> It left behind it false and slipp'ry ground;
> And the more solemn pomp was still deferr'd
> Till new-born Nature in fresh looks appeard:
> Thus (Royall Sir) to see you landed here
> Was cause enough of triumph for a year.

73

The epic simile's elaboration upon the conventional description of rebellion as the flood gives the figure a significance beyond its immediate role in providing a decorative explanatory parallel to the fact that the coronation was held in 1661 and not in 1660. Charles is associated with Noah, who was a major figure in the patriarchalist theory—indeed, he was indispensable to it. At this point there is clearly no theory, patriarchalist or otherwise; but the analogy anticipates the later statement and the wealth of benevolent and paternal images which the poem contains.

Dryden clearly found the idea of the king as *pater patriae* a poetic coin of wide currency, both as an apt expression of certain political attitudes and emotions and in its specifically patriarchalist associations. In addition, there are in these three panegyrics of 1660–2 frequent elaborations of what may conveniently be described as a Bodinian royal monarch. The coronation piece ends with a reference to Charles's martial projects and a picture of his subjects awaiting the outcome of his unilateral decision, which involves sufficient diplomatic considerations to make it a matter of national significance. The taking of the coronation oath by Charles is described earlier in the poem (ll. 65–74) as imposing upon him less of an obligation than his known virtues. The lottery has proved successful, for the nation has drawn a father and no tyrant, although the full extent of this good fortune was to be brought home only by the fire of 1666.

ANNUS MIRABILIS

Annus Mirabilis may be called Dryden's most ambitious poem, not for its length but because its formal requirements were unsuited to the talents Dryden elsewhere displays. His talent for panegyric (and vituperation) is certainly appropriate to the genre of historical poem to which he assigned the work, and Dryden in his prefatory letter to Howard described panegyric and historical poetry as branches of epic. The three genres draw upon the 'same images'; and, we might add, they adopt the same tone, elevated style, and general subject matter: the exploits of great men. But where epic and history arouse admiration principally through sustained narrative, panegyric works through such approved 'places' as the cardinal virtues, illustrating and demonstrating their possession by some great man through the description of selected exploits. These illustrative exploits are consequently linked thematically through the virtues which they separately exemplify rather than by narrative. Few critics of Dryden have failed to remark his 'inability' to maintain a coherent and interestingly diversified story: it is, traditionally, a major charge in the indictment of *Absalom and Achitophel*. But *Annus Mirabilis* is Dryden's only original poem which, by virtue of a clearly identified genre, may be relevantly considered in terms of its success or failure as narrative.

Quite simply, the first two-thirds of the poem, devoted to the Dutch War, are difficult to follow as the history of an event. A single passage may be offered as an example of the kind of incoherence to which I refer, and not, of course, as a complete validation of my remark. An eight-quatrain unit, recalling the units of the *Heroic Stanzas*, is devoted to the English attack on the Dutch East India fleet while it lay in Bergen harbour (ll. 93–124). Although the attack was largely unsuccessful, some of the rich cargo was captured (ll. 121–24), and this conditional Dutch failure after so long a voyage from the Indies leads easily into a skilful adaptation of a passage from Petronius on the vanity of human wishes (ll. 125–40). On the sea of life man is everywhere incident to shipwreck because, in the linking stanza, good and ill, true friends and secret enemies are known only to God; man himself is often deceived. As an example of such deception there is the Bishop of Münster:

> Let *Munsters* Prelate ever be accurst,
>   In whom we seek the *German* faith in vain:
> Alas, that he should teach the *English* first
>   That fraud and avarice in the Church could reign!
>
> Happy who never trust a Strangers will
>   Whose friendship's in his interest understood!
> Since money giv'n but tempts him to be ill
>   When pow'r is too remote to make him good.
>
> Till now, alone the Mighty Nations strove:
>   The rest, at gaze, without the Lists did stand:
> And threatning *France*, plac'd like a painted *Jove*,
>   Kept idle thunder in his lifted hand.
>
>   (ll. 145–56)
>
> *War declar'd by* France [marginal note in the original]

Editors explain that von Galen, the Bishop of Münster, was bribed by England to attack Holland, but came to terms with the Dutch when France entered the war against England. As Dryden refers to the episode (omitting to mention that Charles characteristically neglected to pay the bribe), it seems to be an unimpeachable example of false friendship. What is not at all clear is its connection with the immediately following account of France's entry into the war. The two quatrains devoted to von Galen are, of course, deficient in narrative content—we are not told in what way the Bishop has deceived England—but, even if we accept them as an allusion to an event whose details were well known to all who mattered, they constitute with France's declaration an unexplained inversion of events and a consequently confusing loss of narrative causation. The awkward transition here contrasts with the easy movement of thought from the battle of Bergen through the vanity of human wishes on the sea of life to the treachery of seeming friends. The Münster incident is, then, invoked to illustrate a thematic point, and its place in the story remains unclear.

The passage is illustrative of a general tendency in the poem to work from a proposition toward an illustrative episode, instead of, as in epic, from a narrative sequence toward the general principles that it is found to embody. What appears to have happened in *Annus Mirabilis* is that incidents are ordered to suit a narrative pattern, the history of the war, but are treated in terms of their thematic rather than their narrative significance. There is an incestuous union between those related genres of panegyric and historical poem; *Annus Mirabilis* is the curious issue.

It is a question of length, of course. With some application we can follow the developing argument of a long discursive poem like *Religio Laici* and the developing action of a sustained narrative like *Paradise Lost*. But in verse panegyric there is a limit to the number of discrete episodic pictures that we can apprehend as the total image of a man or group of men acting in accordance with some permutation upon the cardinal virtues. We rely heavily in *Annus Mirabilis* upon the marginal glosses, those brief captions to the stanzaic units informing us that we are reading a description of the first day's battle or his majesty repairing the fleet. Without them it would be difficult to follow the general course of the war and the narrative line of Dryden's poem, although the thematic relevance of the various units is certainly established. As recent commentators have pointed out, however much the action of *Annus Mirabilis* may concern the Dutch War and the great fire, its subject is properly identified as the greatness of England, its glorious scientific and especially mercantile destiny, its intrepid adventurers and courageous seamen; a greatness assured by the bond uniting a paternal monarch with his loyal subjects, by 'victory' in a trade war that removes England's only significant rival on the seas, and by a fire which both purges the lingering sin of civil war and clears the ground for the reconstruction of the capital city into a metropolis more suited to the nation's destiny.

The poem, then, does not lack coherence of a kind—although its lines are not always readily discernible through the over-similar descriptions of the sea engagements, each of them illustrating the same virtues of British loyalty and courage. What it does lack in the first two hundred stanzas is an imaginative excitement in the language. The pleasures of rhetoric are certainly there, although not consistently; and we have only to read the poem's assured opening and close to realize how far Dryden had advanced in his art since the elegy on Hastings. But as simile follows decorative simile, the vehicle illustrating but rarely adding to the point of the tenor, the lack of qualities Dryden elsewhere displays becomes crucial.

Although he described *Annus Mirabilis* as an historical poem, the long account of the Dutch War is provided with no detailed historical parallel that demonstrates its importance. What may now seem the obvious parallel, with the trade war between Rome and Carthage, is accorded only sporadic reference in *Annus Mirabilis*. It is possible that Dryden's usage helped establish the Restoration commonplace of a parallel between the Dutch and Carthaginian wars, a parallel which was most influentially employed a few years later in Shaftesbury's *Delenda est Carthago* speech. But the Carthaginian reference in *Annus Mirabilis* is too brief and infrequent for it to constitute a significant control in the poem. Instead, it becomes but one among the host of discrete allusions and Virgilian echoes with which Dryden tried to amplify his subject, whose significance had principally to be established in terms of itself.

77

The result in the first part of the poem is a consistent subordination of the local illustrations to the themes and events which they set off. Most obviously, the subordination occurs in those similes drawn from classical, especially Virgilian sources. Characteristically, such epic similes depend upon a physical analogy between tenor and vehicle: wounded warriors topple to the ground like trees; the bodies of the slain lie like fallen leaves; the cowardly despoiler of corpses is like a jackal picking over the kill of nobler beasts. There is a general likeness in the pictures suggested by the two halves of the analogy. Occasionally this is augmented, as in the last example, by a similarity in the moral implications of the two actions. But there is no necessity for a detailed correspondence, and the more complete the descriptions of the analogous actions, the less likely it is that a point-for-point correspondence will be possible: the similarities between the movements of a man and a jackal are not very many. In the first part of *Annus Mirabilis* such similes as the following are common:

> The foe approach'd: and one, for his bold sin,
>> Was sunk, (as he that touch'd the Ark was slain;)
> The wild waves master'd him, and suck'd him in,
>> And smiling Eddies dimpled on the Main.

> This seen, the rest at awful distance stood;
>> As if they had been there as servants set,
> To stay, or to go on, as he thought good,
>> And not persue, but wait on his retreat.

> So *Lybian* Huntsmen, on some sandy plain,
>> From shady coverts rouz'd, the Lion chace:
> The Kingly beast roars out with loud disdain,
>> And slowly moves, unknowing to give place.

> But if some one approach to dare his force,
>> He swings his tail, and swiftly turns him round:
> With one paw seizes on his trembling Horse,
>> And with the other tears him to the ground.
>
> (ll. 373–88)

It is difficult to see that the vehicle of the second two stanzas adds much to the physical and psychological relationship of the first two stanzas (and the second line of each of these stanzas supplies, in any case, a brief and effective simile). The general likeness of the lion hunt to Albemarle's retreat is obvious, although a number of its details have no correspondence in the tenor, for the sea lacks the equivalent of shady coverts and ships the equivalent of tails.

For Virgil and his audience, presumably, the general likeness was sufficient. It made relevant the introduction of other material from their world, and the similes thus contributed to the epic's realization of a whole society, civilization, or way of life. For Virgil the amplification was in part at least social or sociological; for Dryden it was wholly literary and his similes were strictly exotic. The point may be illustrated by comparison with a simile a few stanzas before that already quoted:

> Now, at each Tack, our little Fleet grows less;
>   And, like maim'd fowl, swim lagging on the Main.
> Their greater loss their numbers scarce confess
>   While they lose cheaper then the *English* gain.
>
> Have you not seen when, whistled from the fist,
>   Some Falcon stoops at what her eye design'd,
> And, with her eagerness, the quarry miss'd,
>   Straight flies at check, and clips it down the wind.
>
> The dastard Crow, that to the wood made wing,
>   And sees the Groves no shelter can afford,
> With her loud Kaws her Craven kind does bring,
>   Who, safe in numbers cuff the noble Bird?
>
> Among the *Dutch* thus *Albemarl* did fare:
>   He could not conquer, and disdain'd to flie.
> Past hope of safety, 'twas his latest care,
>   Like falling *Cesar*, decently to die.
>
> (ll. 337–52)

The confident 'have you not seen?' emphasizes that the material for the simile is drawn from native sources. If falconry was less widely practised after the civil war than it was earlier, it had still the associations of aristocracy and the noble life that were required in a simile for the courage in defeat of Albemarle. The full aptness of the simile mitigates the lack of correspondence between one or two of the details.

Despite the persuasiveness of recent commentators in arguing the general coherence and felicitous details of *Annus Mirabilis*, it is not clear that the old charge of Mark van Doren has been properly countered: 'the gravity with which . . . the last two lines of a stanza are made to serve up an absurd simile for garnishing the first two is the most lamentable feature of *Annus Mirabilis*. The attention is drawn down full upon the unfortunate comparison.'[27] Although I would wish to moderate the severity of van Doren's condemnation, he has pointed to what I take to be one source of my own dissatisfaction with the first part of the poem. To account for this dissatisfaction I have argued an insufficient narrative coherence, too great a sameness in the accounts of various engagements, a use of exotic similes which draw attention to their merely decorative function, and, indeed, a general tendency of the images to remain subordinate to a statement of literal description. When there are images drawn from the same source, as is the case with the numerous hunting images, their repetition brings nothing to the poem which is not effected by the individual occurrences: the whole set of hunting images is merely the sum of the separate references to hunting, and there is accordingly no meaningful 'pattern'; they are not thematic.

Almost inevitably, it seems, this discussion of *Annus Mirabilis* began with the question of genre: it is a question which insistently raises itself in the discussion of many of Dryden's poems (*Absalom and Achitophel* and *The Hind and the Panther* are obvious cases). However suspect the argument from genre may be and however inadequately it may account for literary excellence, it is none the less helpful at times in providing the terms of negative criticism. Too long for the effective control of its panegyric themes and with insufficient narrative coherence to justify its pretensions toward historical poem, *Annus Mirabilis* fails to provide a compensating imaginative intensity in the stanzas devoted to the Dutch War. What is lacking is any evidence that language is being used creatively to reveal the public values affirmed by the poem: the importance of loyalty, courage, or industry is so often asserted, and then decorated with a classical trope. We are aware, frequently, of a stridency in the tone of amplification. Because the separate figures of elevation do not refer to each other as figures, because the coherence obtains only in the repetition without development of ideas, general propositions, the disparity between tenor and vehicle is constantly emphasized. This charge may seem no more than a barely disguised plea for ubiquitous allegory or extended metaphor, and something of this kind appears necessary to compensate for the lack of narrative development, for the paucity of significant interplay between the episodes as episodes rather than as examples of virtue in action.

Whenever in Dryden's poems the public values inherent in his subject are affirmed in terms of themselves rather than created or re-created in terms of something else, there is a tendency for the praise to become adulatory and for the work to slip into a profusion, and confusion, of similes indicative of what van Doren described as Dryden's Ovidian fancy.[28] This tendency is apparent in many of his formal panegyrics from *Astraea Redux* to *Britannia Rediviva*. One solution was the low style of *Religio Laici*; the other, and more exciting, was through the creative use of analogy which led ultimately to *Absalom and Achitophel*. It is this kind of analogy which dominates the section of *Annus Mirabilis* devoted to the fire of London. The critical importance of the poem is precisely its dual nature, comprising what is best and what produces the least satisfactory in Dryden's work.

The tears of Hastings's smallpox and the tears of the English at Dover expressed the need for a penitential expiation of rebellion and usurpation, and it is a variation upon this belief which establishes in *Annus Mirabilis* the significance of the great fire. Any account of the fire stanzas must necessarily begin from Professor Hooker's illuminating reading of the poem, if only to suggest different emphases in interpretation. The crux lies in the respective weight we give to the purgative and the punitive qualities of the fire in Dryden's account. Professor Hooker stressed the former, and instanced the opening analogy with the cleansing flames of the *Dies Irae* (ll. 845–48), the related vision of London arising like a greater Phoenix from the ashes of a heaven-sent fire (ll. 1169–80), which Dryden took up again in the dedication of the poem, and the Londoners' successful undergoing of a fiery trial of their loyalty to Charles (ll. 1153ff.). But his argument does not seem to require the emphatic statement that the fire was 'not a judgment' and 'was not a wrath aimed to destroy.'

The fire did destroy, and there are many descriptive details of the destruction, while the fact that God wished the destruction is made explicit in a number of places. Most obviously, it is the assumption of the king himself, and his prayer surely represents an important attitude in the poem. It is, in fact, more accurate to say that Dryden allows equal weight to the dual aspect of the fire: the actual description reveals it as primarily punitive and destructive; its aftermath reveals it as a purgative test of loyalty that will be a prelude to the resurrection of a greater city. The transition is effected by Charles's successful intervention with the heavenly author of the flames.

The punishment of fire was visited upon the twenty-year-old crime of rebellion. There are a number of clear references, both in the king's prayer and in such passages as that giving the reason for the destruction of St. Paul's:

> The Dareing flames peep't in and saw from far,
> The awful beauties of the Sacred Quire:
> But, since it was prophan'd by Civil War,
> Heav'n thought it fit to have it purg'd by fire.
>
> (ll. 1101–4)

But the most convincing evidence is afforded by the total suggestions of the analogy Dryden selects to describe the origin and progress of the flames. The epic simile with which he opens his account establishes the terms upon which the whole section is to be read:

> As when some dire Usurper Heav'n provides,
> To scourge his Country with a lawless sway:
> His birth, perhaps, some petty Village hides,
> And sets his Cradle out of Fortune's way:
>
> Till fully ripe his swelling fate breaks out,
> And hurries him to mighty mischiefs on:
> His Prince surpriz'd at first, no ill could doubt,
> And wants the pow'r to meet it when 'tis known:
>
> Such was the rise of this prodigious fire,
> Which in mean buildings first obscurely bred,
> From thence did soon to open streets aspire,
> And straight to Palaces and Temples spread.
>
> (ll. 849–60)

The notes to the Clark Dryden suggest that the dire usurper is 'perhaps a reference to Cromwell, who came from the country and who was an obscure figure until the 1640's.' In fact, Cromwell's origins were so often referred to in accounts of his later life that the details in the last two lines of the first stanza—introduced with such seeming inconsequence—would have been, and are, sufficient to particularize the general comparison of the first two lines. However much it may be ordained in heaven, the rule of an usurper is 'a lawless sway' from a mortal viewpoint; and this glance at the continuing debate upon the nature of *de facto* rule indicates that, while the analogy of rebellion helps establish the significance of the fire, the significance of the rebellion itself is also the concern of this section. In the third stanza it is the fire which aspires (like the politically ambitious) to destroy palaces and temples, but the context of analogy helps recall the direction of the Great Rebellion against monarchy and episcopacy. These three stanzas might, indeed, be advanced as a textbook example of interchange between the two halves of a comparison. The customary syntax of an epic simile—its vehicle introduced by 'as when' followed or preceded by its tenor introduced by 'such'—is complicated here by the fact that the terms describing the tenor contain material even more appropriate to the vehicle, which is consequently developed by the tenor. The analogy established by this simile—of Cromwell, rebellion, and the surprised prince who, like Charles I in all the eulogies, was lacking in power—prepares for its subsequent development and allusive recall throughout the fire stanzas. The pathetic fallacy of the first part of the poem, with its animated winds and waves, seems the merest literary gesture beside the imaginative juxtaposition of the capricious, inanimate fire and the purposeful, animate rebellion. If by the end the fire has seemed the more terrible by its associations with animate purpose, the terror of rebellion has been no less augmented by its association with inanimate caprice.

The rebellious implications of the fire are reinforced by the subsequent description of it as unnatural and criminal. After a stanza describing the trustful sleep of the City, which recalls the earlier reference to Charles I's lack of preparation, Dryden returns to the topic of birth introduced in the account of Cromwell's origin. This time a monster is born rather than an usurper; but both creatures were distinguished by their violation of nature's law: usurpation was a monstrous act, and usurpers, like all rebels, traitors, and seditious opponents of the laws were frequently likened in royalist polemics to monsters, especially the monsters of Africa and the Nile. Where Cromwell was dismissed with a birth and a cradle, Dryden records the generation of the flames by the 'seeds of fire' and their gestation in a 'close-pent room,' as well as the birth and infancy of the monster (ll. 865–72). Just as the dire usurper thrust aside his unprepared prince, so this burning monster is about to usurp the 'silent reign' of the night, beneath which the city is peacefully sleeping (ll. 861–64). But usurpation and rebellion violate civil as well as natural law: they are acts both criminal and monstrous. The rapidly growing fire accordingly undergoes a further metamorphosis: the small room in which it began becomes a 'narrow Jail' (l. 877), and the monster turns into a 'rich or mighty Murderer' (l. 873), reminding us that the Great Rebellion culminated in regicide.

Once free from its confines, the now completely personified fire voraciously stalks across the city, and the parallel between fire and rebellion is emphasized by the vision of the ghosts of regicides and religious fanatics dancing like hags:

> The Ghosts of Traitors, from the *Bridge* descend,
>   With bold Fanatick Spectres to rejoyce:
> About the fire into a Dance they bend,
>   And sing their Sabbath Notes with feeble voice.
>
> (ll. 889–92)

It is not simply that regicides and fanatics are sufficiently ghoulish to delight in the spectacle of destruction, for the metaphoric direction of the passage makes it clear that they are celebrating their moment of triumph seventeen years earlier rather than rejoicing in the immediate calamity. The fanatics were to succeed again in the burning of St. Paul's, a symbolic repetition of the attack upon the established Church, but if the political traitors were thwarted on this second occasion, the analogy once again leaves us in no doubt of their attempt to repeat the overthrow of the monarchy. Later, the rapid movements of the fire are themselves likened to the nocturnal flights of witches (ll. 989–92): that the fire and the traitors can share an analogy in

itself emphasizes their consonance. As it increases, the fire becomes a cavalry charge in which each 'mighty Squadron' seeks
a separate victim:

> Another backward to the *Tow'r* would go,
>   And slowly eats his way against the wind:
> But the main body of the marching foe
>   Against th' Imperial Palace is design'd.
>
> (ll. 945–48)

It is difficult not to recall the part played by the army in the
Great Rebellion.

Finally, the fire is identified, not with the rebels of 1649, but
with the people of 1666:

> No help avails: for, *Hydra*-like, the fire,
>   Lifts up his hundred heads to aim his way.
> And scarce the wealthy can one half retire,
>   Before he rushes in to share the prey.
>
> The rich grow suppliant, and the poor grow proud:
>   Those offer mighty gain, and these ask more.
> So void of pity is th'ignoble crowd,
>   When others ruine may increase their store.
>
> (ll. 993–1000)

The juxtaposition in these two quatrains of the identical activities of the fire and the mob makes it apparent that the application of '*Hydra*-like' to the fire is by no means casual: it would
be difficult to find a more common analogy for the mob than
that of the many-headed monster.

The total suggestions of the developed analogy thus require
that great emphasis be placed upon the fire's punitive qualities.
Dryden is very much concerned to suggest that any divine
judgment has fallen upon the indubitable rebellion of the subjects rather than upon the debatable tyranny of the Stuarts. In
his prayer Charles tentatively presents himself as the man
responsible for God's wrath (ll. 1053–60), but his preceding
recollection of the civil war makes it clear that he accepts the
culpability of the people: his self-accusing alternative merely
argues his piety and humility. By associating fire with rebellion
Dryden not only indicated the destructive tendencies of any
overthrow of monarchy, he also represented the calamity of

1666 as a divinely apt judgment. By means of the analogy, the punishment is made to fit the crime much more accurately than would have appeared from a literal reading of the events: and 'since it was prophan'd by Civil War, / Heav'n thought it fit to have it purg'd by fire.' Professor Hooker was right to emphasize *purg'd*, but *fit* must also take a special emphasis.

Wars of all descriptions have always had an easy connection with fire, because fire customarily accompanies war and they are both instruments of destruction. Dryden's invention could not have been greatly exercised in seeking out this image: it was always likely to occur in seventeenth-century discussions of rebellion. What exercised him was the finding of more and more correspondences between an actual fire and an actual war; and in the working out of these correspondences the stale commonplace becomes imaginatively new: it is poetic originality in the only sense of the word that merits critical currency. But the relationship between the two elements in the historical parallel, the fire and the rebellion, is by no means fixed. The fire is like the rebellion in its overthrow of peace; its progress is like the progress of Cromwell, who is here principally an aspect or particularization of the rebellion. But the fire is also a punishment for rebellion, and purges its lingering sin. At times, as in the ghost stanza, it is difficult to distinguish fire from rebellion; at others their course and significance are almost exactly parallel, as in the opening simile and the stanzas describing the looting; on still other occasions, when the fire punishes and purges the sin of rebellion, the parallel disappears to be replaced by a complementary—here causative—relationship. The fact that such analogies in Dryden indifferently involve identity, simile and complement perhaps explains their large potential for a creative interchange between the roles of the nominal tenors and vehicles.

As is usually the case in Dryden's poems, the point of the analogy can be stated with rather less distortion than often attends such a procedure. Professor Hooker pointed out that part of heaven's design in sending the fire was to tighten the bonds between the king and the people by revealing the nation's dependence upon monarchy in time of crisis. But the analogy takes us beyond this. In 1649 the people rejected their rulers, executing one king and exiling another. Their reward was the political and religious devastation of the land under the 'tyranny' of the Commonwealth and Protectorate. In 1666 the more obvious physical horror of the insurgent fire demonstrated to the people their dependence upon the king, especially when he paternally 'open'd wide / His stores, and all the poor with plenty fed' (ll. 1141–42). The fact that the fire, unlike the rebellion, stopped short of the palace did not prevent the people from fearing that the accomplishment of partial ruin would drive their king away (ll. 1145–48), just as the analogous ruin of 1649 had successfully forced him into exile. Similarly, the remark that the people 'have not lost their Loyalty by fire' (l. 1153) is surely more than unambiguous eulogy: the parallel upon which Dryden has insisted throughout must have enforced a vivid recollection of the manner in which the people lost their loyalty by rebellion.

THE MEDAL

Towards the close of *The Medal* Dryden apostrophizes Shaftesbury in terms that recall God's judgment on the serpent in the Garden of Eden:

> But thou, the Pander of the Peoples hearts,
> (O Crooked Soul, and Serpentine in Arts,)
> Whose blandishments a Loyal Land have whor'd,
> And broke the Bonds she plighted to her Lord;
> What Curses on thy blasted Name will fall!
> Which Age to Age their Legacy shall call;
> For all must curse the Woes that must descend on all.
>
> (ll. 256–62)

Shaftesbury, the Satanic snake of an English Paradise, is cursed for persuading the Eve-like subjects of Charles II to commit the political original sin of rebelling against the authority of their Adamic king. The Satanic suggestions are to some extent anticipated by two apparently casual remarks earlier in the poem. When Shaftesbury abandoned the hopeless task of seducing his virtuous king to tyrannical rule and determined upon the easier course of seducing the people to rebellion, we are told that he showed 'the Fiend confess'd, without a vaile' (l. 81). Still earlier, when Dryden comments upon the length of time required by the engraver to capture a likeness of Shaftesbury for the obverse of the medal, he speculates, with seeming inconsequence, on 'how long Heav'n was making *Lucifer*' (l. 21). The speculation is certainly in itself a satiric gibe at Shaftesbury, and its local effectiveness may obscure its contribution to an analogy that runs throughout the poem.

Recent studies of *Absalom and Achitophel* have accustomed us to Dryden's association of the arch opponent of his king with the arch opponent of God;[30] Dryden himself made the association explicit in the dedicatory epistle to *Absalom and Achitophel*. The sacred aura with which the theory of divine right surrounded a king helped give currency to one part of the formula, while the attempted rebellion of Satan provided the remaining part. Professor Schilling has argued that the biblical associations of serpent and devil were almost unavoidable in Restoration accounts of political deception, and it was perhaps inevitable that Dryden should employ Satanic imagery in *The Medal* so soon after its successful use in *Absalom and Achitophel*.

But in *The Medal*, while still availing himself of the general emotions prompted by such imagery, Dryden extended the theoretic associations of Satan's activities to include at one end a basis principle of ethics and at the other a long-standing dispute over the nature of God. Between these extremes the poem develops a restatement of Dryden's views on true and false government. The connection between ethics, politics, and theology is assisted by the established pattern of correspondences between the control of will by reason, of woman by man, Eve by Adam, subject by king, and mankind by God.[31]

The poem's first seventeen lines contain the well-known description of the City Whigs assembling to marvel at the newly-minted medal celebrating Shaftesbury's release from the Tower after a Bill indicting him for high treason had been rejected by the grand jury. This medal Dryden likens to an idol, which, as a medal, is 'golden to the sight' (l. 8). The biblical overtones of the image of false gods are reinforced a few lines later by the picture of a Whig sheriff pronouncing aloud 'The Word,' *Laetamur* or *rejoyce* (ll. 14–15). Literally, the sheriff does so because *Laetamur* was inscribed on the medal's reverse as a token of Whig jubilation at their leader's release. But in Dryden's imaginary scene the sheriff acquires the stature of a false prophet pronouncing the word of his false god by blasphemously echoing the psalmist's injunction to rejoice in the Lord.

The religious suggestions of these opening lines are confirmed by the fact that the day of Shaftesbury's acquittal, November 24th (1681), is to be established as a 'new Canting Holiday' (l. 17), an annual celebration by hypocritical Puritans, whose doctrinal principles were, for a royalist like Dryden, the religious counterpart of Whiggish republicanism.

In view of the undoubtedly riotous nature of the Whig celebration of Shaftesbury's release,[32] Dryden's imaginary scene is not wholly gratuitous. It is none the less imaginary, whereas the remainder of the poem adheres, if not to unequivocal facts, at least to accepted royalist interpretations of actual events. The fictitious nature of the opening scene, allowing as it does greater freedom to Dryden's satiric imagination, may account for the fact that it is usually regarded as superior to the remainder of the poem. More importantly, perhaps, it permitted Dryden to establish the mood, suggestiveness, and direction of the poem's argument more economically than if he had closely followed the actual events. In *Absalom and Achitophel* the Satanic associations derive naturally from the Old Testament setting; it is perhaps not too much to say that the imaginary opening scene performs for *The Medal* much the same function as is performed for *Absalom and Achitophel* by the biblical fable.

What the opening scene establishes is that Shaftesbury is a false god and a false king who has issued in the medal, with its depiction of title, face, king, and palace (ll. 10–11), a counterfeit coinage (l. 9) rivalling the currency of the true king. His seditious and dissenting supporters follow the false god, which is also a 'Monster' (l. 4), with the overtones it had in *Annus Mirabilis* of a creature that departs from the law of nature in much the same way that a rebel departs from the law of the land. The analogy between rebel and monster was frequently drawn, and Dryden later makes use of one of the more common versions when he compares the seditious London merchants with the monstrous fauna of Africa by converting the Thames into another Nile (ll. 171–74). The terms of these opening lines; the concentration upon Shaftesbury, the Whigs, and the Puritans, anticipates the division of attention in the remainder of the poem, while the specific association of Shaftesbury with a false god develops into a complex of Satanic imagery that is central to the poem's meaning.

The golden idol of the opening lines is quickly and specifically replaced by Lucifer (l. 21). But the context of this Satanic reference is Dryden's speculation on the many changes in Shaftesbury's character and intentions during his career, and, when we recall the allusive employment of *Paradise Lost* in *Absalom and Achitophel*, it is not difficult to see a parallel between the metamorphoses of Milton's Satan and those of Dryden's political devil. Just as Satan whispered to the sleeping Eve in the guise of a toad, so Shaftesbury was a 'Vermin, wriggling in th'Usurper's Ear' (l. 31), and the common analogy between court favourite and earwig gains added point from the Miltonic echo. Satan disguised himself as a 'stripling Cherube' (III, 636) to deceive Uriel, and his action was specifically that of 'Hypocrisie' (III, 683); Shaftesbury 'cast himself into the Saint-like mould' (l. 33), although his 'Hypocritique Zeal' (l. 38) was less successful than Satan's in that it was discerned by men as well as God. When his Commonwealth aspirations were thwarted, Shaftesbury bowed to the restored king:

> Pow'r was his aym: but, thrown from that pretence,
> The Wretch turn'd loyal in his own defence;
> And Malice reconcil'd him to his Prince.
> Him, in the anguish of his Soul he serv'd.
>
> (ll. 50–53)

Satan, 'rackt with deep despare' (I. 126), was particularly subject to anguish and malice, and the turn in Dryden's last line is strikingly Miltonic. When Ithuriel and Zephon discover Satan, 'Squat like a Toad, close at the eare of *Eve*' (IV, 800), a touch from Ithuriel's spear reveals the disguise: 'So started up in his own shape the Fiend' (IV, 819). When Shaftesbury abandons the direct struggle with the king, apparently hoping to depose Charles after first rendering him odious to the country, and determines upon the more cunning course of corrupting the people, we are told that he 'shews the Fiend confess'd, without a vaile' (l. 81).

In *Paradise Lost* Satan makes two distinct attacks upon God, one direct and in heaven, the other indirect and on earth. Dryden's account of Shaftesbury's career also divides into two main endeavours: a direct attempt to overthrow the ruler while he held office prior to 1673 and an indirect attempt to persuade the people to rebel against their king during the Exclusion crisis. The first and direct attempt of both Satan and Shaftesbury met with total failure; their second and indirect attempt met with the partial success of a fortunate fall by Adam and Eve and (it may be) by the people of England. Just as the descendants of Adam and Eve had to suffer for the sin of the first parents, until they were redeemed by the Son of God, so (if Shaftesbury should succeed) the descendants of rebellious Englishmen will suffer 'the Woes that must descend on all' (l. 262) for the political crimes of their forbears, until their return to 'a rightfull Monarch's Breast' (l. 322) brings redemption from the anarchy of faction, dissent, and endless revolution (ll. 289–319). The closing prophecy of *The Medal* thus finds a counterpart in the prophecy delivered to Adam by Michael at the end of *Paradise Lost*.

In *Absalom and Achitophel* the Miltonic references appear to function in part at least as a means to lend the poem epic dignity. But in *The Medal* the lack of a formal narrative makes a similar function unlikely, although it is true that as an essay in satiric vituperation, and therefore of inverted panegyric, *The Medal* would for Dryden be akin to epic in its choice of subject and tone. The chief function of the Satanic and related references in *The Medal* seems to be, in fact, to provide a visual and metaphoric background to the theoretic discussion and therefore to provide a poetic justification for it. It is because Dryden chooses to consider disloyalty, rebellion, and treason to some extent at least in terms of their theological implications that the divine and Edenic imagery is central to the poem.

The polemic point of *The Medal* is that any argument to justify the overthrow of a king must be based upon a particular (and, for a royalist, erroneous) view of the nature of royal authority. But since the king is God's deputy with an authority analogous to the divine, that erroneous view of royal authority must comprehend or imply a similarly erroneous view of God's authority. Such a paraphrase reveals the fallacy in Dryden's argument; for it assumes that the republican shares the royalist's view of a meaningful analogy between divine and kingly rule, whereas republican attempts to limit or eliminate royal authority were chiefly based upon an assumption that no such analogy between God and king existed: the king rules not because he is

God's deputy, but because his authority is delegated to him from the people, to whom he is responsible for the administration of his office.

To justify his employment of a republican divine analogy to balance the royalist divine analogy Dryden accordingly made use of what is, strictly, a logical fallacy. This fallacy is introduced in a manner typical of what might be called Dryden's technique of insinuation, whereby a point is first presented figuratively or humorously and then assumed to have actual validity in the succeeding argument. By this means a reader's surprised rejection of a logical fallacy is checked and even obviated, since, once he has agreed to accept the point as a figure or sarcastic aside, he is less likely to reject the point when it later appears with an assumption of validity. Dryden frequently employed a version of this technique in his panegyrics, where the person praised is first superficially likened to some divinity or hero by means of epic simile and then assumed to possess further qualities of that divinity or hero.

In *The Medal* the insinuation is made possible through sarcasm rather than simile. When Shaftesbury abandons the direct assault on Charles II's virtue and turns to the more easily corruptible people,

> He preaches to the Crowd, that Pow'r is lent,
> But not convey'd to Kingly Government;
> That Claimes successive bear no binding force;
> That Coronation Oaths are things of course;
> Maintains the Multitude can never err;
> And sets the People in the Papal Chair.
>
> (ll. 82–87)

Dryden is offering a fairly accurate, if undeniably contemptuous, statement of the republican theory of popular sovereignty, concluding with the natural deduction that the people are always right. For the seventeenth century whoever possessed the ultimate sovereignty must be legally incapable of wrong, because the possessor of ultimate authority on earth could not be impeached for crimes except before the court of God. Thus, the royalist theory of direct donation from God to king entailed the corollary that 'Kings can doe no wrong,' as Dryden himself asserts later in the poem (l. 135). Similarly, if a republican view of sovereignty is adopted, then the people, whenever they act as a body, can legally do no wrong. Whoever possesses the ultimate sovereignty is, by virtue of being human, quite capable of moral wrong or political injustice. Royalists were prepared to admit that a king may be evil, may be a tyrant, but insisted that because he was sovereign he could not be held legally culpable (even though a scapegoat minister like Strafford might well be).

Logically, therefore, once Dryden has agreed for the sake of argument to accept popular sovereignty, he should follow the theory that such an acceptance entails. But a few lines later he sarcastically questions the 'right' of the people in their pursuance of contradictory acts: 'to kill the Father, and recall the Son' (l. 100). Even if the people were wrong, it is apparent that by the theory of popular sovereignty they were so on moral grounds alone, and no qualification of their legal infallibility could be implied by their actions. That Dryden's gibe does not appear irrelevant is made possible by his conversion of legal into moral right through a sarcastic insinuation. Dryden follows his statement of republican popular sovereignty with an explanation:

> The reason's obvious; *Int'rest never lyes;*
> The most have still their Int'rest in their eyes;
> The pow'r is always theirs, and pow'r is ever wise.)
>
> (ll. 88–90)

Dryden is giving what is, for his purposes, the real reason that lies behind rationalizations about the divine donation of sovereignty to the people, but if we accept the validity of Dryden's reason, we must also, as royalist sympathizers, reject the validity of republican divine sanction. Dryden, however, proceeds to couple his 'reason' with a false divine sanction:

> Almighty Crowd, thou shorten'st all dispute;
> Pow'r is thy Essence; Wit thy Attribute!
>
> (ll. 91–92)

When he speaks of the power of the people, he is doing no more than echo the royalist view that subjects have the ability to confer *de facto* recognition of a king's rule. But when he ironically deifies the people as an 'Almighty Crowd,' he is providing them with a divine analogy which is, in political terms, only appropriate to a king. On the one hand his explanation of the people's infallibility by way of might is right implicitly denies the divine analogy, while on the other hand his deification of the people explicitly supplies it. If we accept the charge of self-interest as a sarcastic revelation of what the crowd is like in practice, we are less likely to be alert to the false logic of the crowd's deification, which assumes the theoretic as well as the practical validity of the charge.

By means of the insinuation Dryden is in a position to balance his discussion upon two opposed views of sovereignty, each with a divine analogy: against a genuine royalist theory of God and the king we have a largely fabricated republican theory of the people, authority, and God. The fact that it is not wholly fabricated naturally lends Dryden's argument greater plausibility. The opposition thus established derives from a long-standing dispute over the nature of God which it would be both tedious and unnecessary to recount in detail. Tedious because it has been well-documented elsewhere, and unnecessary because Dryden's usage, as might be expected, depends upon a simplified distinction that ignores theological subtleties.

The difference may be most compendiously described as a dispute over whether the faculty of reason or of will should be allowed pre-eminence in God and man.[33] By the intellectualist theory of Aquinas and later of Hooker, God's actions are an expression of his infinite wisdom and justice; because they are so men ought to be obedient to them. Moreover, an ethics dependent upon this theology subordinates the desire of the good and the will to achieve it to the judgment of the reason. It is through reason that man most fully realizes his specifically human potential in the ultimate contemplation of the rational harmony of God. In the sphere of politics a Thomistic God easily suggests the concept of a king *de jure divino* who should be obeyed because that is the just, reasonable, and pious thing to do, although it is important to remember that Aquinas himself adopted the more republican view of a divine donation of sovereignty to the people, who delegate it to the ruler. Aquinas exemplifies that however much the early republicans may have assumed an analogy between God and man, they did not assume a direct analogy between practical political rule and the rule of God.

Opposed to Thomistic intellectualism was the voluntarism of

Scotus, Ockham, and, later, of Hobbes. Scotus felt that God's acts were just, reasonable, and to be followed by man because God had willed them and because the strength of his will was greater than that of anyone else. An ethics dependent upon this theology entails, as it does in Hobbes, a view of the good not as something selected and approved by the reason, but as something desired by the will. Since it is the will which provides our effective power of action, the contingent politics emphasized the ruler's power or ability to maintain his position, rather than his just right to do so.

In its original terms the dispute resolves itself into a question of what is the divine essence and what are the divine attributes. Both Scotus and Aquinas realized that it is false in an absolute sense to discuss the essence and attributes of God, but from the human point of view some distinction could be drawn. The Thomistic God is pure existence, but for the purposes of man's obedience God's essence is his pure wisdom or intelligence, his attribute is the power of his wilful act. On the other hand, and still from this mortal viewpoint, the essence of the Scotist God consists in his irresistible will: what God wills is to be obeyed because he is omnipotent. The Scotist God wills in accordance with his own infinite wisdom and to that extent divine understanding precedes divine will. But since divine will cannot err, it is in a sense true that it does not need the divine wisdom to direct it. To a point, then, intelligence is an attribute of the Scotist God, although such a formulation grossly oversimplifies the subtle doctor.

As might be expected, the arch opponent of Dryden, as of any orthodox royalist at this time, was Hobbes; to be more precise, perhaps, it was Hobbism, that theory of supreme authority based upon extracts from the more voluntaristic passages in *Leviathan*. As far as the Stuart apologists were concerned, Hobbes was a Hobbist, and they were willing to adduce evidence to prove it. They could point to passages in which reason is given only a subordinate role in the business of living, passages in which Leviathan is permitted his sway only as long as he is physically able to retain it.[34] What the orthodox royalists appeared most to fear from Hobbism was a sanction which, when logically considered, opened the way to a succession of usurpers as first one man or party and then another seized the supreme power that carried with it the right to govern. The closing prophecy of *The Medal* presents the anarchy of such a succession, and it is, for Dryden, no vision because the progress of events detailed there follows closely the course of the Great Rebellion from the first proffering of the Covenant to the eventual restoration of Charles II.

Power, ethically the will to act, theologically the divine omnipotence, was politically a largely material factor. The word itself is no more than an abstract of strong arms and military force, and bigger muscles or a better equipped army can obviously overcome it. But both justice and reason are intangible and absolute: true justice cannot be defeated by truer justice, nor can right reason be subdued by reason more correct.

The whole ethical rejection of Shaftesbury and the Whigs is based upon the charge of self-interest. When what is desired is the good, the way is open to a wilful indulgence of the appetites; in terms of gluttony, to 'long for Quails' (l. 131) and to loathe the manna which is here, as elsewhere in Dryden, an image for patriarchalist royal bounty and beneficence. Chiefly, however, this self-indulgence is presented in terms of the greed that is permitted by the opening concentration upon the pecuniary aspects of the medal. It was earlier pointed out that Dryden treats the Whig medal as an issue of counterfeit coinage, and this suggestion is recalled by a later couplet in which attempts to limit royal sovereignty are likened to the act of clipping legal tender within the circle surrounding the king's head (ll. 228–29). Both counterfeiting and clipping were high treason and were accordingly punishable by death; and both serve to emphasize the pecuniary ambitions of the opposition. These ambitions were observable in Shaftesbury as early as the Protectorate, when he could be seen 'Bart'ring his venal wit' to Cromwell in return for 'sums of gold' (l. 32). His love of pelf he shared with the Puritans, who piously refused to engage in legitimate trade, but did not hesitate to engage in secret traffic without licence (l. 41). The apparently casual suggestions earlier in the poem are collected and discharged in the address to London, 'thou great *Emporium* of our Isle' (l. 167). Shaftesbury's love of material gain was early converted into an unmitigated concentration upon power (l. 50). But the City Whigs are attracted to the notion of popular rights because of its possibilities for material aggrandizement. The benefits of trade which they should bring to the whole nation are instead converted into a concentration upon personal riches. Because that concentration represents the City's unethical *summum bonum*, everything which contributes to it is virtuous as far as they are concerned.

The natural political extension of this selfish ethic is either a tyranny or an anarchy reminiscent of the Hobbesian state of nature. Dryden makes use of both versions in his rejection of Whiggism. The seventeenth century understood a tyrant to be any ruler who consulted his self-interest to the neglect of the good of his people: his actions were arbitrary in the strict sense. For Dryden, it is the people who have become an 'Arbitrary Crowd' (l. 142), and their anarchy of individualistic self-interest is revealed in his picture of the London merchants cheerfully defrauding each other (ll. 191–94) and in his representation of the extreme Whigs, who

> grinn and whet like a *Croatian* Band;
> That waits impatient for the last Command.
> Thus Out-laws open Villany maintain:
> They steal not, but in Squadrons scoure the Plain:
> And, if their Pow'r the Passengers subdue;
> The Most have right, the wrong is in the Few.
> (ll. 240–45)

Similarly, the identification of Shaftesbury with Jehu, the most famous of the biblical usurpers (l. 119), and the implicit identification of him with Cromwell (ll. 129–30) together make clear what are those political ends that Shaftesbury's 'greedy Hopes devour' (l. 274). Like Satan, Shaftesbury aspires to usurp the throne of his ruler. Like Satan, Shaftesbury takes as his political excuse his ruler's pronouncement upon the succession, and at least like Milton's Satan,[35] Shaftesbury makes the mistake of assuming that his ruler is most properly defined in terms of his *de facto* power and can therefore reasonably be challenged and ultimately deposed by a superior power.

Just as in its ironic deification the crowd has power as its essence and wit or intelligence as its attribute (ll. 91–92), so in its Shaftesbury-inspired view of kingship the crowd defines its ruler in terms of his power to govern, not in terms of his inherited right to do so. Since the 'Almighty Crowd' expresses a

divine analogy, its view of the king must imply a similar analogy
by way of voluntarism:

> If Sovereign Right by Sovereign Pow'r they scan,
> The same bold Maxime holds in God and Man:
> God were not safe, his Thunder cou'd they shun
> He shou'd be forc'd to crown another Son.
> Thus, when the Heir was from the Vineyard thrown,
> The rich Possession was the Murth'rers own.
>
> (ll. 213–18)

When it is recalled that Satan's revolt was immediately inspired
by his jealousy at the presentation of the Son of God, while the
attempted Whig revolution of those years accepted as its rally-
ing cry no popery and the contingent exclusion of James, it is
obvious that Dryden is fashioning a close parallel between the
mortal and angelic rebellions, which was, in more general
terms, conventional royalist doctrine. The attempted exclusion
of the Son of God is, in any case, immediately translated into the
human terms of the biblical parable, which Dryden slants toward the political situation by emphasizing the vineyard (possession of which was in those years one of the most common
representations of individual freedom) and by omitting Christ's
use of the parable to prophesy his crucifixion and the subsequent
wrath of the Father. The passage, in fact, like the poem as a
whole, maintains a careful balance between the divine and the
human, the theological and the political, which intensifies the
crimes with which Dryden charges Shaftesbury without re-
moving the discussion altogether from the realm of men.

Dryden is engaged in illustrating the political commonplace
that sedition and open rebellion transgress divine and natural
law: Shaftesbury and his followers rush toward tyranny and
anarchy (ll. 119–22), allowing neither 'Faith nor Reason' to
check their impetuous progress (ll. 93–94). Because their king,
unlike their God, is not omnipotent, it is more than likely that
their impious endeavours will meet with temporary success:
they had done so, after all, in the deposition and execution of
Charles I. But because their king and his title to government
were a manifestation of divine wisdom and justice, it was inevitable that their temporary success should result in a return
to a hereditary monarchy more firmly established than be-

fore, just as it had in 1660. Shaftesbury and the Whigs merely take their places in the roll-call of those who have vainly attempted to subvert the form of government most natural to man, and who, as the royalists never seemed to tire of pointing out, serve the interests of the monarchic system they would overthrow by demonstrating its inevitability and indispensability.

Closely interwoven in the poem with the wilful irrationality of the political factions is the irrational inspiration of the Puritan sects. In strictly sociological terms such a connection was justifiable, since the association of the country party with dissent had been adequately demonstrated during the Great Rebellion. In the context of the poem there is further justification. The lineal descent of Presbyterian and Congregationalist from Calvinism manifested itself in their postulate of a *deus absconditus* who had withdrawn from the world leaving only the Bible as an indication of his will.[36] The dependence of Anglican and Catholic alike on the light innate of natural reason as well as on the infused or revealed light of scripture rendered their position hostile to the Puritans. Calvin agreed that God's wisdom was manifested in the Creation, but insisted that man's postlapsarian will was so infected that without the aid of faith the divine manifestation was of small help in man's ascent to God.[37] As far as man was concerned, the Calvinist doctrine of predestined election or reprobation could appear as no more than the wilful act of an arbitrary God—a tyrant, as Dryden calls him in *The Medal*:

> A Tyrant theirs; the Heav'n their Priesthood paints
> A Conventicle of gloomy sullen Saints;
> A Heav'n, like *Bedlam*, slovenly and sad;
> Fore-doom'd for Souls, with false Religion, mad.
>
> (ll. 283–86)

The Puritans were 'mad' because they rejected the support of reason, rejected the possibility that the rational pursuit of virtue could have any influence upon the arbitrary decision of their God.[38]

In *The Medal* the Puritans are no longer the amusingly pathetic 'Host of dreaming Saints . . . / Of the true old Enthusiastick breed' that they were in *Absalom and Achitophel* (ll. 529–30).

They are hypocrites (l. 38), 'puft up with spiritual Pride' (l.298) who 'plead a Call to preach, in spight of Laws' (l. 157) that deprived all those who refused to accept the Anglican Prayer Book of the livings to which they had been appointed during the Interregnum. Ethically, their much-boasted 'Godliness' is represented as a mere disguise for personal advancement (l. 34). Theologically, their God is a tyrant. Politically, their argument that impious kings (kings, that is, who do not hold their tenets) may lawfully be deposed is conventionally associated with the similar teaching of some of the Jesuits (ll. 199–204), for both old priest and new presbyter insisted upon some version of the popular sovereignty that was so inimical to the Stuart theory of divine right. Dryden can thus remark with particular significance—as well as a pun—that the doctrine of popular sovereignty 'sets the People in the Papal Chair' (l. 87).

Consolidating the activities of Puritan and Whig is the Satanic Shaftesbury, the idol and the monster, the god of the sects (l. 269) and the lord of the factions (l. 144). Shaftesbury's personal god—for he too must have a divine analogy—is the very Satan with whom Dryden metaphorically identifies him in the course of the poem, for his is a god

> That unconcern'd can at Rebellion sit;
> And Wink at Crimes he did himself commit.
>
> (ll. 281–82)

The epigraph to *The Medal* refers to King Salmoneus, who aspired to be worshipped as Zeus by his subjects and who was destroyed by Zeus for his impiety. Shaftesbury is already king of the mob, of the brisk boys of Wapping, but he wishes for the even greater power of usurping monster and idolatrous deity. His incitement of the sects is intended to lead, however, not merely to the deposition of the king but to the abolition of kingship itself (ll. 203–12). If the Shaftesbury of Dryden's poem is aiming at any particular title (and Dryden is admittedly not explicit) it is that of Lord Protector, a king in everything but name. The direction of Shaftesbury's personal ambition is further suggested by the opening reference to the 'Polish joke': the report, greeted with royalist derision, that Shaftesbury had intrigued for the electoral throne of Poland when it fell vacant a few years before. The medal is a '*Polish Medall*' because it makes clear Shaftesbury's aspirations to rule by its pretension to rival—and to counterfeit—the royal currency. Poland, as Professor Wasserman has pointed out, is identical with England, or at least with the England of Shaftesbury's ambitions.[39]

As an upholder of order, of course, Dryden would have preferred that Shaftesbury be checked before his ambitions reached a stage that necessitated the rather lengthy and certainly painful process of correction detailed in the closing prophecy. To the royalists it had seemed possible that Shaftesbury's appearance before the grand jury in November 1681 would be the initial step in a move to check his activities. Shaftesbury's acquittal and the subsequent Whig jubilation argued the need for further efforts to obviate what must have seemed an imminent civil war. Dryden's poem does not merely satirize the medal, for it reviews much of the evidence presented at the Old Bailey hearings on the bill of indictment.[40] The grand jury's unsurprising reluctance to accept the testimony of the infamous Irish witnesses (borrowed or hired from the Popish Plot trials) is attacked by Dryden almost as strongly as Shaftesbury's reputed leadership of the Protestant Association for altering the succession, which had comprised the circumstantial part of the evidence at the Old Bailey. Dryden's poem, then, may be in part described as a restatement of the evidence for Shaftesbury's treason in the light of his supporters' activities during the months following the trial. For this reason *The Medal* is an attack on both Shaftesbury and his supporters, and it is important to remember this fact when reading the opening lines.

If the topical context is borne in mind, there are grounds for seeing the poem as a poetic version of forensic oratory in which Dryden, as royal advocate, reopens the case against Shaftesbury. In these terms, Dryden's argument begins with a *narratio* or statement of the case that is amplified by reference to the past sedition of Shaftesbury and his followers in order to render the current charge more plausible (ll. 1–144). Then follows a proof consisting of an attempt to discredit the previous adverse verdict by attacking the grand jury and of an examination of the treasonable implications of the proposed Association (ll. 145–255). Because no overt act of treason could be charged against Shaftesbury to secure indictment under the statute of 25 Edward III, Lord Chief Justice Pemberton invoked at the Old Bailey hearings the treason act of 1661, which required proof only of an intention to kill or overthrow the king. As Dryden puts it:

> In vain to Sophistry they have recourse: ⎫
> By proving theirs no Plot, they prove 'tis worse; ⎬
> Unmask'd Rebellion, and audacious Force. ⎭
> Which, though not Actual, yet all Eyes may see
> 'Tis working, in th'immediate Pow'r to be.
>
> (ll. 219–23)

Although there is no need for a formal refutation in a prosecution speech delivered before the defence has been offered, the final cursing of Shaftesbury is strikingly similar to a *refutatio* based simply upon the disgust excited by the charges (ll. 256–72). The closing prophecy is, of course, a peroration that focuses attention upon the nation-wide implications of Shaftesbury's actions. If the work possesses an exordium, it must be sought in the prefatory epistle, much of which is given over, in the approved fashion, to a tacit recommendation of the advocate as properly instructed and as motivated by worthy principles.[41]

The rhetorical pattern entails no restrictive or unpermissive framework. It exists as the means to the oratorical end of Dryden's philippic: to demonstrate that Shaftesbury and his supporters are guilty of high treason. Beyond that, it provides continuous opportunities for the illustration of the poem's main proposition that any attempt to overthrow the hereditary monarchy of England constitutes an offence against reason, against the country, and against God. The validity of this tripartite proposition is urged by multiple restatement and illustration. Of the illustrations, those associated with the divine analogy are the most striking and have therefore been considered in some detail, although no full reading of the poem can safely ignore those images associated with the argument from nature.

Taken together, the illustrative analogies reinforce a thematic unity in the poem which is first stated in the imaginative opening description of the medal, and this circumstance is perhaps sufficient justification for the title. When seen as a form of forensic oration, the poem exhibits an argumentative progression toward a demonstration of the treason of Shaftesbury and his followers. One indication of their criminality is the striking of the medal, an act which becomes in the poem equivalent to the treasonous issuing of counterfeit coin, and this 'indication' of the Whigs' continued treason after Shaftesbury's acquittal is further justification for the title. The rhetorical pattern checks the tendency of the satire toward rambling discursiveness, while the analogies and the tripartite proposition generalize the limiting specificity of the philippic. *The Medal* derives part of its coherence from a skilled handling of verse argument, yet the advocate presents his case, not in a courtroom, but in a strange country compounded of England and the multifarious analogies of political debate. It is a country where Salmoneus jostles Satan, where golden idols are worshipped in the market-place, and where royal Adam experiences domestic difficulties with his subject Eve. The capital city straddles an estuary on whose muddy shores a horde of seditious reptiles is engendered; while overhead the admonitory thunder of celestial battles may be heard as another serpent displays his art by the banks of a different Nile.

The Kingdom of Adam

O F the materials available to the encomiast of politicians and great men those derived from the classical and Christian myths of a golden age were perhaps the most obvious and were certainly among the most frequently employed. The idea of a society of ideal innocence from which man had degenerated readily suggested a pattern of praise based upon a prophecy of the ruler's ability to restore to his people the conditions of this lost age. These conditions were not, it is true, to be literally restored, for the panegyrists envisaged neither the bucolic communism of Hesiod and Ovid nor the nude horticulture of Adam and Eve. The new golden age was to be the civilized version of the *pax Romana* vision in the sixth Aeneid. It was to recover lost innocence rather than lost simplicity, to recover the true justice of Astraea, last of the goddesses to leave the earth with the advent of the iron age of crime.

Some version of political millenarianism seems always to be with us, however modestly, crudely, or outrageously it may be phrased. Those better things around the corner, the jam tomorrow and pies in the sky point less to the cynicism of politicians than to the ubiquitous need for an assurance that the future will improve upon the present and past. In some respects and on some occasions, such visions and promises do issue in social improvement. But the poet is concerned less with advancing a programme than with recording and realizing aspects of experience (although one important aspect of experience concerns what it is like to hold or advance a moral or political programme). His task is the creation and re-creation of myths and images that can convey the universal experience in terms appropriate to his age. For the poets of the seventeenth, as for those of earlier centuries, future prosperity was characteristically represented by a restored golden age. The euphoric close of *Astraea Redux*, the vision of a Caroline millenium, has its counterpart in the wild jubilation with which the king was greeted at his restoration—so wild, indeed, that even Charles II was moved to issue a *Proclamation against vicious, debauched, and prophane Persons* the day after his return.

The familiar process by which parallel myths of Graeco-Roman and biblical origin were linked in suggestive poetic harmony was followed as efficiently as ever during the Restoration. Dryden himself provides a clear and successful example within the space of three couplets in his lines to Congreve:

> Strong were our Syres; and as they Fought they Writ,
> Conqu'ring with force of Arms, and dint of Wit;
> Theirs was the Gyant Race, before the Flood;
> And thus, when *Charles* Return'd, our Empire stood.
> Like *Janus* he the stubborn Soil manur'd,
> With Rules of Husbandry the rankness cur'd.
>
> (ll 3–8).

In this brief history of England in the seventeenth century the strong sires are the Jacobeans and the flood conventionally represents the Great Rebellion and Interregnum, as it does in the panegyric on Charles II's coronation. In the earlier poem Charles II is directly associated with Noah, whereas the Congreve address likens Charles to Janus, who was, according to mythographers and exegetes, the Roman counterpart of Noah. In fact, he was not the counterpart of the Noah who rode out the flood, but the Noah who cultivated vineyards. Noah's association with vineyards and their produce is certainly of doubtful panegyric value, but the change from biblical to Roman material is principally justified because Janus was better known than Noah as a cultivator and civilizer: he lived in the golden age of Italy and introduced laws and coinage as well as husbandry, while the opening and shutting of his temple to indicate war and peace is appropriate to the change from rebellion to Restoration. Janus, then, provides a more suggestive panegyric analogy without breaking the movement from giants to flood.

The connections between Eden and the golden age were far richer and more varied, and depended less upon the speculations of mythographers and exegetes than the Janus-Noah association. For a poet of Dryden's interest they were chiefly established by the political significance of the two myths. The major contribution of the classical tradition was the figure of Astraea and the true justice that she represented. The biblical tradition contributed a large literature concerned with the relevance of Edenic economy for constitutional theory. In England the potential value of Astraea for poetic panegyric was most fully exploited during the Elizabethan age, when the sex of the monarch facilitated identification with the goddess.[1] When Dryden early indicated his nostalgic affinity with the Elizabethans in *Astraea Redux*, the Astraea who is brought back is not so much an anthropomorphic goddess of justice as the concept and practice of justice exemplified by Charles II: the poem does not seek to establish an analogy between king and goddess. This troublesome matter of gender is not present in the political interpretation of Eden, for the king can readily be associated with Adam as the terrestrial ruler of creation.

Although Dryden never abandoned the long-established practice of conflating biblical and classical materials, it is none the less possible to detect in his poetry a shift in emphasis from Saturnian times to the Garden of Eden; more accurately, perhaps, the matter of Eden makes significant appearance only in the mature poetry from 1680 onwards. Such poems as *Annus Mirabilis* and the coronation panegyric make extensive use of the familial analogy, of the patriarchal relationship between king and subjects, but the relationship is largely generalized and never presented in terms of the first father. But in 1681–82 he three times in six months made use of the kingdom of Adam as an analogy for England: in *Absalom and Achitophel*, *The Medal*, and the Prologue to *The Unhappy Favourite*. In *The Medal* the oblique reference in the cursing of Shaftesbury is a variation upon the poem's major control in the plots of a Satanic Shaftesbury to overthrow his God-like king. Eden also enters indirectly by way of the poem's allusive reference to *Paradise Lost*; and a similar reference operates in *Absalom and Achitophel*. In each poem it is Satan's temptation of Eve which receives emphasis, while in the Prologue to *The Unhappy Favourite* Eve has no specific role.

The Prologue (which is among Dryden's most successful

applications of the form to political discussion) begins with the opening analogy of the coronation panegyric: the rebellion as flood, the restoration as the ark's landfall and the pledge of peace. This analogy controls the poem's first twenty-six lines until it is succeeded by a second and related analogy:

> Our Land's an *Eden*, and the Main's our Fence,
> While we Preserve our State of Innocence;
> That lost, then Beasts their Brutal Force employ,
> And first their Lord, and then themselves destroy:
> What Civil Broils have cost we know too well,
> Oh let it be enough that once we fell.
>
> (ll. 27–32)

Characteristically, the analogy edits and reinterprets the biblical material to make it yield the required political sense. If we insert the details that Dryden omits, if, that is , we try to expand the analogy by further reference to the biblical source, the result is an inevitable failure in correspondence. Political innocence guarantees a golden age of peace and prosperity; the political sin of rebellion converts the subject beasts of the field into dangerous beasts of prey in a manner which recalls at once Hobbes's anarchic state of nature and the omens of the eagle and lion turned hunter in *Paradise Lost* (XI, 182–90). But to read the lord whom they destroy as Adam (in addition to Charles I) produces obvious difficulties; and it is similarly difficult to determine to whom in Genesis the fallen 'we' correspond. Analogy here functions as simile rather than as historical precedent. Metaphysically, man can fall but once; politically, he can fall as often as rebellion breaks the just bonds between subject and ruler. Inevitably, then, Dryden's use of the myth involves the paradox that man, while metaphysically fallen, can be politically unfallen. Philosophically, the paradox is unresolvable; but, by eliminating metaphysical reference, the force of the myth in Dryden's poem is to suggest that a political fall is at once sufficiently like the original Fall to invoke its contingent religious sanctions and, by implication, sufficiently unlike it for the people to lose and regain paradise as often as they rebel against and restore their king. That the myth could be given political application without metaphysical overtones was a commonplace, for, as Ralegh remarked, 'good and golden

Kings make good and golden Ages: and all times have brought forth of both sorts.'[2]

The view, held by royalist and republican alike, that the forms of authority were first developed in families was used to support far more than the idea of the king as *pater patriae*. Even for a moderate royalist it indicated the universal relevance of an analogy between the government of a family, a village, or a country. Oxford could provide for Dryden, both as town and university, a meaningful analogy with the kingdom at large.[3] Microcosmically, as Plato argued, the patterns of government were analogous to the rational control of the will and appetites. Since, moreover, the faculty of reason was more developed in man, while in woman the lower faculties were more apparent, familial government was wholly patriarchal: a man ruled his wife as well as his sons. In *The Medal* these correspondences permitted Dryden to conduct his case on ethical, political, and theological grounds. But beyond this, some royalists were willing to argue not the analogy but the identity of familial and national rule. The Old Testament patriarchs were kings and the first king was Adam in Eden: Adam ruled over Eve as well as the beasts of the field. His authority, in accordance with divine and natural law, was the prototype of all monarchic authority; the right of kings to rule was descended to them from the first ruler on earth.

The dubious historicity of this view moved some royalists to admit a difference between Edenic and postlapsarian rule. The difference was based on the distinction between directive and coercive authority, between instruction and compulsion. Adam's prelapsarian authority was wholly directive, because his instructions could be nothing but reasonable and proper and because Eve unfallen could not fail to see them as such and to obey them unquestioningly. One result of the Fall was to introduce in subject Eve and her descendants an element of perverse obtuseness, and coercion inevitably became necessary from time to time. On the other side, the suspect nature of the royalist thesis suggested to republicans that monarchy was one of the (more lamentable) consequences of the Fall. The first king was not Adam, in or out of Eden, but Nimrod, who set the pattern for all subsequent monarchy by tyrannously arrogating to himself authority over neighbouring family groups. In *Paradise Lost*

Michael assures Adam that, chastened by divine severity, men will live

> Long time in peace by Families and Tribes
> Under paternal rule; till one shall rise
> Of proud ambitious heart, who not content
> With fair equalitie, fraternal state,
> Will arrogate Dominion undeserv'd
> Over his brethren, and quite dispossess
> Concord and law of Nature from the Earth;
> Hunting (and Men not Beasts shall be his game)
> With Warr and hostile snare such as refuse
> Subjection to his Empire tyrannous:
> A mightie Hunter thence he shall be styl'd
> Before the Lord, as in despite of Heav'n,
> Or from Heav'n claming second Sovrantie;
> And from Rebellion shall derive his name,
> Though of Rebellion others he accuse.
>
> (XII, 23–37)

In view of the republican claim that monarchy was a consequence of the Fall, that before it Adam and Eve shared the government of the beasts, the eagerness of royalists like Filmer to insist upon a prelapsarian monarchy is readily understandable.

No one, presumably, would now care to take sides in this dusty dispute on its own terms. But even from a position of detachment it is easy to see the rich potential of the examples most often used in it. Filmer once chastised a treatise advocating a mixed or parliamentary monarchy by remarking that 'it hath so much of fancy, that it is a better piece of poetry than policy.'[4] Whatever the justice of this rebuke, it has undeniable relevance to its author's own account of the kingdom of Adam, for it is difficult to read the pages Filmer devotes to this subject without being reminded of its poetic possibilities. It is a quality which Filmer shares with many of the apologists for monarchy (one recalls those passages in which Hobbes expresses his fear of civil disorder, or Bodin his reverence for his elevated monarch); a quality which is perhaps best felt in contrast with the prosaic pages of Locke's *Two Treatises*.

The events in Eden had for long been given a political interpretation by commentators on the Bible,[5] but this interpretation was commonly ancillary to the largely theological issues that the story was held to involve. Their transfer from the learned tradition into the common political typology of the Restoration was principally effected by the works of Sir Robert Filmer. Filmer's major work was the *Patriarcha*, an essay designed to prove the origins of monarchy in the rule of Adam. Although *Patriarcha* remained unpublished during Filmer's life, he extrapolated many of its main arguments for use in a series of tracts published during the five years that preceded his death in 1653. These tracts apparently occasioned little comment at their first appearance, and his theories were widely debated only after the posthumous publication of all his works, including *Patriarcha*, between 1679 and 1685. The conservative reaction to the constitutional crisis of the Popish Plot and Exclusion Bill often took the form of support for an increase in the royal prerogative to the extent of virtual absolutism. The chief practical manifestations of this reaction were Charles II's refusal to call another parliament after the dissolution at Oxford early in 1681 and the suspension of the charters which gave to many towns and cities a large measure of self-government and consequent independence of the central authority. These actions were assumed to prove the old royalist contention that the privileges of parliament and the city charters were held by the gracious permission of the king and were not the inalienable constitutional rights of the people. In this context the reissue of Filmer's earlier tracts and the publication of *Patriarcha* have obvious point. Filmer was perhaps the most militantly reactionary royalist of the century and his works offered the theoretical justification for the violence of the royalist response to the attempted Whig revolution of 1679–82. Inevitably, the republican retort in such works as Sidney's *Discourses*, Locke's *Two Treatises*, and Tyrell's *Patriarcha non Monarcha* and *Bibliotheca Politica* succeeded, among other things, in popularizing the terms of the debate; and the politics of Paradise provided ready material for discussing the constitution of England.

The poets also inherited the traditional panegyric 'places' of the classical golden age with its restoration at the return of the virgin goddess of justice. They inherited, too, the idea that the Fortunate Isles, the paradise of heroes, could be identified with Great Britain;[6] and the Fortunate Isles were linked with both Eden and the golden age of Saturn because all three were remarkable for a harmony between man and nature whose most important manifestation was the unlaboured fertility of the land in a condition of perpetual spring. England could well be in Gaunt's speech 'this other Eden' and an Adamic ruler of the palace garden could appropriately imitate the king's own government of the land. Dryden himself was the first writer of importance to appreciate the practical use of the large poetic resources of *Paradise Lost*: within seven years of its publication he had turned it into an opera (which was never staged), and seven years later in *Absalom and Achitophel* and *The Medal* (a year after the first edition of *Patriarcha*) he made the first important entries in the long schedule of allusions to *Paradise Lost*.

The very confusion and contradictions of this material, the possibilities for combinations and permutations that differ in significant details, meant that individual poets had a large responsibility as well as a large freedom in the coherent re-creation of the myths within a poem. There can be no question of critic or reader exclaiming at a reference to Adam and assuming an identification with the king which may or may not be required by the poem. If the author was drawing upon the political debate he would know that for some persuasions Adam was an absolute king, for others a co-ruler with Eve; only the terms in which the poet chooses to present his Adam can make his emphasis clear. A knowledge of this material is chiefly of value in keeping us alert to the possibility of its use in individual poems, in prompting us to ask what may turn out to be the right questions about the principles of coherence in the work.

Sometimes, it is true, the Edenic analogy will be in the form of an expanded simile, and the poet will, as it were, explicate his own image. Dryden (perhaps because he aimed at a wider audience than Milton's) frequently spelled out the implications of his analogies (and thus expanded their reference). A clear example occurs in *Eleonora*, when he praises the deceased Countess of Abingdon in the following way:

> A Wife as tender, and as true withall,
> As the first Woman was, before her fall:
> Made for the Man, of whom she was a part;
> Made, to attract his Eyes, and keep his Heart.
> A second *Eve*, but by no Crime accurst;
> As beauteous, not as brittle as the first.
> Had she been first, still Paradise had bin,

And Death had found no entrance by her sin.
So she not only had preserv'd from ill
Her Sex and ours, but liv'd their Pattern still.
Love and Obedience to her Lord she bore,
She much obey'd him, but she lov'd him more.
Not aw'd to Duty by superior sway;
But taught by his Indulgence to obey.
Thus we love God as Author of our good;
So Subjects love just Kings, or so they shou'd.

(ll. 166–81)

Eleonora is the pattern of wifely submissiveness, which was first
seen in Eve's submission to Adam before the Fall. But because
true wifely submissiveness also provides the pattern for the
people's obedience to the king, subjects should, like this second,
incorruptible Eve, defer to their Adamic ruler. Since *Eleonora*
was published within three years of the Glorious Revolution of
1688–9, there is special point in the implication that subjects
have a regrettable tendency to follow the dangerous path of the
first Eve.

Clear though it is, the passage in *Eleonora* provides no in-
fallible gloss upon Dryden's other and more allusive reworkings
of the Eden story. The closing analogy of the Prologue to *The
Unhappy Favourite* obviously applies the myth rather differently,
for there the roles of Adam and Eve are combined and modified
instead of kept distinct. There is a similar conflation in *The Hind
and the Panther* (I, 245–90), where the patterns of just monarchy
and tyranny, of religious tolerance and intolerance are traced
through an account of the Creation, the Fall, and its consequences. The passage constitutes a characteristic instance of the
fertility of Dryden's invention in drawing out more and more
significance and correspondence from the terms of an established analogy. Hunting and the preying of one beast on another provide the pattern of tyranny, while man's benevolent
dominion over nature before the Fall provides the pattern of
just monarchy, of kings on coronation day. The Fall occurs
when

knowledge misapply'd, misunderstood,
And pride of Empire sour'd his balmy bloud.
Then, first rebelling, his own stamp he coins;
The murth'rer *Cain* was latent in his loins.

(I, 276–79)

Because it was a rebellion against God's commands, the Fall sets the pattern for all subsequent rebellion. As a variation upon the fact that man was created in the image of God, the idea of coining his own image is wholly appropriate; but it further emphasizes the condition of rebellion by recalling that it was high treason to counterfeit coinage or, as Shaftesbury was charged with doing in *The Medal*, to issue a coinage rivalling the king's and bearing the head of the traitor instead of the king's head. The passage concludes with an assurance that James II is in the process of restoring the prelapsarian conditions of benevolence and tolerance to his faction-ridden and sect-torn subjects. The variations between the use of the analogy in the Prologue, *The Hind and the Panther*, and *Eleonora* are such that, while all three usages keep within the terms of the same general debate, the precise significance of each can only be apprehended from its own context. In poems where the point is not made in explanatory commentary, it is important to pay close attention to the exact terms in which the analogy is presented and to be alert to the way in which one analogy may develop out of another while retaining the values established by the first. Throughout his works, but especially in his later poems, Dryden reveals an ability to generate poetic excitement by realizing in the body of the poem the possibilities of images and allusions which had earlier been offered with seeming inconsequence.

TO THE DUCHESS OF ORMONDE

There is one overriding reason why the late address to the Duchess of Ormonde may be considered Dryden's most successful attempt at formal verse panegyric upon a person of elevated rank. His rival works in this genre: *Astraea Redux*, the lines upon the coronation and Clarendon, *Threnodia Augustalis* and *Britannia Rediviva*, are inferior chiefly because they fall short of the Ormonde address in the poetic justification of the analogies through which they function. They all accept, to some extent, the poetic adequacy of a convention that the exploits of great men are properly amplified by comparison with the deeds of gods and heroes. They do not work to validate in the ordering and expression of their subject the selection of this god rather than that hero as an amplifying analogy. This circumstance accounts for the sense these works convey of a dizzy accumulation of comparisons. Even their controlling analogies, the golden age of *Astraea Redux* for example, depend heavily upon the conventions of praise as a justification for their presence. When these conventions lose their force and currency, the weakness of the poems in justifying their selection becomes, not more crucial, but certainly more apparent.

As with so many of Dryden's poems—*The Medal* is an obvious example—it is essential to pay close attention to the opening lines of the Ormonde address. We are so accustomed to thinking of Dryden as the master of memorable openings, that we may be in danger of overlooking the way in which the opening prepares for what is to follow. Because the address also serves to dedicate Dryden's version of the *Knight's Tale* to the Duchess, he begins by insisting that the Chaucerian original at least is a poem worthy the attention of the great. Chaucer sums up and extends the poetic achievement of Homer and Virgil. This rash critical assertion is to be accepted, partly because it is inspired by patriotic pride, but chiefly because it is expressed in terms of topics common to the three poets: love and arms. In this general form the proposition[7] permits the establishment of an epic context which will be fully exploited later in the poem and which could certainly not have been introduced with such economy from the *Knight's Tale* alone.

There is an additional reason for the excellence of Chaucer's poem: the martial prowess it records was inspired by the fair eyes of Emily, whose beauty is like that of the Duchess of Ormonde herself. The compliment is too conventional to be exceptionable. Because there can be no possible reason for disagreement, we are all the more receptive to the next step in Dryden's speciously logical insinuation, and the next step is crucial:

> If *Chaucer* by the best Idea wrought
> And Poets can divine each others Thought,
> The fairest Nymph before his Eyes he set;
> And then the fairest was *Plantagenet*;
> Who three contending Princes made her Prize,
> And rul'd the Rival-Nations with her Eyes:
> Who left Immortal Trophies of her Fame,
> And to the Noblest Order gave the Name.

Like Her, of equal Kindred to the Throne,
You keep her Conquests, and extend your own.

(ll. 11–20)

The conditionals ensure a tone of undogmatic fairness. Dryden asserts neither that Chaucer modelled his Emily upon the most beautiful woman of his age nor that Dryden at the end of the seventeenth century is gifted with some special insight into the creative processes of a fourteenth-century poet. He merely suggests that if these things are so, then Chaucer's model for Emily was the Fair Maid of Kent, who was 'married for the third and last time to Edward the Black Prince . . . and [was] commonly believed to be the Countess of Salisbury from whom the Order of the Garter, according to the well-known story, derived its name.'[8] When she married the Black Prince, the Fair Maid accompanied him during his nine-year governorship of the English domains in France, and thus may reasonably be said to have ruled 'with her Eyes' the 'Rival-Nations' of England and France. The Fair Maid was Edward I's granddaughter and married in the Black Prince John of Gaunt's brother, while the Duchess of Ormonde was descended through her father from John of Gaunt, himself the great-grandson of Edward I. This intricate genealogy is absent from Dryden's poem, but it is available as a (rather dubious) support for the assertion that the Duchess and the Fair Maid are of 'equal Kindred to the Throne.'

All this depends upon two large conditions: that Chaucer modelled Emily on an actual woman and that Dryden can read Chaucer's thoughts. It is presented as the natural consequence of these conditions, but the 'discovery' that the Fair Maid and the Duchess are linked by genealogy as well as beauty implies the actuality of the conditions. Emily is like the Duchess because both are beautiful; Emily is also like the Fair Maid (if we follow the conditions), but there is other evidence to show that the Fair Maid is like the Duchess; therefore Dryden is quite correct to divine the Fair Maid as the inspirational original of Emily. The semblance of logic is necessary to imply that a likeness between three beautiful women (an unexceptionable and unexciting proposition) is no accident but the result in one case of imitation and in the other of heredity. Likeness, in fact, is verging upon identity; and it is to complete the movement toward identity that Dryden embarks upon an epic simile whose immediate occasion is to explain how it is that the Duchess keeps the conquests of the Fair Maid and extends her own (just as Chaucer summed up and improved upon the achievements of Homer and Virgil):

> As when the Stars, in their Etherial Race,
> At length have roll'd around the Liquid Space,
> At certain Periods they resume their Place,
> From the same Point of Heav'n their Course advance,
> And move in Measures of their former Dance;
> Thus, after length of Ages, she returns,
> Restor'd in you, and the same Place adorns;
> Or you perform her Office in the Sphere,
> Born of her Blood, and make a new Platonick Year.
>
> (ll. 21–29)

The strict justification for this verse paraphrase of the *Timaeus* is that it provides a simile for the fact that the Duchess, born of the Fair Maid's blood, continues the ancestral tradition of governing with her beauty the court of England and thus, by extension, England itself. But the simile is actually applied in very different terms: either the vehicle illustrates a tenor of metempsychosis or the vehicle is itself the tenor, and the star originally inhabited by the Fair Maid, having returned to its starting point in the heavens, is now inhabited by the Duchess. The transmigration of the Fair Maid's soul into the Duchess, her restoration in her descendant, is certainly one (metaphorical) way of expressing the strict justification for this unconventional epic simile. But if we prefer it to an apotheosis into the angelic ruler of a planet, we are then committed to the virtual identity of Duchess and Fair Maid. Moreover, no choice is made between the alternatives (which are far more than different ways of saying the same thing); therefore the existence of each is evidence that the other is not categorically stated, while the existence of both is a double source of compliment. The Duchess is now provided with an alarmingly rich context of heavenly bodies, the return of a female figure and a new platonic year— that is to say, a new golden age.

Having established that Emily is modelled upon the Fair Maid and that the Fair Maid is, in effect, the Duchess of Ormonde, Dryden is in a position to complete his circular argument:

> Had *Chaucer* liv'd that Angel-Face to view,
> Sure he had drawn his *Emily* from You:
> Or had You liv'd, to judge the doubtful Right,
> Your Noble *Palamon* had been the Knight:
> And Conqu'ring *Theseus* from his Side had sent
> Your Gen'rous Lord, to guide the *Theban* Government.
> Time shall accomplish that; and I shall see
> A *Palamon* in Him, in You an *Emily*.
>
> (ll. 32–39)

Because the wheel is full circle, we are in a position to explain why Emily's eyes sparkled like the Duchess's. The model, the idea for Emily was, in effect, the Duchess herself, and what began as unelaborated simile ends as literal explanation. The Duchess becomes Emily, and Emily the Duchess. The *Knight's Tale* is extended to enable Theseus/William III to send Palamon/Duke of Ormonde to Thebes/Ireland with Emily/the Duchess. Palamon returns to his native Thebes, Ormonde to his ancestral home in Ireland: his family had been hereditary butlers of Ireland for some five hundred years and had provided the country with a number of lieutenant-governors. The Duke of Dryden's poem had for several years made little secret of his wish to hold this post, and Dryden's assurance that time would see his ambition fulfilled is both an advisory hint to the government and, as it turned out, an accurate prophecy. The Ormondes had already made to Ireland a visit of political consequence; the Duchess, therefore, had ruled the 'Rival-Nations' of England and Ireland, just as this new Emily, having judged 'the doubtful Right' in Athens, was now to exercise her power in Thebes. But it was the Fair Maid who originally ruled the 'Rival-Nations,' and her exploits are recalled by addressing the Duchess as a 'true *Plantagenet*' (l. 30). Prehistoric Athens thus finds common ground with the England of both the fourteenth and the seventeenth centuries, while the Duchess of Ormonde is both Emily and the Fair Maid and herself; she appropriates their conquests and adds them to her own.

The movement of this opening section depends upon the poet's making an assertion which must be defended or explained, and in the course of explanation making a further assertion that must be defended. This process of continual justification inevitably imparts to the lines a semblance of logic, by which each analogy, each panegyric 'place,' is tested, as it were, and shown to be appropriate to the Duchess in the very moment of its application. Dryden is certainly observing the advice of rhetoricians to praise illustrious ancestry and the virtuous employment rather than the mere possession of such 'accidental advantages' as health and wealth (the Duchess, by attraction from the other women, is not merely beautiful; her beauty inspires acts of fortitude and martial prowess). But the poem creates its own justification for the use of such topics. The precepts of rhetoricians, which Dryden observes throughout this panegyric, are strictly irrelevant to the poem, because they are not needed to justify the terms of his praise.

The simile of the platonic great year is but one step in this process of argument, whose immediate end is the poetic identification of the three women for the purpose of encomium upon the Duchess. But the simile also works to posit a series of values and assumptions that permit the poet to raise his ensuing account of the Duchess's previous visit to Ireland to the level of myth. The idea advanced by Plato in the *Timaeus* that 'the complete number of Time fulfils the Complete Year when all the eight circuits [of the planets and stars], with their relative speeds, finish together and come to a head'[9] suggested an easy connection with the millenial prophecies of classical antiquity, and these in turn were associated with the Christian apocalypse. Virgil's *Pollio*, with all its accretions of commentary and imitation, was the acknowledged precedent for the conflation of the great year and the return of the golden age, just as it was the precedent for marking the return of the golden age with the return of Astraea. Moreover, in some accounts the end of one platonic cycle was marked by a purgatorial fire or flood, phenomena which had an obvious biblical counterpart.[10]

In his application of the simile Dryden observes that 'after length of Ages, she returns, / Restor'd in you,' and his placing of *returns* and *Restor'd* in the positions of emphasis and in a context of the great year has obvious overtones of Astraea's return and the restoration of the golden age. Strictly, of course, it is the Fair Maid who returns and is restored; but she does so in a manner and in terms that recall Astraea's return, and Dryden's lines consequently establish what may be called an Astraean potential. When realized, this potential reveals the Duchess as a person who restores—or at least inspires the restoration of—peace, order, harmony, justice, concord. The means by which discord will be banished will still be the Duchess's beauty, and in this important sense the Duchess will surpass the achievements of Emily and the Fair Maid, whose beauty chiefly worked to inspire contention, rivalry, and martial prowess. The long middle section of the poem (ll. 40–145) is an elaboration upon the harmonious effects of her beauty upon nature, the state, and the body.

The account of the earlier visit to Ireland is introduced to justify the prophecy of Ormonde's appointment to the lieutenant-governorship: the success of the earlier visit is an argument for the success of a permanent administration. The political motive for the visit of 1697 had been a hope that the head of one of the leading Irish houses would be able to persuade his countrymen to become reconciled to an England which had confiscated much of the Catholic property and had severely repressed the Jacobite rebellion that broke out after the accession of William III. The visit was a success to the extent that it demonstrated the continued popularity of the Ormondes. In 1697 the Duchess had preceded her husband by several months, and although her crossing of the Irish Sea was rough and much delayed, its unpleasantness was forgotten in the 'exuberant welcome' she received: 'the day of her arrival was described as "one of jubilee," the streets being strewed with leaves and flowers and guns and bells sounding a welcome.'[11]

The rough crossing was not to Dryden's panegyric purpose, and he accordingly converts it into what Professor Hoffman has aptly called 'a miniature of the full epic voyage' replete with Virgilian echoes.[12] The conspiracy of the deities of land and sea to provide the Duchess with a smooth crossing is also an instance of her beauty's miraculous ability to bring harmony to the elements. She is greeted, furthermore, with unaccustomed submission by the 'sturdy Kerns' (l. 58), and although this submission is inspired by reverence for the whole house of Ormonde, the general praise is quickly appropriated to specific encomium upon the Duchess. In line 62 she is still receiving homage in the name of her husband, and in the next line the situation is described by analogy: the Duchess precedes her husband as Venus, the star of morning, precedes the sun, or—to apply the astrology—as beauty comes before the prince. In a panegyric upon a beautiful woman it is perhaps surprising to find the entrance of the goddess of beauty so long delayed. When she does appear, it is to provide more than a conventional simile, for it is the beauty of the Venus-Duchess which marks the end of martial destruction. By implication, moreover, she inspires the restoration of the agricultural arts neglected during rebellion (l. 65). This Venus, then, is not merely the patroness of beauty and love but a beneficient deity whose 'kindly Care' is 'Nature.'[13] She is, in fact, the Venus Genetrix of Lucretius, who is thus addressed in Dryden's translation:

> Mean time on Land and Sea let barb'rous discord cease,
> And lull the listning world in universal peace.
> To thee, Mankind their soft repose must owe,
> For thou alone that blessing canst bestow;
> Because the brutal business of the War
> Is manag'd by thy dreadful Servant's care:
> Who oft retires from fighting fields, to prove
> The pleasing pains of thy eternal Love.
>
> (I, 41–48)

The peace brought by this Venus prompts an analogy with the olive branch brought by Noah's dove, and the transition is further justified because the dove was also the bird of Venus:

> As when the Dove returning, bore the Mark
> Of Earth restor'd to the long-lab'ring Ark,
> The Relicks of Mankind, secure of Rest,
> Op'd ev'ry Window to receive the Guest,
> And the fair Bearer of the Message bless'd;
> So, when You came, with loud repeated Cries,
> The Nation took an Omen from your Eyes,
> And God advanc'd his Rainbow in the Skies,
> To sign inviolable Peace restor'd;
> The Saints with solemn Shouts proclaim'd the new accord.
>
> (ll. 70–79)

The voyage of the ark provides an important complement to the earlier description of the Duchess's crossing in Virgilian terms. In fact, Dryden's lines establish that the ark is here an Ireland that has been tossed upon the flood of civil war. The sign that the waters have abated is the arrival of the peace-bearing dove of Noah and Venus, and the continued presence of the Venus association is apparent from the fact that the Irish take the omen from the Duchess's eyes, from her beauty. They also take it, as inhabitants of the ark, from the rainbow by which God marked his covenant with man. But God, said the commentators, chose the rainbow precisely because it is very beautiful.[14] The complexity of these lines owes much to the fact that, although the epic simile is formally divided into vehicle and tenor by 'as when . . .' and 'so when . . .', material strictly appropriate to the other half is included in each part of the comparison. Thus, the rainbow of God's covenant occurs in the nominal tenor instead of the vehicle, and the biblical matter is reintroduced as if it were part of the events in Ireland. Similarly, it is reasonable that the men and women in the ark would open a window to allow the dove to re-enter; as a security measure they might well open every window, although the Bible is silent on this point. But every window would certainly have been open when the Duchess made her triumphant progress through Ireland.

It is just possible that the rich exegetical traditions surrounding the dove of Noah and the rainbow of the covenant, traditions associating them with the Holy Ghost and with Christ, are brought to the surface by Dryden's immediately proceeding to allude to the second coming. In any case, the introduction of the Christian millenium inevitably recalls that it was traditionally ushered in, as in Dryden's poem, by a purgatorial fire or flood. With this millenial prophecy (ll. 80–89) the poet can reap a full harvest of tradition and association from the analogies he earlier introduced. The new platonic year with its overtones of an Astraea who returns with a restored golden age is recalled with the Venus Genetrix who can inspire the spontaneous fertility of the golden age and the terrestrial paradise in a passage that echoes with the tropes of Virgil and Lucretius. Moreover, just as the earlier 'discovery' that the Duchess was descended from the Fair Maid argued the probability that the Fair Maid was Chaucer's model for Emily, so too the recollection that Ireland had in long tradition been associated with the venomless earthly paradise and the Islands of the Blest[15] increases the poetic probability of the Duchess's ability to restore to it the conditions of the golden age. With this recollection Dryden completes his account of the Duchess's power to inspire harmony into the sick body politic of Ireland. By bringing back the dove analogy, this time as an emblem of fragility, he permits himself a smooth transition to the Duchess's restitution of order to her own sick body, in which the elements had rebelled (l. 117) with results analogous to the waste produced in Ireland by civil war. This conventional parallel between political and bodily ill health is reinforced by the analogy in which Dryden couches his plea to the Duchess not to venture abroad until she is fully recovered:

> A Subject in his Prince may claim a Right,
> Nor suffer him with Strength impair'd to fight;
> Till Force returns, his Ardour we restrain,
> And curb his Warlike Wish to cross the Main.
>
> (ll. 107–10)

The terms of the analogy are drawn from the stormy parliamentary debates in the last years of the century over William III's proposal to maintain a large standing army. Both Whig and Tory members agreed that after the Treaty of Ryswick in 1697 the military forces should be disbanded, and there were grounds for suspecting that the king's demands for a large standing army would lead the country into a further continental war. The parliamentary debate spilled over into a series of tracts that at least brought the issue to wide public notice.[16] The immediate purpose of Dryden's allusion is, then, to bring home the analogy between the political and human bodies as a major control in his poem. But its further function is to collect together the earlier references to 'Conqu'ring *Theseus*' and his associations with contentious rivalry, and to the 'Foreign Hand' which had, by implication, ruled in Ireland before Ormonde's arrival (l. 59). Ireland was the scene of James II's last important resistance to William III, who defeated the Jacobite forces at Boyne in 1691, and it was the harsh Williamite punishment which necessitated the Ormonde visit of 1697. William III, then, the foreigner, the conqueror, and the warlike prince, promoter of discord and strife is present in the poem—by indirection and allusion—as the antithesis of the peace-bringing Ormondes, with their long

ancestry in the land, their kinship to the throne, their hereditary association with the high chivalric order of the Garter,
their demonstration of the values of the succession (ll. 146–47,
166–68). Just as satire in its largely negative attack upon vice
and folly will often take time to touch briefly upon the opposed
positive or virtue, so its rhetorical converse of panegyric may
properly set its celebration of virtue into high relief by touching
upon the opposed vice.

The examination of the Duchess's sickness for panegyric
topics is conducted under the headings of its cause, course, and
cure. This section (ll. 111–45) repeats the earlier techniques of
linking the various analogies it employs by a semblance of logical argument and enquiry and of multiplying and making
reasonable the terms of praise by presenting them as unresolved
alternatives. If in imaginative suggestion its falls below the re-
creation of the earthly paradise in Ireland, its own effectiveness
and the poem's integrity is increased by the allusive recall of the
Irish venture in the account of the Duchess's sickness. Both
require that she assuage the destruction of civil war, and both
involve miracles, for the special providence that (may have)
preserved her in sickness (l. 141) is similar to the whole series
of miraculous events that accompanied the Duchess on her
visit to Ireland. At its height, the progress of the sickness is like
the Romans' sacrilegious burning of the temple at Jerusalem
(ll. 122–26), and the 'Holy Place' of the Duchess's soul reminds
us that the ship which carried her to Ireland, no doubt sancti-
fied by her presence, was a 'sacred Vessel' (l. 50). Similarly, the
holy place, the sanctuary of the temple, was so because it contained the ark of the law, while the Irish ark was also, traditionally, the 'Holy Isle' of line 85.

The incidental allusive recall in the passage on the Duchess's
sickness is succeeded by a conclusion whose point is quite obviously and appropriately to resume the main analogies and topics
of the whole poem. Like Venus, the Duchess is accompanied by
the Graces, and just as the Fair Maid inspired Chaucer so the
Duchess is the muse of Dryden (l. 150). The beauty that is her
inherited right makes her a true daughter of the rose (l. 151),
the flower at once of Venus and the Plantagenets, and here the
Tudor rose that composed the strife of York and Lancaster. Her
beauty is a paradise where no further fall may be feared (ll. 155–

56). Chaucer's heroine returns by implication from the concluding references to the Fair Maid, especially her traditional
association with the Garter (l. 168). Penelope and Dido appear
as amplificatory compliment upon the Duchess's needlework
(ll. 157–62), and further ensure the reunion of the opening
poets' triumvirate: Chaucer, Homer, and Virgil. The poem begins with 'The Bard who first adorn'd our Native Tongue' and
ends with the promise of an infant Ormonde 'To fill in future
Times his Father's Place, / And wear the Garter of his Mother's
Race.' The poet's task is indeed to adorn his native tongue by
recording the triumphs of his nation's great. The epistolary convention that a significant relationship be established between
writer and recipient is here modified to suit the formal requirements of panegyric upon someone of elevated rank: the writer
remains subordinate, someone inspired to praise the great.[17]

TO DRIDEN OF CHESTERTON

The success of the panegyric upon the Duchess of Ormonde
depends upon the poem's justifying the analogies it adopts
through a semblance of logical argument. Dryden's lines to his
cousin, published with the Ormonde address in the volume of
Fables, similarly depend for their effectiveness upon a process of
what may be called continuous translation. The values established by one topic of praise are retained in the consideration of
subsequent topics because the subsequent topics are introduced
as metaphors for the first. Most notably—and crucially, perhaps, for the poem's integrity—the extended praise of Driden's
rude good health is finally summarized by metaphor: 'You
hoard not Health, for your own private Use; / But on the Publick spend the rich Produce' (ll. 117–18). Retrospectively, the
physical advantages of good health are given metaphoric expression as economic advantages, but because the poem then
proceeds to enquire into the economy of England, the metaphor
also works to ensure the continued relevance of the earlier
praise. The metaphor is, in fact, reversible into its more familiar
form: the economic health of the nation is analogous to the
bodily health of an individual; or, in terms that more accurately
describe the poem's assumptions, bodily health is the rural
equivalent of economic health in the nation. It is in working

out all the implications of this equivalence that Dryden achieves, what he had never quite managed before, a compellingly original turn upon the ancient analogy between the human and political bodies.

The process of continuous translation inevitably entails a high degree of sequaciousness, and this quality in turn dictates a reading which follows quite closely the developing argument of the poem. It is useful, however, to describe briefly the general organization of the poem before considering its details in their proper order.

The fact that Driden was both a country squire and a member of parliament explains the major structural division of the poem into two almost equal parts, the division occurring between lines 116 and 117. The poem at once insists upon the connection and the separateness of Driden's rural and urban activities. The connection is established chiefly by the repetition of key terms and similar relationships; separateness is emphasized by the repetition with differences of the image of activities in Paradise. The opening lines promise an encomium, in the manner of Horace, upon the pleasures and values of retirement to the country, and the voice of Horace may be heard intermittently throughout the enumeration of rural delights.[18] It is Horace with a difference, however; for what chiefly engages the poet's interest is the relevance of these rural activities for the administration of national affairs. The Driden who studies peace at Chesterton and who devotes much of his attention to the promotion of concord among his tenants is one with the Driden who is to speak out in London for the peaceful pursuit of trade in opposition to the military policies of the king and his ministers. Driden's role of magistrate (either official or unofficial) in the society of Chesterton enables him to obviate a situation 'Where Suits are travers'd; and so little won, / That he who conquers, is but last undone' (ll. 12–13). At the level of international affairs this situation finds a parallel in the poet's fears for the ruinous effects of war, by which 'Ev'n Victors are by Victories undone' (l. 164).

Driden's role at Chesterton, in fact, is consistently presented as magisterial, in the sense that he supplies his rural community with executive government. Even his hunting becomes, by simile, a judicial activity, for the foxes that he successfully pursues are humanized into 'Felons' who are punished for the 'murd'rous Deed' of killing lambs (l. 57). In addition, Driden meets a major requirement of paternal rule by his charitable benevolence toward his dependent community and relatives (ll. 36–49). One important function of the rural encomium on his executive ability is to present Driden's experienced qualifications for legislative and advisory office in parliament. This function associates the poem with the recommended technique for a deliberative oration, which was the rhetorical form for advising on a course of action to be adopted in some present emergency or state of affairs. Sometimes the advice would simply be to entrust the matter to a worthy man, whose worthiness would be established through a statement of his qualifications in the form of encomium upon them. At other times the orator would outline the situation and then offer his own detailed solution, although he would first establish himself as a man worth listening to in an introductory exordium. In this poem the two possibilities are combined, and Driden of Chesterton is presented as a type of the man best able to extricate England from its difficulties, while the course he will follow is, strictly speaking, the advice of the poet as orator.

One of Driden's most important qualifications is, rather surprisingly, his celibacy; and it is in the process of justifying its inclusion that the poet introduces the analogy with Eden which is finally to provide one of the major controls in the poem. The couplet which introduces the topic (ll. 17–18) is an excellent example of the way the poet makes capital out of his particular verse form. The first line: 'Promoting Concord, and composing Strife,' is retrospective in its epigrammatic summary of the preceding account of Driden's magisterial activities, which are serene, like his mind. The second line: 'Lord of your self, un-cumber'd with a Wife,' is a prospective introduction to the discussion of marital disputes. Together the two lines act as an obvious transitional device, but because they are joined by rhyme into a couplet unit they imply that Driden's virtuous social activities are a result of domestic freedom: Driden composes strife in his dependents because he is not subjected to it at home. But the word *strife* reminds us that Driden's serenity of mind equally derives from the civil strife which he avoids by living in the country. In fact, the strife, the anxious cares and civil rage which result from engaging in the public life of England are strikingly similar to the long penitence, the ill-matched minds, and the cursed pairing of Adam and Eve (ll. 21–22) which leads to the two wrestlers who pull each other down (l. 30). The poet is not at all explicit about the civil rage which his cousin shuns, but the most obvious connotation of the phrase would be some form of constitutional dispute, a connection that is further suggested by the description of Driden's rural activities in governmental terms.

The following proposition may be advanced: the first thirty-five lines of the poem, down to the end of the praise of celibacy, establish a double contrast. Driden of Chesterton is able to practise a system of peaceful government because he avoids the strife of both civil and marital engagement. The parallelism of the two varieties of strife effects a potential equation between activities in England at large and the unscriptural elaboration of Adam and Eve's activities in Eden. This equation or parallelism is to some extent emphasized by verbal repetition: the retired countryman *shunning* civil strife in line 3 is picked up in the congratulation of Driden in line 34 for having *shunn'd* the married state and repeated in line 122 with the information that Driden *shuns* the 'Common Care' of initiating government policy.

This potential equation remains to some extent in abeyance while the poet fills in the details of his cousin's parochial rule in descriptions of his charity and his hunting. In line 71, however, we embark upon a long discussion of health and medical aid which lasts until the conclusion of the first part of the poem in line 116. The discussion is introduced with the observation that hunting of the kind in which Driden engages was once the way of life long ago in the time of the patriarchs of Genesis, before the advent of doctors. The meaning of the observation is made clear in lines 88–93, which contrast the superior health gained from hunting with the health to be purchased from doctors. This connection of health, hunting, and long-lived fathers echoes back to the opening mention of youth and age in line 4 that was elaborated in the hunting passage proper with its comparison of Driden's approach to field sports in early and late life (ll. 58–61). Early and late hunting, however, are alike productive of the common good (l. 53), just as the equal enjoyment of age and youth is a result of shunning civil strife. Health becomes, in fact, a metaphor for the peace and harmony of Driden's mind, which are productive of the same qualities for the common good of the society he governs. If, then, we bear in mind the suggestive parallel between civil strife and the marital strife of Adam and Eve, with its double converse in the serenity Driden achieves from his retirement and his celibacy, and if we further bear in mind the value of health as a metaphoric expression of that serenity, we should be prepared for the explicit connection with the situation in Eden:

> The Tree of Knowledge, once in *Eden* plac'd,
> Was easie found, but was forbid the Taste:
> O, had our Grandsire walk'd without his Wife,
> He first had sought the better Plant of Life!
> Now, both are lost: Yet wandring in the dark,
> Physicians for the Tree, have found the Bark:
> They, lab'ring for Relief of Humane Kind,
> With sharpen'd Sight some Remedies may find;
> Th' Apothecary-Train is wholly blind.

(ll. 96–104)

The connection between celibacy and Eden that was earlier expressed in negative terms is now given positive statement. If there had been no Eve, Adam would have sought the tree of life instead of the tree of knowledge, and would thus have guaranteed his health, to say nothing of his immortality. But this is precisely what Driden of Chesterton has achieved: he guarantees his health by hunting, his serenity by celibacy and retirement, and he is, finally, to be accorded a species of immortality through the poet's verse (l. 209). Health is both the metaphoric expression of peace and serenity and the lot which would have befallen Adam if he had remained unmarried, while celibacy is equally conductive to peace and serenity. The circularity of the proposition ensures the relevance of each element in it to all the others. What we have, then, is a continuous opposition between two conditions. On the one hand there is a line running from country life, through peace, retirement, long life, serenity of mind, celibacy, hunting, natural health, to Adam without Eve, and the tree of life; the values of this line are attached to the figure of Driden. On the other hand there is a line running from strife, through civil rage, the quarrels of Adam and Eve, opposed wrestlers, the approximate and largely fortuitous health provided by physicians, to Adam with Eve, and the tree of knowledge. The line associated with Driden is implicitly presented as a prelapsarian state because it is conveyed in terms of an Adam who avoids the tree of knowledge, the eating of whose fruit led to the Fall. The opposed line is explicitly presented as a postlapsarian state because it is conveyed in terms of an Adam and Eve who fall by pulling each other down and are lost by eating the fruit of knowledge, and because it is a condition which leads to the rise of physicians, who search forbidden truths and thus repeat the sin of Adam and Eve which led to the Fall (l. 76).

Eden in the poem, then, differs radically from the scriptural Paradise, because it functions as an image for the body politic. Driden's community at Chesterton is an unfallen Eden, ruled absolutely by a benevolent and solitary Adam, and inhabited by an Israel host (l. 49) who maintain the health of their own bodies and of the body politic by engaging in the hunt. England at large is a fallen Eden, fallen because the lordly Adam was encumbered with an unsubmissive Eve, fallen because their civil strife pulled each other down, and, because it is fallen, forced to seek an imperfect health from the physicians, while running the risk of being altogether destroyed by the unqualified ministrations of the greedy apothecaries. The Eve who in lines 25–26 should have maintained a position subordinate to her lordly husband Adam, but did not and therefore contributed to the country's loss of peace and health, thus takes her place in the conventional political debate as the type of the subjects or their parliamentary representatives, while Adam takes his place as the type of the king. The marital struggle between Adam and Eve is the familiar type of the struggle between king and parliament experienced by the Stuarts. Just as the line of peace and serenity is associated with Driden, so the opposed line of strife and civil rage is associated with the princes of lines 67–70:

> Thus Princes ease their Cares: But happier he,
> Who seeks not Pleasure thro' Necessity,
> Than such as once on slipp'ry Thrones were plac'd;
> And chasing, sigh to think themselves are chas'd.

A. W. Verrall long ago suggested that these lines refer to the exiled James II hunting in the forest of St. Germain and sighing to think himself *chassé*, driven away from England.[19] Although the reference is certainly generalized by the plural form of *princes*, Verrall's suggestion is almost certainly correct in some respects. Actually, the syntax of the four lines (if not that of the second couplet alone) implies that the prince's hunting takes place while he is still on the throne, and his sighs are for the fact that he is in turn hunted by the political enemies who are trying to push him off his slippery eminence, for, as James I tersely observed, 'the highest bench is sliddriest to sit upon.'[20] It is important that the hunting passage proper, with its killing of the fox, is followed by five lines devoted to an emblematic hare:

> The Hare, in Pastures or in Plains is found,
> Emblem of Humane Life, who runs the Round;
> And, after all his wand'ring Ways are done, ⎫
> His Circle fills, and ends where he begun, ⎬
> Just as the Setting meets the Rising Sun. ⎭
>
> (ll. 62–66)

We move, in fact, from a description of the triumphant hunter to an account of the hunted, just as we are later to see the prince both chasing and chased. As an emblem of human life the hare runs in a circle, but the last image suggests a further analogy with the course of the sun. Although there would normally be no reason to regard this sun as anything more than an emblem of declining age, the immediately following reference to princes would tend to bring to the surface its always latent associations with kingship. Just as the hunter Driden gives way to the hunted hare, and the chasing prince is chased himself; just as the hare runs in a circle, and the setting sun of age meets the rising sun of youth; so too the deposed prince meets his heir or rival ascendant. The circle of the hare, the revolution of the sun, and the slippery thrones of kings combine to suggest that behind these lines there is a circle greater than the hare's and as slippery as thrones; the circle, in fact, of fortune's wheel, with kings ascending, seated at the top, and tumbling down the other side into the limbo of failure. That there is a specific allusion to James II seems most probable: in 1699 the fall of princes would almost inevitably recall the fate of the exiled Stuart.

We may say, then, that Driden as landowner embodies the theoretical values of Stuart rule, absolute and benevolent, still existing in him by virtue of his isolation, but lost to them by the ingratitude of subjects, which was perhaps the inevitable result of human nature and the indulgence of the king, a king who is hunted from his throne much as the unwary Adam's failure to shun the bait leaves him, in an important prefiguration of the hunting passage, struggling in the snare of marriage (l. 33). In Driden of Chesterton paradise is retained; in James II it was lost; the second part of the poem is devoted to the attempt to regain paradise, or at least to establish an imitation Eden.

The opposed wrestlers of the first part are paralleled by the opposed country and court parties of the second (l. 128). These become the parliamentary opposition and the king, each with its respective right to privilege and prerogative:

A Patriot, both the King and Country serves;
Prerogative, and Privilege preserves:
Of Each, our Laws the certain Limit show;
One must not ebb, nor t'other overflow:
Betwixt the Prince and Parliament we stand; ⎫
The Barriers of the State on either Hand: ⎬
May neither overflow, for then they drown the Land. ⎭
When both are full, they feed our bless'd Abode;
Like those, that water'd once, the Paradise of God.

(ll. 171–79)

In the first part of the poem Adam and Eve were themselves associated with the rivers of Eden, Eve's being tributary to Adam's (l. 26). Because she is no longer tributary and sub-ordinate, a barrier is required to effect an approximation of Edenic bliss. Similarly, because when left to themselves the two wrestlers pull each other down, an umpire is needed, one who will 'steer betwixt the Country and the Court' (l. 128). This umpire is the true patriot of lines 171, 184, and 195, who will devote himself to the good of the whole realm, which consists in the maintenance of a due balance between parliamentary privi-lege and royal prerogative. It is because there are and will be bad parliament men, just as there will be a Williamite son of Jove to squabble for military renown (l. 163), that there must be a judicious patriot to moderate between them. Such a man would be a true physician to the body politic, and if he cannot guarantee the Edenic health of Driden's community, he can at least offer a measure of well-being that is the most that can be expected in an England which has chased its rightful king from paradise and been forced to follow him.

Just as the disinterested Garth with his free dispensary for the poor brings a measure of health to the postlapsarian bodies of his patients, so the disinterested Driden with his incorruptible integrity will bring a measure of health to the fallen body politic of England (ll. 126–30). The generous Garth 'prescribes and gives' (l. 107); the just fiscal policy enacted by Driden will ensure 'That Kings may be supply'd, the People thrive' (l. 136). Conversely, the greedy apothecaries (ll. 104–14) and the bad physicians, Maurus/Blackmore and Milbourne (ll. 83–87), are as destructive of physical and spiritual health as bad parliament men are destructive of the country's political health. The analogy between human and political bodies was frequently extended to consider the role of the physician to the sick state, sometimes with a parallel attack upon false state physicians, the mountebanks of politics. Driden's most obvious mark of disinterestedness is the health he has gained in his Edenic community, a health he will share with the less fortunate remnant of the population by dedicating his services to their well-being (ll. 117–18).

The government to result from this judicious medical care will differ from the lost Stuart absolutism, for political disease has entered England with its fall from Edenic rule. Parliament is no longer seen as the supporter and helper of the king, but as his equal partner in government, with patriots like Driden on hand to settle their constitutional squabbles. The closest analogy the poet can find for this situation is that of the Roman republic with its consuls of moderate power in peace even if with a dictatorial *dux bellorum* is war-time (ll. 180–83). The analogy further emphasizes the shift from the predominately scriptural associations of the first part to the predominately Graeco-Roman context of the second, with its references to senates, to Alexander and Hannibal, and to consuls and dictators.

The advice on state matters contained in lines 131–70 can, as editors have noticed, properly be set in the context of the dispute in the last few years of the century over the merits of a large standing army; a dispute, it will be recalled, which also provided the Ormonde address with an important analogy. The stream of tracts during the closing years of the century arguing for and against the standing army contained many that advocated an alternative development of the navy, especially the merchant navy, with a view to establishing England's position as a leading mercantile nation. Dryden's support for the mercantilist view recalls his earlier interest in maritime trade in *Annus Mirabilis*, the address to Walter Charleton, and the dedication of *All for Love* to Danby.[21] It was confidently expected that the army-navy issue would be a major topic when William's fourth parliament met in 1700, a parliament to which, of course, Driden had been returned. The poem can therefore be seen in the light of a common journalistic practice of the age: that of issuing just prior to the assembling of a parliament tracts variously called a letter or advice to a member of parliament setting forth a course of action to be followed with respect to the issues that were to be raised. Dryden observed in a letter that his poem contained a character of a good parliament man,[22] and such was, in fact, a common variation on the tract or letter of advice, as the 'character' usually remarked that the good member would support this proposal and attack the other. The 'character' version was particularly appropriate in 1699, as William's third parliament had closed the previous year amid criticism of its proceedings and the corruption of its members. The poet's advice is no more detailed than that commonly offered by the journalists; he contents himself with stating the main lines of the international role most appropriate to England, just as the bulk of the poem is concerned to establish the domestic or constitutional role appropriate to the current circumstances of England.

Similarly, the specific attack on apothecaries, the introduction of the dispensary controversy, affords a measure of satiric detail to the poem, but is at the same time generalized by its association with the Edenic analogy and the constitutional burden. Much the same is true of Dryden's resumption in lines 83–87 of his critical squabble with Milbourne, the Norfolk rector who attacked Dryden's *Virgil* and offered in comparison his own translation of the first Georgic, and with Maurus/Blackmore, the court physician and poet who had attacked Dryden in the preface to *Prince Arthur*. In themselves these details are wholly topical and petty, but they are worth mentioning if only to see how Dryden uses them and transcends the topicality. Garth the good physician to sick people parallels Driden the good physician to the sick state. Blackmore and Milbourne are bad physicians, the one to sick bodies the other to sick souls, who parallel the mountebanks of politics implicit in the negative terms of the praise for good senators. Garth the good poet, the author of the mock-heroic *The Dispensary*, also parallels the good poet Dryden, and together they oppose the bad poets Blackmore and Milbourne. A major rhetorical end of the poem is to bring together the implications of the title, To my Honour'd Kinsman, John Driden of Chesterton, and the linking of poet and politician in the peroration: 'One to perform, another to record' (l. 204). Ultimately, the poem is about both its author and its recipient. The passage on the physicians, then, so far from being the unrelated disgression that it might at first appear, is totally integrated and is, indeed, essential to the movement of thought and suggestion. It ensures the relevance of the rural encomium to the urban advice by way of the health observable in each place. By selecting physicians who were also poets it further ensures that the two cousins stand to each other in the public relationship of poet and politician as well as in the private relationship of the title. Because the combination of physician and poet in one man was uncommon even in the seventeenth century, specific examples were needed to avoid the arbitrary effect of presenting the combination in wholly general and hypothetical terms.[23]

The lines to his cousin appropriately contain Dryden's last as well as his most interesting use of the analogy with Eden. What is appropriate is that the analogy here thoroughly implicates the recurring political fall with the unique metaphysical Fall, and thus denies the possibility of a new golden age in government. The hunting of the prince from his slippery throne has about it the irrevocability of the eating of the forbidden fruit itself, and this sense is emphasized by the concern with death, age, declining health, and defeated hopes. But affairs of state permit little time for elegies upon lost causes, and the task of curbing Dutch William must be attended to promptly and vigorously. This general change in attitude is a reminder that the complexity of the lines derives only partly from their allusive richness, for they also exhibit a controlled fluctuation of tone between panegyric and satire, elegy and argument. What controls these changing tones is the process of continuous translation from analogy to topic to analogy, a process which also helps draw together the poem's multiple references (to poets, commons, physicians, king, army, and navy), and thus to assure integrity in the work. The process guarantees, in fact, that strong sequaciousness which more perhaps than any other quality signals the fulfilment of Coleridge's requirement that a poem contain within itself the reason why it is so and not otherwise.

The Kingdom of Letters

M ORE clearly perhaps than in any other part of his work we are aware in reading Dryden's verse addresses to his fellow poets of his multiple claim upon our attention. They are poems that discuss the grounds of literary creation and judgment in terms that recall the critical essays and in a context that relates literary achievement to political events. Dryden in them is most obviously a man of letters: poet, critic, and historian; and we shall be in less danger of misreading these works if we keep in mind the coincidence of talents. Quite often they have been treated as ancillary or equivalent to the critical essays: their specifically literary discussion is emphasized and detached from its context of compliment. There is no reason to impeach such a procedure, since it does not claim to be reading the poems as poems. Dryden himself established the form of such commentary when he elected to defend in an essay his Epilogue to the second part of *The Conquest of Granada* as if it were solely a document of sociological criticism without a context of studied compliment to his audience. This approach is analogous to the practice of seeking evidence of Dryden's religious and political position indifferently in his poems, plays, and prefaces. There is a large conceptual element in *The Medal* which can be related to the wholly conceptual Postscript to *The History of the League*; but this element can also be related to the total poetic context of *The Medal*. Similarly, the literary judgments of the compliments to fellow poets can properly be related to their immediate context by considering the internal as well as their external reference. In several of these works the internal reference effects a meaningful analogy between affairs in the kingdom of letters and affairs in the kingdom of England.

Dryden was not the first to use this analogy: he found it in the long tradition of the commonwealth of poets that was, in part, an imitation of the political state. Taking its probable origin from the pastoral contests of the Sicilian poets,[1] and gaining impetus from the obvious parallel between the poet laureate and the crowned king, the developed tradition produced such variations as the Parnassian sessions of the poets, the parallel between *translatio studii* and *imperii*, and the kingdom of dullness in *MacFlecknoe* and *The Dunciad*. Similar to the kingdom of poets was the humanistic concept of the republic of letters, which lies behind the two parts of *Wits Commonwealth* by Bodenham and Meres—anthologies of learned axioms—and which is presumably the ancestor of the more modest community of scholars that is still invoked occasionally. It was a concept that led naturally to the formation of societies of antiquarians and historians, to the Royal Society itself, to Academe and an Academy. It attracted to itself, in fact, the whole classical heritage of a university, which, as a corporation, was analogous to the kingdom at large, for a communal body is the body politic in little.

The analogy was, then, so conventional that the difficulty was not to justify its employment (this metaphor was never in danger of becoming catachresis), but to give it a compellingly new expression; its implicit challenge to the poet was perhaps as great as that contained in the analogy between human and political bodies. Inevitably, it seems, an outstanding poet *ruled* his fellows by the example he set them, and a censorious critic *tyrannized* over dramatists. Donne, we know, ruled over 'the universal monarchy of wit'; and Jonson can be praised by Neander in the *Essay of Dramatic Poesy* because 'he invades authors like a monarch, and what would be theft in other poets is only victory in him.'[2] Professor Hoffman has pointed out Dryden's frequent use of the analogy in his prologues and epilogues as a source of value terms for critical propositions.[3] Thus, the converse to the praise of Jonson is provided by the Prologue to *Albumazar*, where plagiarizing hacks are described as creating an 'Anarchy of witt' in which they freely plunder the work of other authors (ll. 17–18). Not only did the vocabulary of politics provide a rich source of metaphor for literary discussion, but —as Professor Hoffman remarks—it provided an especially appropriate source of metaphor in an age of constitutional debate, when the vocabulary of politics was inevitably so often on men's lips.

It was this sense of special appropriateness that indicated one important way in which the old analogy might be revitalized. As long as its use was restricted to such general words as monarch, kingdom, empire, dominion, and tyrant it was always likely to verge upon and perhaps become a cliché metaphor, because the political terms of the vehicle were important only in so far as they illustrated the literary tenor. When the general words were either replaced or augmented by words that directed attention to the specific political events of the age, the vehicle became interesting in itself and its point was reciprocally illustrated by the nominal tenor. Professor Hoffman thus comments on the following couplet from the Prologue to *The Kind Keeper* (1680), 'Let them, who the Rebellion first began, / To wit, restore the Monarch if they can' (ll. 11–12): '*them who the Rebellion first began*, used here for aesthetic disvalue, strikes upon strongly resonant surfaces in the political realm, the late deposition and execution of Charles I.'[4] The word which permits the specific allusion is *restore*—as it so often is in Dryden's poetry. Particularization of this kind might be achieved punningly, as with the play upon the plots of dramatists and traitors in the Oxford Prologue of 1680 (l. 16). More striking and certainly more daring is the complicated play that Dryden introduced into his lines to Granville in 1698. After reworking his compliment to Congreve of four years before by ceding his poetic laurels to Granville, Dryden proceeds to illustrate the current stupidity of the London theatre by the practice—which also provided material for *The Medal*'s energetic opening—of exhibiting a monster:

> And in Despair their Empty Pit to fill,
> Set up some Foreign Monster in a Bill.
>
> (ll. 21–22)

Coming as it does immediately after an account of the succession from the old monarch Dryden to the young prince Granville, the couplet probably refers to more than a poster advertising some exotic creature designed to draw an audience. The bill, in fact, is both a poster and the parliamentary bill eventually enacted as the Declaration of Rights in 1689, by which

William, the foreigner from Holland, was declared (set up as) king to fill the 'vacancy,' as it was called, created by the 'abdication' of James II. Since, for an orthodox Stuart loyalist, this procedure inevitably represented a departure from the law of succession, a monster would be its obvious counterpart in nature.

If particularization could help the poet find fresh correspondences between the terms of the ancient analogy, a sociological view of literary achievement as conditioned by the state of the nation and contemporary culture could 'justify' the use of the analogy in the moment of its application. The Epilogue to the second part of *The Conquest of Granada* argues that the superiority of Restoration to Jacobean dramatists is a consequence of the later age's improvement in manners, conversation, ethical norms, and critical refinement. Dramatists are simply the particular beneficiaries of a general raising of standards in society. They benefit by their dedication to a mimetic view of literature and their consequent imitation of the patterns and assumptions of living that they can observe around them. In the Epilogue the analogy of kingdoms is not present, but its general view of the dependence of literature on society or environment becomes of special note when, as so often in Dryden, it is expressed in terms of Stuart fortunes.

We are familiar with Dryden's celebration of order in the peaceful art of government and the peaceful art of letters. We are also familiar with his complementary attack upon the disorder of war and rebellion and the consequent lowering of artistic standards in unsettled times. The restoration of Charles II is doubly important for the writer: as a citizen he benefits from the national peace, security, and prosperity that is ensured by the establishment of a legitimate monarch; as a writer he additionally benefits because these are the most favourable conditions for the pursuit of learning and the arts. It is not that in himself Charles Stuart is a better man or ruler than Oliver Cromwell—he may be, but that is not the point. Charles Stuart is the current embodiment of Marvell's 'great work of time,' the long-developing English constitution with its divine right of hereditary succession to the monarchy. Whatever the imperfections of the legitimate ruler's natural body, his incorruptible political body, the continuity of his office, ensures the due transmission of the nation's ancestral wisdom in a way denied to Oliver Cromwell, however good the man or just the ruler. The constitutional assurance that comes when a Stuart is on the throne is thus of special importance to the writer—if he is a royalist—while the fact that the age had seen and was to see again years when the rightful Stuart was banished inevitably prompted a frequent celebration of due succession and an attack upon its opponents.

It is not for nothing that *the Restoration* refers both to the events of 1660 and to—at least—the whole reign of Charles II. Nor is it for nothing that we automatically consider Dryden the major literary figure of the Restoration, despite the fact that the period also saw the publication of Milton's last and greatest works. The particular restoration of 1660 with all its consequences and implications dominated political consciousness for at least twenty-five years, and it further provided its major man of letters with an enduring frame of evaluative reference. As late as 1684, Roscommon can be praised for restoring by his *Essay on Translated Verse* the empire of the muse in the reign of Charles II (ll. 28–29): his learned achievement is analogous to the Caroline restoration and therefore gains in importance. But, by implication, the Caroline restoration created a situation favourable to the muse's restoration, and the importance of the former is thus itself augmented. In the years immediately following 1660 the extent and variety of allusions to the restoration were inevitably at their height. *Astraea Redux* was but one among a host of poems saluting the king's return; justice and settled government but two of the panegyric topics prompted by the event. The panegyrists, in fact, rapidly established a central bank of viable topics and analogies, with the restoration itself as their chief capital but with numerous subsidiary assets, among which some of the more valuable were the presentation of Charles II's wanderings as a storm-tossed sea voyage comparable with that of Aeneas and of his eventual restoration as a divinely ordained landfall on the coast of a new Italy. When in his panegyric upon Clarendon in 1662 Dryden included a barely disguised hint for patronage, it was in terms of the Aeneas analogy phrased to point the dependence of arts (and church) upon settled monarchy:

When our Great Monarch into Exile went
Wit and Religion suffer'd banishment:
Thus once when *Troy* was wrapt in fire and smoak
The helpless Gods their burning shrines forsook;
They with the vanquisht Prince and party go,
And leave their temples empty to the fo:
At length the Muses stand restor'd again
To that great charge which Nature did ordain;
And their lov'd Druyds seem reviv'd by Fate
While you dispence the Laws and guide the State.

(ll. 17–26)

The circumstance that restoration is both a condition and a specific event; that the restoration took place in 1660 and lasted for twenty-five years, frequently involves those of Dryden's poems that refer to it in an artificial present, bounded by the moment of the restoration on one side and the time of their composition on the other. Such at least is the implication of the Aeneas parallel in the Clarendon address of 1662, for the verb tenses indicate that the past of the poem is concerned with Charles's exile and ends with the moment of his restoration in 1660, which inaugurates the poem's 'present.' Past and present, in fact, point to historical ages. Because this is so, the monarchic values introduced at the specific restoration can be constantly reaffirmed throughout the Restoration age. Its special importance for affairs in the kingdom of letters is equally observable in the verse compliments to Howard in 1660, to Charleton in 1662, and to Lady Castlemaine in 1663 at the earliest.

TO DR. CHARLETON

Professor Wasserman's reading of the address to Charleton argues the integrity of the poem's dual concern with scientific achievement and political events. Dryden's full title is 'To my Honour'd Friend, Dr Charleton, on his learned and useful Works; and more particularly this of Stone-Heng, by him Restored to the true Founders.' The poem served as introductory compliment to Charleton's *Chorea Gigantum; or . . . Stone-Heng . . . Restored to the Danes*, a treatise which attempted to rebut Inigo Jones's theory, published in 1655, that Stonehenge was a Roman temple by asserting that it was instead a palace in which Danish kings were elected. By substituting 'Restored to the true Founders' for Charleton's 'Restored to the Danes,' Dryden frees the phrase from specificity and thus establishes a potential reference to the recent restoration of Charles II, the current representative of the true founders of English monarchy. This potential is fully realized by the conclusion of the poem, in which Charles's coronation is imaginatively re-enacted at Stonehenge. Because Charles had tarried at Stonehenge after his defeat at Worcester in 1651, Inigo Jones's theory was in a sense correct, for, in the poem's final couplet, Charles's *'Refuge* then was for a *Temple* shown: / But, *He* Restor'd, 'tis now become a *Throne.'* Professor Wasserman justly remarks that 'in a significant sense the total poem exists in order to bring about the identification of the "Restored" of the title with the "Restor'd" of the final line.'[5]

Because its analogies occupy a status ultimately indistinguishable from the overt topics which they illustrate, the lines to Charleton may be described as possessing six major concerns: scientific, geographic, medical, mercantile, constitutional, and historical. In musical terms, these concerns are the themes of the poem, which is divided into three movements, the first dealing with Aristotle and scholasticism, the second with English scientists in general, the third with Charleton's treatise. Each movement makes use of all six themes, although the constitutional note is most clearly heard in the first and third.

The first twenty lines, dealing with the reign of Aristotle, are characterized by slavery, repression, constriction, rigidity, and falsity. The twelve lines devoted to the English introduce freedom, expansion, movement, and truth, while the final section contrasts some of the characteristics of the first two. An incidental motif is that of light. The light of free enquiry is at first replaced by Aristotle's jealous torch (l. 4), which, fearful of competition, drowns the sun within its own geographic limits (l. 18) and denies the existence of southern stars (ll. 19–20). In contrast, Charleton's fame travels as far as light itself (l. 35), because he, like his fellow Englishmen, has shaken off the old restrictions on free enquiry. The opposition between the small pool of illumination cast by Aristotle's torch and the limitless domain of light itself is thus one expression of the contrast between constriction and expansion.

The same contrast occurs in the commercial theme. Economic matters under Aristotle were handled by the issue of monopolies; patents, that is, authorized by the stamp of the Great Seal bearing his arms (l. 8). Such a system meant that 'onely one suppli'd the State' (l. 5). The inevitable abuse resulted: the commodity authorized for sale by monopoly became 'scarce, and dear,' while lack of competition enabled the patent holder to 'sophisticate' or adulterate his goods (l. 6). The first blow to this corrupt system was the voyage of Columbus, and although it has no immediate economic overtones, its obvious implications for mercantilism are picked up in the second section, where Gilbert's contribution to knowledge proves invaluable to English trade (ll. 25–26). Commerce under Aristotle is centripetal, under the English it is centrifugal. At this level, it is impossible to separate the geographical theme from the commercial. Aristotle's reign permits no international trade because his realm extends only to the edge of the classical Ocean: it is bounded by the western seas (l. 17). But the discoveries of Columbus have revealed a 'boundless Ocean' (l. 26); consequently, Charleton's fame need not be 'circumscrib'd with *English* ground' (l. 34), and his works discover 'rich veins of Ore' (l. 39)—just as the voyage of Columbus led to the discovery of the West Indian gold-mines.

Closely combined with the commercial theme is the medical, for the goods sold under Aristotle's patent are quack medicines: 'Emp'rique Wares, or Charms' (l. 7). In addition, Harvey's discovery of circulation is implicitly connected with the theme of trade by virtue of the '*Circling* streams' (l. 29), a term equally applicable to blood and the Ocean. The circulation of trade under mercantilism contrasts with the old 'pools' of restrictive monopoly, although the commercial implications of Harvey's discovery are dependent upon the general context for their suggestiveness.[6] Charleton's other role as physician permits an appropriate use of the medical theme, but it should be noticed that his curing of books follows from and is paralleled by his discovery of mineral resources in other authors. In fact, the change of imagery at this point marks the transition from the economic aspects of government to the constitutional.

The opposition between true and false knowledge which runs throughout the poem and which is variously expressed in terms

of medicine, geography, and economic practice is finally resolved by the opposed theories of Jones and Charleton about the
origin of Stonehenge. Charleton can find Stonehenge to have
been a place where kings were crowned because the restoration
of Charles II has renewed the relevance of coronation, while
Jones in 1655 was 'correct' to see the monument as a temple,
because, as Professor Wassermann points out, Charles was then
only king *de jure*, possessed of a 'Sacred Head' but without *de
facto* authority in the land. The recent change in England's constitution is thus the final factor that makes possible Charleton's
'discovery.' This change takes its place in a series of enabling
factors, operating in similar ways and with similar effects, from
the general level of Western civilization through the general
contribution of the English to the specific event that Dryden
celebrates.

Because the unhealthy theory of Jones, which Charleton has
now cured, resulted from its being propounded during the
Interregnum, it follows that an Interregnum which can produce
this diseased knowledge is analogous to the rule of Aristotle with
its similarly adulterated truth. The values established earlier
in the poem in terms of Western civilization are thus operative
in the final, specific opposition between Interregnum and
Restoration. Their relevance is all the more likely because the
progress of learning had been expressed in terms of the conventional kingdom of letters. Sick knowledge results from a
tyranny in this kingdom, while a discovery like that of Columbus shakes the tyrant's throne, and consequently, by the climate
theory of government, converts the torrid zone of tyrannical
or despotic rule into a temperate zone characterized by a monarchy coexisting with popular liberties—with free-born rights
to parallel the 'free-born *Reason*' that had been betrayed to
Aristotle (ll. 2–3). Because the poem has already explored fully
the constitutional implications of tyranny and its overthrow in
the kingdom of letters, the final account of the enthronement of
the legitimate king of England has no further need to elaborate
upon the constitutional opposition. Activities and their consequences are parallel in the two kingdoms because the same
analogies serve to describe events in each and because the
practical contribution of learning to medicine and commerce
has identical consequences in both kingdoms. By the end of the

poem, in fact, analogy has been replaced by identity: England is the kingdom of letters.

The art of the poem is to bring about this identity, for it cannot be assumed from the beginning. The very fact that the analogy was a commonplace, that learning, like poetry, was conventionally described in political terms, would militate against immediate topical reference. Professor Wasserman's argument that Aristotle's tyranny refers however implicitly to the administration of Cromwell thus depends upon a doubtful inference. There is no reason to suppose specific allusion precisely because the general analogy was so unexceptional. While it is true that '*our* Ancestors' in the second line can ambiguously suggest both a Western and a specifically English inheritance, the force of *Ancestors*, while not, it is true, precluding a reference to the Interregnum, scarcely helps focus attention upon the immediate past. Moreover, the commercial handling of Aristotelean learning by monopolies would not, in historical terms, point chiefly to the Interregnum, since the abuse had been largely restricted by the Monopolies Act of 1623. Even more important is the fact that the poem itself in the second movement conducts its survey of English science in terms that ignore any parallelism with the recent fortunes of English government; for the discoveries of Gilbert and Harvey predated both Interregnum and Restoration.

By taking Aristotle's rule as an exact paradigm of Cromwell's, Professor Wasserman is led to assume a more detailed contrast between Charles II's reign and Aristotle's than the poem in fact supports, and to argue that the association of Charles with the Danes involves Dryden in praising the restoration of a limited Stuart monarchy after a period of Cromwellian absolutism. The Danish monarchy had been elective until 1660, and Professor Wasserman argues that elective monarchies were understood in the seventeenth century to involve limitations upon kingly power that effectively guaranteed the rights of subjects. In fact, elective monarchy was as susceptible to conflicting interpretations as any other political belief of the age. For Bodin, election implied an absolute donation of sovereign power to the king reminiscent of the Hobbesian covenant.[7] Sanderson agreed with Bodin, and although he assumed a popular election in which a prince is chosen by the 'free *suffrages* of the people' he insisted that the people only '*designate the person* who is to govern,' the authority to govern is given by God alone.[8] Filmer, as might be expected, rejected popular election and insisted that the right of choice is restricted to an aristocratic diet; he admitted a theoretical limitation on the king's power, but argued that in practice the king is absolute. For Filmer, moreover, elective monarchies evolved from an act of grace by an originally hereditary monarch who wished to demonstrate his piety and good intentions.[9] Against these royalist interpretations of elective monarchy as virtually absolute must be set the 'Gothic' evidence cited by Professor Wasserman. Samuel Kliger has pointed out that elective monarchies were instanced by those who opposed Norman absolutism; the so-called Germanic heritage argued an original restriction on royal authority that was imposed in practice by governing through the High Court of parliament. It is this conception of the High Court which is presented by the author of *A Plea for Limited Monarchy* when he describes government as consisting in 'the senate proposing, the people resolving, the magistrate executing.'[11] If, then, elective monarchy could be indifferently interpreted as absolute or limited, it becomes essential to ask whether the poem directs our reading to one or the other.

The mere fact of the king's official inauguration at the time of his coronation did not necessarily imply constitutional limitations upon his authority. On the other hand, it is possible that Dryden is transferring to Charles's rule some of the values implicit in the ancient ceremony described by Charleton. It is certainly true that lines 47–52 make use of part of Charleton's treatise, for the ruler is placed on a high stone as a symbol of his election and inauguration. But Charleton did not make any constitutional deductions from the fact of popular suffrage, other than the conditional remark that it was 'As if the Place and Ceremonies were essential parts of his Right to soveraignty, and the votes of his Electors much more valid and authentique, for being pronounced in that *Forum*.'[12] Elsewhere, Charleton's treatise tends rather to minimize than to accentuate any idea of restriction. When he describes the newly elected king standing on the high stone, he adds that the reason for this prominence is to enable the king to receive from his people 'their joyful Acclamations, wishes of felicity, and other *testimonies of submis-*

sion and fealty.'[13] It is this note which Dryden catches in his reference to the 'wondring Subjects' (l. 49), just as the elevation of the king and the fact that he will 'rule the Land' (l. 52) is a greater indication of absolutism than limitation. Moreover, a major reason for the specific introduction of Charles at this point is apparently that a compliment is to be made on his royal bearing. Just as the warlike Danes at the inauguration of their kings were 'Joy'd with their Stature, and their Princely meen' (l. 50), so Charles (who was certainly tall) can inspire like emotion in his own subjects.

In an earlier chapter it was pointed out that some royalists believed it unnecessary to place limitations upon the king *ab externo* in order to guarantee the rights and liberties of subjects. Freedom was as much a condition of the royal monarchy as it was of the constitutional. Dryden, it was further suggested, seems to tend in other poems toward the Bodinian ideal rather than that of, say, Hunton and Henry Parker, both of whom Filmer attacked in *The Anarchy of a Limited or Mixed Monarchy*. In the lines to Charleton, however, Dryden seems concerned not so much with questions of absolutism or limitation as with legitimism and usurpation. After all, if we agree that the restored Danes of line 45 are analogous with the Stuarts, then the Saxons of the next line must, by Professor Wasserman's argument, be an analogy for the Interregnum. But in 'Gothic' terms Saxons and Danes were indistinguishable, for their constitutions both reflected the Germanic heritage of parliamentary monarchy. It seems worth noting, moreover, that the introduction of the Saxons has nothing to do with Stonehenge as a temple: Inigo Jones's theory had assigned the monument to the Romans. The justification of their presence is apparently that Charleton attempted to date the construction of Stonehenge to the temporary decline in Alfred's fortunes when the Danish invaders controlled nearly all of southern England. When Alfred was able to marshal his forces, he expelled the Danes, who left behind them the curious monument to their leisure activities.[14] Charleton's work has restored the Danes, who now become identified with royal legitimism and the 'mighty Visions' (l. 56) that testify to their warlike spirit.

A reading of the lines to Charleton would suggest, then, that it is for the poet and his poem to release the potential for topical reference which was always latent in accounts of the kingdom of letters. By releasing this potential the poem re-creates or renews the well-tried analogy, and a reading is properly directed to the process by which this is achieved. The fact that somewhere in the poem there will usually be a passage of explicit topicality directly relating literary to political events does not justify our indiscriminate application of its special values elsewhere in the work. To do so would convert the poems into political allegories, whereas their poetic mode is quite clearly that of analogy which, in the passages of explicit topicality, becomes virtual identity. It is true that in such poems the general political analogy will usually be phrased in a way that prepares for the specific application, for in no other way can the poem's sequacious logic be maintained. But this preparation, this planting of potential reference, does not necessarily convert a general into a specific analogy. In the lines to Charleton the passage of explicit topicality concludes the poem, and considered strictly as topical allusion the bulk of the poem therefore has only potential reference. But, of course, the point of the poem is not to effect a wittily dark conceit; what happens in the kingdom of letters is important in itself as well as in relation to analogous events in the kingdom at large. There is always a danger that works of this kind will become merely ingenious testimonies to the poet's skill in talking about two realms at once: something like this seems to be true of Dryden's lines to Lady Castlemaine. Only when the poem makes us feel that the two realms are dependent upon and revelatory of each other, that the literary event has a significance and weight equivalent to the political, is it likely to avoid this danger.

TO SIR ROBERT HOWARD

The most striking difference between the lines to Howard and those to Charleton is that the latter poem, unlike the former, makes consistent use of political terminology which leads naturally into the topical explicitness of the close. The address to Howard confines its political terminology almost exclusively to lines 45–54 and the explicit references of the final twenty lines. The remaining two-thirds of the poem are given over to general critical praise for Howard's verse. In fact, lines 45–54 effect a parallel between the history of recent poetic taste and recent political events, while the closing lines can become explicit because Howard included panegyrics upon Monck and Charles II in the little volume of verse to which Dryden's lines served as introductory commendation. If the critical criteria can assume in lines 45–54 an analogous relationship with recent history, there is some point in enquiring whether the poem prepares for such a relationship from the start.

It is clear from even a casual reading that the poem's movements or sections correspond quite closely with the contents of Howard's volume. The first forty lines offer general observations on the nature of Howard's poetry and on how it achieved its astonishing excellence; they comprise the first movement. The second movement, from lines 41 to 54, concerns itself with Howard's 'easier Odes,' which are apparently the 'Songs and Sonnets' which immediately follow the panegyric to Charles in Howard's volume. Dryden omits Howard's next offering: 'The Blind Lady, A Comedy,' and proceeds to items 4 and 5, the translations of the fourth Aeneid and the *Achilleid* of Statius. The whole passage on Howard's translations, extending to line 86, may be taken to comprise the third movement. The fourth, lines 87–100, deals with Howard's opening and closing items, the panegyrics on Charles and Monck. The last six lines of the poem contain Dryden's prophecy, and may be called the coda. From this brief analysis it can be seen that the passage of specific topicality and the historically explicit close are contained within a more general structure that binds them closely to the critical discussion. It is possible, moreover, to divide the poem into smaller units, for each movement consists of two parts. In the third and fourth sections the division results from Dryden's discussion of two related items in Howard's volume: the two panegyrics and the two translations. The opening section of general comment concerns itself for sixteen lines with the qualities of Howard's verse before moving to a discussion of how poetry, especially Howard's, is composed. The second section deals specifically with the 'odes' for only four lines before turning to a general discussion of the qualities that make them analogous to certain political values.

When consideration is given to recurrent themes, it becomes clear that the first three movements offer a series of oppositions and double standards. The general qualities of Howard's poetry are epitomized by the couplet on Samson's riddle (ll. 15–16). The qualities of sweetness and strength refer back to the opening images of the poem. Sweetness alone is possessed by the untutored bird of 'unfrequented shades' (l. 3), and presumably refers, therefore, to the melody that Dryden claims to have detected in Howard's verse. Both sweetness and strength are possessed by Howard's river muse—Aganippe perhaps—but their necessary mutation into calmness and depth suggests that the quality of strength has something to do with content. In the couplet that forms the transition between the two parts of the first section the strength and depth become 'weight' (ll. 17–18). Dryden, then, is proposing to praise Howard's verse on the double criterion of its melody and content. In the brief discussion of the 'odes' the two terms assume their familiar dress; melody provides delight, the content provides instruction (ll. 41–42). Melody is *dulce*; content is *utile*. When he comes to Howard's translations the double criterion undergoes a further change, for, not satisfied with cautious praise for a spirited version that captures the flavour of the original, Dryden surprisingly asserts that the knight has improved upon his authors. The soft submissiveness of Virgil's Dido is made commanding. Her speech is now 'eloquent' (l. 60), forcibly expressed that is, and inspires obedience in Aeneas, or it would have had the narrative not required that he leave. In other words, Howard has strengthened the sweetness of Virgil. Conversely, he has softened the undue harshness of Statius. Achilles is made more feminine, just as Dido was made more masculine, and the breach of decorum that this achievement seems to entail makes it look as if Dryden is satirizing rather than praising Howard. In the fourth section of the poem Dryden suddenly abandons his double critical standard and contents himself with applauding Howard's good taste in eulogizing Charles and Monck. Once again, it seems pertinent to ask whether the change is quite so abrupt as it seems, and to determine the answer it will be necessary to consider lines 45–54.

> Of Morall Knowledge Poesie was Queen,
> And still she might, had wanton wits not been;
> Who like ill Guardians liv'd themselves at large,
> And not content with that, debauch'd their charge:

Like some brave Captain, your successfull Pen
Restores the Exil'd to her Crown again;
And gives us hope, that having seen the days
When nothing flourish'd but Fantique Bays,
All will at length in this opinion rest,
'A sober Prince's Government is best.'

As Professor Wasserman pointed out in his discussion of the Charleton address, Howard's 'successfull Pen' has restored poetry to its rightful kingdom of 'Morall Knowledge' just as the 'brave Captain'—General Monck, that is—has restored Charles to the throne of England. The analogy thus established is by no means based simply on the fact that Howard published what Dryden chose to regard as a volume of accomplished verse in the year of Charles's restoration, for the analogy elaborated in lines 49–54 depends on the fact that both Charles and Howard's poetry restored sobriety to their respective dominions. Within the course of the next decade few Englishmen would have selected their monarch as the ideal converse of 'wanton wits,' and the reputation of Charles for licentiousness has survived unimpaired to the present day. But it should be remembered that in 1660 Charles was virtually unknown to his countrymen, since he had been in exile from the age of nineteen to the age of thirty. Moreover, the people's curiosity about the personality of their new king had been comprehensively satisfied by a wealth of eulogistic 'characters' that enumerated Charles's compendious virtues.[15] He was a skilled linguist, diplomat, and conversationalist, and was remarkable for honesty, piety, sobriety, and general integrity. Dryden's analogy thus tenders one of the more negotiable assets of the bank of common praise, and would presumably have been accorded nothing but ready acceptance in June 1660.

Howard's poetry bears an analogous relationship to Charles himself, because both are marked by gravity and sobriety. These qualities in the poetry are a sign of its strength, depth, and weight, and it seems possible that we can find a latent historical theme beneath the manifest concern with criticism and poetry. At this point in the poem it is apparent that during the period of exile and Interregnum poetry was perverted by too great an emphasis on delight and a neglect of instruction. Moreover, the concern with delight led to an abuse of trust. The 'wanton wits' of the Interregnum have corrupted poetry and by implication have driven it from the land, for Queen Poesie becomes successively the debauched ward of 'ill Guardians' and the exile who is restored to 'her Crown' by Howard's pen. A series of analogies may be assumed. Moral knowledge is to England as poetry is to Charles. Poetry's rule over moral knowledge and Charles's government of England further contrast with Interregnum misrule, which included the abuse and expulsion of Charles and poetry. Clearly, for all its emphasis on delight, the Interregnum was characterized by violence. In terms of the double critical standard the abuse of sweetness manifests itself in an abuse of strength.

It will be recalled that in *Astraea Redux* (a poem written within weeks of the Howard address) Dryden addressed Charles in the following terms:

> You, whose goodness your discent doth show,
> Your Heav'nly Parentage and earthly too;
> By that same mildness which your Fathers Crown
> Before did ravish, shall secure your own.
> Not ty'd to rules of Policy, you find
> Revenge less sweet then a forgiving mind.
> . . . .
> Your Pow'r to Justice doth submit your Cause,
> Your Goodness only is above the Laws;
> Whose rigid letter while pronounc'd by you
> Is softer made.
>
> (ll. 256–61, 266–69)

Royal mercy is modified by such epithets as 'sweet' and—in its comparative form—'soft.' Moreover, Charles I's undue mildness and clemency led directly to the rape of his office, just as the 'ill Guardians' of the Howard address 'debauch'd their Charge.' Charles I's mildness gave way to the unbridled, intemperate power of the Interregnum. Charles II, on the other hand, has both power within the law and mercy above it, he combines within himself the extreme qualities of the preceding rules to produce the ideal king.

Because the political debate of the early Restoration so often coupled sweetness, strength, softness, and violence with law, equity, and justice, it may be suggested that critical praise of Howard's verse in terms of its (morally instructive) strength and (melodic) sweetness possesses a potential relationship with the power and mercy of Charles II. It is an intention of the poem to realize that potential in order to show how the quality of poetry is dependent upon the nature of government and to find in even the most detailed of literary phenomena an image of political events. The first forty-four lines of the poem are concerned, then, to establish its critical criteria in terms that make appropriate the subsequent coupling of literary and political matters. The coupling is marked in line 45 by the transfer of the critical discussion to the kingdom of letters, which is in turn quickly associated with the kingdom of England. Before that point political reference is only potential. Syntactically, the formula governing the first forty-four lines is 'in poetry'; in lines 45–54 the formula becomes 'as in poetry, so in politics.' But the values established 'in poetry' are identical with those 'as in poetry' and hence are relevant 'in politics,' not, it is true, at the moment of their introduction, but only at the moment of their political application. The account of the coronation in the Charleton address had no need to detail the rejected qualities of the Interregnum because those qualities had already been established in terms of the Aristotelean tyranny. The lines to Howard can practise a similar economy, although they undoubtedly pose greater problems for an accurate critical description of their poetic mode. The potential political reference of the opening praise is best revealed by relating the qualities and conditions operative 'in poetry.' to the similar qualities and conditions operative 'as in poetry.' Such a relation is required by the approximate nature of criticism; it is not meant to imply that the potential of the opening lines is convertible into an actual reference to political theory and recent history.

The first eight lines establish that Howard's verse possesses a rude melodic sweetness similar to that of birds who sing in 'unfrequented shades' away from 'home.' This sweetness is 'native,' and hence is both untouched by art and belonging to the birds by right of birth. Similarly, when Queen Poesie was forced into exile what she lost was her dominion over 'Morall Knowledge,' her instructive strength, but she was by implication able to retain her beauty and capacity to delight during the period of exile. Howard's poetry possesses in addition to 'native sweetnesse' the depth and strength of 'mighty Rivers' (ll. 9–14). In fact, it has restored 'the Exil'd' Queen to her rightful dominion, just as the 'sober' Charles has been restored to the dominion of England (ll. 50–54). Howard's river muse also exhibits sobriety in its 'even calmnesse' (l. 10), and this quality contrasts with a poetry disfigured by high-swelling and dangerously bold metaphors. The violence of this second river is picked up in the violence of the 'ill Guardians,' the 'wanton wits' responsible for the 'Fanatique Bays' of the Interregnum, who 'debauch'd their charge' and apparently drove her into exile (ll. 47–50). The qualities of sweetness and strength, separately observable in the bird and the river, are finally combined in Howard's verse as they had been only once before in Samson's riddle of the lion and the bees.

Howard, then, has brought back the paradigm of true poetry, just as Charles II has been brought back as the true ruler of the land. The exact analogy ensures that Charles becomes, on the political level appropriate to him, the paradigm of the prince possessed of innate sweetness and the acquired but rightful strength of dominion: native mercy combined with *de facto* power produces the true justice that can be expected in the best of governments. If we give Samson's riddle its more usual seventeenth-century interpretation (which Dryden does not, of course), Charles is both the lion of effective power and the bee of clemency. Moreover, one of the great commonplaces of the age was the analogy between government and a river, with multiple variations upon the controlled flow of justice, the due limitation provided by the banks, and the tyrannous or rebellious consequences of overflowing those banks. Dryden, it will be recalled, made effective use of the analogy in the lines to his cousin. In the Howard address he stops short of explicit political reference, but only just short, for the dangerous boldness of metaphoric aspiration in the false river muse is described in terms equally appropriate to a rebellious overthrow of government, and its qualities are consequently all the more relevant to those of the 'ill Guardians' of poetry during the Interregnum.

Howard's achievement, it is quite clear, is not only similar to recent political events, it is conditional upon them. The return of a sober prince ensures the return of poetry to its ancient moral eminence. It was the lack of a moral guardian during the Interregnum which encouraged nothing but 'Fanatique Bays': the versification of individual religious inspiration with its royalist suggestion of a challenge to church and hence to national government.

An opposition is thus established between the true poetry of Howard's restored muse, at once sweet and strong, and the false poetry that flourished during the Interregnum, with its violent abuse of strength forcing sweet poetry into exile. This opposition is then adapted to the praise of Howard's translations, for Howard has brought strength to Virgil's Dido and sweetness to the Achilles of Statius. Because the political implications of the critical criteria have been drawn out in the lines immediately preceding praise for the translations, the relationship between Howard's versions and his originals can reflect or at least parallel the course of recent political events.

Virgil's Dido is reminiscent of Charles I, who was characterized, as all the royalists agreed, by undue lenity in his dealings with parliament. If he had been more commanding, parliament would have obeyed him instead of invoking a divine dispensation to rebel:

> *Elisa*'s griefs, are so exprest by you,
> They are too eloquent to have been true.
> Had she so spoke, *Æneas* had obey'd
> What *Dido* rather then what *Jove* had said.
>
> (ll. 59–62)

Howard's muse, as the type of Charles II, suggests what would have happened if the son had been faced with his father's difficulty, for the parliamentary opposition of Aeneas would inevitably have submitted to the true combination of power and mercy. Achilles is an extension of Aeneas because he shares a couplet and an obligation with him:

> But if *Æneas* be oblig'd, no lesse
> Your kindnesse great *Achilles* doth confesse.
>
> (ll. 67–68)

Achilles exemplifies Interregnum government in general and Cromwell in particular. The actual conditions of the Interregnum are shown in Statius's original to have been 'too bold,' and 'lamely rough, / Each figure stiffe as if design'd in buffe' (ll. 69, 73–74), dressed, that is, in the leather jerkins of the seventeenth-century army. 'The Buff' was an accepted term for the army, and here suggests the Interregnum stratocracy, Cromwell's dependence upon army support.[16] From his Restoration vantage point Howard is able to correct the abuse of strength in Statius and the Interregnum, for his translation reveals, in effect, what would have happened if Charles II had succeeded his father *de facto* as well as *de jure* in 1649. The relationship between Howard's translations and his originals is thus similar to Charleton's curing of error in Inigo Jones's treatise by giving the corrected Restoration version of 1649 and the Interregnum, which were accurately described by Virgil and Statius.

Although the political reflection is no more than implicit in Dryden's lines, the implication is permitted, not only because literary and political matters are explicitly coupled in the immediately preceding lines, but because the translations are considered in terms of the characters' ability to command and to meet the requirements of their position. In fact, the fashioning of an implicit parallel seems to result in forced ingenuity at one point, for, while praise for the commanding eloquence of Howard's Dido effectively applies the earlier critical criteria, it does so at the cost of hinting at a breach of narrative decorum: even in Howard's version Aeneas obeyed Jove, not Dido, and Howard's representation of character has therefore contradicted the course of the action. A further reason for considering the political suggestion of the translations is that Dryden's account of them ends with a metaphor which is then almost immediately given its conventional political application in the historically explicit section dealing with Howard's panegyrics on Charles and Monck:

> Your curious Notes so search into that Age,
> When all was fable but the sacred Page,
> That since in that dark night we needs must stray,
> We are at least misled in pleasant way.
> But what we most admire, your Verse no lesse
> The Prophet than the Poet doth confesse.
> Ere our weak eyes discern'd the doubtfull streak
> Of light, you saw great *Charls* his morning break.
>
> (ll. 83–90)

Howard's (pedantic and uninteresting) annotations upon his Statius serve, then, as guide to an age of 'dark night' just as

Charles II's return brings back the sun to an England of benighted rebellion. The original of Statius is thus once more implicitly related to the Interregnum. Moreover, the reference to the Bible's 'sacred Page' seems oddly gratuitous in an account of a Roman poet, until we recall that in the Interregnum Puritans triumphed and justified their actions by scriptural reference. In the realm of poetry such conduct produced the 'Fanatique Bays' of line 52.

In addition to the major concern with the qualities of Howard's verse there is in the second half of the opening section a subordinate enquiry into the secret of Howard's composition. Dryden is proposing, in fact, to discover why Howard has been able to restore Queen Poesie to her rightful domain:

> Is it Fortune's work, that in your head
> The curious Net that is for fancies spread,
> Let's through its Meshes every meaner thought,
> While rich Idea's there are onely caught?
> Sure that's not all; this is a piece too fair
> To be the child of Chance, and not of Care.
> No Atoms casually together hurl'd
> Could e're produce so beautiful a world.
> Nor dare I such a doctrine here admit,
> As would destroy the providence of wit.
>
> (ll. 25–34)

The rejection of the mechanistic theory of composition as 'Fortune's work' and the contrary celebration of creative imagination as 'the providence of wit' further prepares for the alignment of poetry with politics. Just as Howard's providential wit has brought Queen Poesie into her own again so Charles II has been restored to his patrimony. The terms and values established in lines 25–34 make it clear that, as in *Astraea Redux*, Charles has been restored by providence. Howard's 'successful Pen'—which in fact brings back the Queen—is not merely a metonymy for Howard himself. It is specifically the agent of his providential wit, just as Monck the 'brave Captain' is the agent of the divine providence, an office identical with that assigned to him in *Astraea Redux* (ll. 151–52).

Implications, suggestions, and potential references are by their very nature difficult, perhaps impossible, to describe accurately. As soon as explication moves on from what is explicit in the poem only a modicum of critical scepticism is required to prompt at least some dissatisfaction with the terms of analysis. The critic's problem is notoriously to demonstrate the poem's subtlety and not his own. If he is not to confine himself to what is obvious, he must risk the latter in order to approximate the former. But every reading should be centred upon some probability. In the lines to Howard I take that probability to be the integrity of the poem's simultaneous concern with poetry and politics. Values established in literary terms are translatable into analogous political values because they share the same adjectives and the same attitudes to order and disorder and because the quality of poetry is conditioned by and hence an expression of the political situation of the land. At the end of the poem the earlier parallel between the Caroline restoration and Howard's restoration of poetry is recalled in Dryden's prophecy:

'This Work by merit first of Fame secure
'Is likewise happy in its Geniture:
'For since 'tis born when *Charls* ascends the Throne,
'It shares at once his Fortune and its own.'

Charles II's elevation to the throne places his star in the ascendant over the fortunes of England, while Howard's volume has the good luck to be born or published at the time of the king's return, thus fixing a beneficent influence in its horoscope. It is because Howard's poetry reflects the fortune of Charles while maintaining its own that Dryden's lines on Howard's poetry must recognize its public significance as well as its artistic merit. Professor Wasserman argued that the lines to Charleton work to identify the *restored* of its title and final line. We may say that the lines to Howard work to demonstrate the validity of the concluding prophecy by implicating Howard's poetry with the fortunes of the restored Stuart.

TO LADY CASTLEMAINE

On a Thursday afternoon early in February 1663 Dryden's first play, *The Wild Gallant*, was presented at the Theatre Royal in Vere Street. A confiding Prologue informed the audience that the author, dubious of the play's success, had commissioned him to seek the advice of fortune-tellers. In an excess of gregarious-ness the friendly Prologue invited the audience to accompany him, whereupon the curtain was drawn to reveal two astrologers who presented the play's horoscope:

> *First Astrol. reads.* A Figure of the heavenly Bodies in their several Apartments, *Feb.* the *5th.* half an hour after three after Noon, from whence you are to judge the success of a new Play called the *Wild Gallant.*
> 2. *Astrol.* Who must Judge of it, we, or these Gentlemen? We'l not meddle with it, so tell your Poet. Here are in this House the ablest Mathematicians in *Europe* for his purpose.
> They will resolve the question e'r they part.
> *1. Ast.* Yet let us judge it by the rules of Art.
>
> (ll. 13–21)

The further discussion of the astrologers revealed that the heavens were undecided about the fortunes of *The Wild Gallant*, although they warned that its reception might be adversely influenced by the success of a rival play. Unperturbed by this zodiacal uncertainty, Prologue referred the matter back to the audience, confident of their favour. Such good nature did not deserve to be abused, but the irresponsible judges of the pit apparently damned the play. Nevertheless, a few weeks later the ubiquitous Pepys went to Court,

> And there got good places, and saw 'The Wilde Gallant,' per-formed by the King's house, but it was ill acted, and the play so poor a thing as I never saw in my life almost, and so little answer-ing the name, that from beginning to end, I could not, nor can at this time, tell certainly which was the Wild Gallant. The King did not seem pleased at all, all the whole play, nor any body else. . . . My Lady Castlemaine was all worth seeing tonight.[17]

Lady Castlemaine apparently did more than receive admira-tion, for she took the fledgling playwright beneath her powerful wing to such good effect that Dryden reported six years later in the preface to the published version of the play that, despite the general condemnation of the town, *The Wild Gallant* 'was received at court; and was more than once the divertisement of his Majesty, by his own command.'[18] If Pepys's estimate of the king's reaction is correct, it seems likely that the chain of com-mand did not begin with his Majesty. By the end of 1662

Barbara Villiers, Countess of Castlemaine, was firmly established at Court in the dual role of mistress to the king and lady of the queen's bedchamber. It was a trifling request of her royal lover to ask that he occasionally sit through the performance of a dull play.

In return for this presumed office, Dryden wrote his lines to Lady Castlemaine, and when he did so he had recourse to the alternative sources of favour proposed by the two astrologers: mortal applause and heavenly approval. The first forty-four lines develop a contrast between the condemnation of the town and the gracious recognition of Lady Castlemaine. Human reaction is associated with stormy 'misfortunes' (l. 4), 'ill success' (l. 7), the 'Worlds applause' (l. 14), 'empty Fame, and Praise' (l. 17), 'vain men' (l. 19), the stars (ll. 25, 38), and 'Natures Laws' (l. 28). Lady Castlemaine attracts to herself an increasing number of divine attributes until she finally becomes 'Some God' who 'descended and preserv'd the Play' (l. 44). In the course of thanking her for her favour, Dryden successfully compliments Lady Castlemaine upon her undoubted beauty and upon her more suspect 'Innocence' and 'Virtue' (ll. 30, 32). The unsurprising circumstance that Lady Castlemaine has been subjected to the hostile gossip of Court intrigue allows her to appreciate the analogous plight of Dryden's 'much-envy'd Muse' (l. 5). Her defeat of her opponents by the simple expedient of confronting them with her innocence is an argument that Dryden's play will be similarly vindicated. Her triumph ensures his because she is his protector, and her 'great Fate' has more influence than the lesser stars which govern Dryden's customary lot (ll. 37–38). The relationship is similar to that which Dryden prophesied would exist between the fortune of Howard's poem and the fortune of Charles II. To this single cumulative movement Dryden appended a fourteen-line coda that isolates the Countess's beauty for special attention.

The manifest simplicity of the poem's matter contrasts sharply with the complexity of the Charleton address, but the metaphoric amplification of commonplace events may constitute an invitation to place them in a wider context. Whether such an assumption is justified is best determined by an immediate consideration of the suggestive historical analogy in lines 9–12:

Once *Cato*'s Vertue did the Gods oppose,
While they the Victor, he the Vanquish'd chose:
But you have done what *Cato* could not do,
To chuse the Vanquish'd, and restore him too.

In terms of the poem's surface meaning what is troubling about
this passage is the seemingly gratuitous introduction of a victor
to be set beside the vanquished muse or play of Dryden, or, indeed, the vanquished playwright himself. Moreover, it is
reasonable to ask to what Dryden has been restored. *The Wild
Gallant* was his first play, and its failure could not therefore have
robbed him of previous dramatic importance. In view of the
unavoidable associations of *restore* and the fact that Barbara
Villiers's power is superior not only to Cato's but also, by implication, to the pagan gods', it is clear that there is a conventionally allusive reference to the providential restoration of Charles
II. The adaptation of Roman history to the recent past of England thus provides a series of implicit parallels and identifications. The vanquished Pompey is both Dryden and Charles II
in 1649 as the representative of the temporarily defeated House
of Stuart. The victorious Julius Caesar is not only a superfluous
successful playwright but also the parliamentarians in general
and Oliver Cromwell in particular. Barbara Countess of Castlemaine is the divine providence responsible for the restoration,
just as it will become apparent in the succeeding lines that the
pagan gods are responsible for the transitory whims of fortune.
Thus, Dryden can remark later in the poem: 'Well may I rest
secure in your great Fate, / And dare my Stars to be unfortunate' (ll. 37–38). Lady Castlemaine's 'great Fate' is her providential care of her favourites, and it is explicitly opposed to star-
governed fortune. It may be recalled that one of the basic controls of the *Heroic Stanzas* is the implicit identification of Cromwell with Julius Caesar. The identification was a commonplace
and was sometimes expressed in terms of the passage from
Lucan's *Pharsalia* that Dryden adapts to the praise of Lady
Castlemaine. Dryden, moreover, employed in his praise of
Cromwell precisely that passage of Roman history which is here
applied to royalist ends:

Fortune (that easie Mistresse of the young
But to her auncient servants coy and hard)

> Him at that age her favorites rank'd among
> When she her best-lov'd *Pompey* did discard.
>
> (ll. 29–32)

The murder of Pompey implies the elevation of Caesar, and because it represents an overthrow of an established *de jure* rule for *de facto* government it also implies the execution of Charles I. For the purpose of encomium upon Cromwell the intrusion of Charles II would be disastrous, and Pompey is therefore representative only of Charles I in the *Heroic Stanzas*. After the restoration any mention of Charles II would be the reverse of disastrous and far from an intrusion; and Pompey can represent Charles during his exile. In fact, the Pompey of the Castlemaine address is both Charles I and Charles II. As he was vanquished he is a type of the defeated House of Stuart, by which both father and son are implied; as he was murdered he is specifically Charles the Martyr; but, as he was, in Dryden's adaptation, restored, he is specifically the ultimately triumphant son.

Having posited the figure of Cromwell as foil to Charles, Dryden develops the implicit political contrast through the course of the next eight lines. The nameless successful playwright depends (like Cromwell) on three things: his intrinsic merits and deserts, popular applause, and the favours of fame, who is, we should remember, traditionally connected with fortune, by virtue of the fickle womanhood they share. In the *Heroic Stanzas* Dryden coupled them in a single line when he remarked of Cromwell that 'He fought secure of fortune as of fame' (l. 53). Fame and fortune are representative of the vicissitudes of the human lot; in themselves they typify merely mundane approval or disapproval, and they are opposed to the divine and enduring sanction essential to kingship and right rule. Dryden's providence, as in the poems discussed in an earlier chapter, is not the general prescience of God, but the special providence which manifests itself by a direct and supernatural intervention of the divine into a world otherwise ruled by fortune, for the purpose of protecting some favoured individual who is invariably royal or connected with royalty. True kings, kings by divine right, are, like the 'True Poets' of line 17, the particular care of heaven, whereas other men are merely mortal and hence the natural fools of fortune. The popular applause that the rival playwright relies upon represents a false sanction to be set against the valid divine sanction. The earlier allusion to Lucan, the deliberate equation of theatrical and political matters, helps to align this false sanction with the anti-royalist view that rulers are dependent upon the general choice or election of the people. What is left to the rival playwright and *de facto* ruler alike is their merit, and as this is a wholly mortal quality it is fittingly rewarded by the mortal agencies of justice, fame, and popular applause. 'True Poets' may also have merit, but not only is merit inessential, it is irrelevant to the awarding of the 'Prize.' That prize is a smile (l. 18), the mark of a special favour, but it is also, at the end of the poem, a 'soveraign smile' (l. 58), for this special favour is the bestowal of sovereignty and true title upon the 'Happy' recipient. (There is, in addition, an obvious pun upon the twenty-shilling piece that is appropriate to the context of debt and receipted bills.) Only a clearly divine figure who sits 'above' and sees 'vain men below' (l. 19) can bestow that sovereignty, no matter how much mere mortals may delude themselves into thinking that it is something they can fight for among themselves (l. 20). The graceful self-deprecation of these lines thus gains point by being couched in terms reminiscent of the constitutional debate of the Restoration.

In two later passages (ll. 25–30, 37–44) Dryden elaborates his basic opposition between fortune and providence. As God, Lady Castlemaine is fittingly provided with her 'own Heav'n' (l. 26), and is distinguished from the realm of 'Natures Laws' by her 'Knowledg,' her divine omniscience, that is (l. 28). The inferior stars are associated with the realm of nature and, traditionally enough, with the individual fortune of mortals (l. 38). Dryden as Charles has providence on his side and can reasonably challenge the stars of fortune to do their worst (l. 38). Moreover, the 'Cause' of the divine Lady Castlemaine is 'Nobler' (l. 27) than that of 'Natures Laws' because it is the first cause, while theirs is a second cause. The lady's beauty is her 'Inheritance' (l. 22), but since she is born to her own heaven, her beauty is but one more aspect of her divine self-sufficiency, and as such can be a metonymy for it. Thus, while all men are religiously bound to God (all men, that is, who recognize the supremacy of God, and, of course, of 'Beauty'), God has freed Dryden—just as he had freed Charles—not, certainly, from theological bondage, but from the bondage of depending upon popular acclaim, in the theatre as in the state. But it is for lines 41–44 that Dryden reserves his most successful representation of providential deliverance:

> Posterity will judge by my success,
> I had the *Grecian* Poets happiness,
> Who waving Plots, found out a better way;
> Some God descended and preserv'd the Play.

The invoking of the Euripidean epiphany or *deus ex machina* provides an explicit parallel with his theme of special providence at the same time that it is generated by the whole theatrical context and the overt occasion of the poem. This divine lady does not only 'sit above,' she descends and directly intervenes for the preservation of a play that has been staged both in Vere Street and throughout England, for the manifest God has dismissed the plots of dramatists and rebellious subjects alike, and produced a better way in the restoration.

When we turn to the opening epic simile we can see that it is not simply one more voyage upon the sea of life. Dryden is appropriating to himself and his muse that image of a storm-tossed sea voyage culminating in a prosperous landfall which was so often specified as the wanderings of Aeneas and which was nearly always associated with the exile of Charles II and his eventual restoration. Inasmuch as the weighty political potential of this simile is immediately realized by the *Pharsalia* allusion—adapted to suit the restoration context—it is true to say that the political suggestiveness of the poem is established so firmly by the opening twelve lines that it can be invoked allusively throughout the remainder of the poem. Thus, the (apparently casual) parallelism of line 15: 'Let Merit Crowns, and Justice Laurels give,' suggestively links poetic and political success. Consequently, the detailed account of Dryden's debt to Lady Castlemaine carries a constant implification of Charles II's debt to providence.

The closing lines of the poem afford a graceful, if unduly extended play upon the physical beauty of Barbara Villiers and that beauty as, I have argued, an aspect of her divinity. The underlying political sense of the lines is that, whereas kings have long honoured the divinity by basing their claims to rule upon its sanction, the divinity has heretofore neglected to give open approval of their submission. The providential restoration of Charles II has discharged the debt by conferring sovereignty upon an exiled king, and Dryden's 'Acquittance' of Lady Castlemaine is also Charles's acknowledgment of divine favour. The poem is both Dryden's panegyric upon the Countess and Charles II's hymn of praise and thanks to God. The poem's integrity may be judged by the fact that the accents of both panegyric and hymn can be heard throughout. It seems impossible that this little piece was not intended for the eyes of the king as well as for those of his mistress.

It must be admitted, however, that integrity does not conclusively demonstrate the poem's merit. The suggestion of forced ingenuity in Dryden's handling of Howard's translations is ubiquitous in the lines to Lady Castlemaine, for the working out of a parallel between muse and monarch is pursued as evidence of its author's witty cleverness. The implication of theatrical and political events is not supported, as it is in the Howard and Charleton addresses, by any suggestion of the actual dependence of literary upon political affairs. Lacking that suggestion, the tone of the lines is merely gallant, and the poem merely a flattering similitude with which the reader might well be inclined to call a truce. Because the poem makes no attempt to justify its exploitation of the analogy, it leaves an impression of empty cleverness. But it is a cleverness which was, no doubt, likely to be well received at Court so many years before the Popish Plot and so many before the second and final exile of a Stuart.

TO MR. CONGREVE

When James II fled across the Channel to France he carried with him the ark of divine right, which was jealously guarded at St. Germain, and passed in succession to his son and grandson. His departure marked the beginning of Jacobitism, a cause illuminated by the glow of defeat and the past. It seemed for a few years that William's infant government might not survive the nursery, as non-juror and Jacobite remained loyal to the House of Stuart for a variety of reasons. The defeat of the Irish expedition at Boyne, the alignment of James with Louis XIV, the great enemy of England and of William's ambitious Grand

Alliance, merged into the Channel skirmishing of Tourville and Russell. The war in the Lowlands led to the treaty of Ryswick and the Act of Settlement barring male Stuarts from the succession. The real political threat of the few years following the Glorious Revolution developed within a decade into the ritual gesture of declaring the Chevalier de St. George James III of England on the death of his father in 1701. The subsequent invasions of the Old and Young Pretenders left as their legacy an insubstantial glory, some songs of touching beauty, and an enduringly popular liqueur.

Nearly five years after the flight of James II Dryden addressed to Congreve a verse compliment on his second play whose manifest subject is the state of English drama and the beneficial effect that the works of the rising young playwright have had and will have upon it. In illustration of this subject Dryden drew upon his favourite comparison between the Jacobean and Restoration theatre. An obvious approach to the poem is to cross-reference it to the parallel discussions in the *Essay of Dramatic Poesy*, the *Essay on the Dramatic Poetry of the Last Age* written in defence of the Epilogue to the second part of *The Conquest of Granada*, and the prologues to *The Tempest*, *Aureng-Zebe*, and *Troilus and Cressida*. Additional parallels can be found in the lines to Southerne, Granville, and Motteux. The result of this labour would be an anthology of Dryden's views on Jonson's judgment, Fletcher's easy grace, and Shakespeare's genius. The address to Congreve could take its place in this anthology as evidence of the persistence (or early ossification) of Dryden's critical judgments. The only disturbing element would be a growing realization that the critical discussion of the Congreve address is based upon a few poetic qualities that are variously applied to different authors in a manner contradictory of the apparent argument.

The first nineteen lines appear straightforward enough in terms of the literary criticism. A clear opposition is established between Jacobean and Restoration playwrights, the former being possessed of 'wit' and 'strength' and the latter of 'skill.' Wit is most consistently modified by its connection with strength (ll. 3, 12, 16, 19); it is 'boistrous' (l. 10) and appears to be synonymous with native genius (l. 13). The Janus image connects skill with cultivation in its social as well as its horticultural sense (l. 11). Skill is an art (l. 10) which proceeds according to the rules (l. 8) and results in the civilized virtue of 'manners' (l. 9), because it tames the wild or natural virtues of wit, whose luxuriance has become rank (ll. 8–9). Skill produces grace (l. 19) and beauty (l. 16). The general opposition is, then, between the native genius of Jacobean wit, with compelling force as its chief virtue and unpolished excess as its chief weakness, and the tutored skill of Restoration art, with refinement and paucity of genius as its complementary virtue and defect. The Jacobean virtue is more highly regarded than the Restoration: wit will conquer without art (l. 4), but to lack genius is to creatively 'curst' (l. 13). To apply Dryden's own architectural analogy, the Doric columns will stand without the Corinthian capitals, but the capitals must have the support of the columns. Although art is a virtue inferior to genius, it has its value, and in Congreve may be observed the realization of the ideal. The merits of neither column nor capital are overlooked.

Against this division into opposed ages must be set the fact that Dryden goes on to refer to the ease of Fletcher and the strength of Jonson (ll. 20–25). Their virtues are complementary, and Congreve's combination of them is clearly akin to his combination of Jacobean strength and Restoration grace. The general contrast between the two ages is thus mirrored in the particular contrast between two authors which implicitly denies the validity of the general opposition because both authors belong to one age. A similar process is observable in the triplet discussing Congreve's contemporaries (ll. 28–30). The beauties or virtues of Etherege and Southerne are specifically those of the Restoration; the language used to describe Wycherley's achievement associates his virtues with those of the Jacobeans. Wycherley is to Jonson what Etherege and Southerne are to Fletcher, while the first pair are to the Jacobean age what the second three are to the Restoration. The general opposition between ages both contains and conflicts with the particular comparison with individual authors. The argument of the first thirty lines is thematic rather than logical.

Later in the poem Dryden returns to the critical discussion, and praises Congreve more as a Jacobean than as a Restoration playwright. He has innate genius (l. 60), but has yet to master the dramatic rules of the three unities (ll. 58–60). It is true that he can learn those rules, but the burden of the earlier opposition between ages would suggest that he, like his contemporaries, has already mastered them. As a final confusion, Congreve's achievement reveals abilities exactly equal to Shakespeare's (ll. 62–63), while the whole point of the poem's second line would appear to be that Congreve has surpassed his predecessors as well as his contemporaries.

It should be apparent that Dryden is not concerned to versify one or more of his critical essays. His use of judgments and terms common to those essays can easily suggest that such is the purpose of the poem, but the irreconcilability of his general opposition with his specific comparisons is not a typical feature of his prose discourse. The lines to Congreve are a complimentary address, and as such they partake of the nature of panegyric. The movement of the poem becomes clearer if we see the comparisons with other authors as examples of epideictic *amplificatio*, whereby the recipient of praise is compared with men of known worth and found superior to them. In fact, the praise is subsumed into a slightly different rhetorical end. The passage beginning at line 41 urges that Congreve should have succeeded to the laureateship which Dryden had (perforce) resigned at the accession of William and Mary. The overtones of a deliberative oration's counsel to a particular course of action give greater rhetorical point to the opening praise. The matter at issue is the succession to the throne of wit. The first forty lines offer a *narratio* of Congreve's abilities and qualifications and argue his superiority to his rivals. From these facts Dryden asserts the justice of Congreve's claim, dismisses the present incumbent as temporary, and prophesies the eventual success of his favourite (ll. 41–54). He briefly considers the objection against Congreve's inadequate grasp of the unities, and refutes it by reference to the example of Shakespeare (ll. 55–64). The closing peroration assumes as demonstrated the just succession of Congreve and charges him to extend *pietas* towards Dryden. The poem is not a deliberative oration any more than *The Medal* is a forensic oration, but both works rely upon rhetorical precept for aspects of their structure, argument, and point.

The deliberative point of the poem, the succession to the laureateship, explicitly introduces the kingdom of letters, and, as always in Dryden's use of the analogy, it is worth enquiring whether it is phrased in terms appropriate to recent events in England. Each of the three poems discussed earlier in this chapter contains a passage which aligns the literary topic with the return of Charles II. This analogical centre, as it may be called, signals its occurrence by the presence of the charged word *restore* or its variants. In 1693 the constitutional equivalent of the restoration was the termination of James II's reign and the accession of William III. When Dryden turns to the matter of the laureateship in the lines to Congreve, he presents it in terms of hereditary succession, deposition, and the unjust accession of a ruler without legal right to the throne:

> Oh that your Brows my Lawrel had sustain'd,
> Well had I been Depos'd, if You had reign'd!
> The Father had descended for the Son;
> For only You are lineal to the Throne.
> Thus when the State one *Edward* did depose;
> A Greater *Edward* in his room arose.
> But now, not I, but Poetry is curs'd;
> For *Tom* the Second reigns like *Tom* the first.
>
> (ll. 41–48)

On June 10th, 1688, James II's second wife, Mary of Modena, gave birth to a son. Because the new prince would obviously be brought up a Catholic, it appeared that a Catholic succession was assured. When James II came to the throne he was old enough to give his opponents hope that his reign would not be insupportably long. The succession at his death would pass to his Protestant daughter, Mary, whose marriage to William of Orange assured an alliance with the leader of the anti-Catholic coalition in Europe. Beyond Mary was Anne, the High Church sympathizer. The birth of a son to the Catholic rulers checked the Anglican hopes, and there is a certain inevitability in the immediate charges of the prince's illegitimacy. The multiplication of anti-government pamphlets claiming that James was trying to foist either bastard or foundling on the nation was answered by an assertion of the prince's legitimacy. Dryden's laureate contribution was *Britannia Rediviva*, a poem celebrating the birth of the prince, but also concerning itself in part with a vindication of James II's rule and in part with countering the charge of illegitimacy (ll. 118–33).

When, after the flight of James and the Catholic members of

his family, the Convention Parliament met early in 1689, it occupied itself with a number of possibilities for the settlement of the throne. During a debate on the state of the nation held on January 28th the major issue was the interpretation of James II's flight and its significance for the country. If James left under duress he had been deposed; if he left voluntarily his action involved either abdication or desertion. Whatever name was given to his flight, it was important to decide whether it had created a vacancy on the throne. If it had not, the Convention Parliament was unconstitutional, because it had not been summoned by the king. One group argued that the constitution was based upon contract between king and people; James II had broken the agreement by attempting to impose Catholicism, and his departure represented an abdication. Throughout the debates the only point of agreement was that James should not be allowed to return, but the fact that he was still alive produced a number of sophistical arguments over who should be granted the executive power. From time to time explicit or implicit reference was made to the claim of the infant prince, but even strong supporters of instantaneous succession were reluctant to press this claim. The twin issues of illegitimacy and fear of Catholic domination effectively eliminated Prince James from consideration. As Sir Robert Howard phrased it, 'a regency and the king are all one. . . . To talk of preserving the Succession as sacred, is to suppose the title of the Prince—a thing well cozened. If the young gentleman beyond the seas should die, the king of France will find another for you.'[19] Some suggested that because James II was still alive his heirs could not inherit, and parliament was therefore free to elect what monarch they pleased. To soothe the Lords' fears of a dangerous precedent, the Commons assured them that election was merely expedient. Once an inadequate dynasty or branch of that dynasty had been removed, the principle of succession could be readopted.

In support of this proposal parliament appealed to the precedent of history. Throughout the debates reference was made to the deposition of Edward II and Richard II and to the flight of Edward IV before the hostile advance of the Earl of Warwick. The case of Edward II was felt to justify their procedure in declaring the throne vacant, but the contingent accession of Edward III provided an unwelcome parallel that caused parliament to refer but sparingly to this precedent. The fact of Edward IV's eventual return and resumption of the crown made that instance similarly unpopular, and the major support was found in the 'abdication' of Richard II and the subsequent acclamation of Henry IV as king. The precedents utilized by the Convention Parliament were chiefly drawn from the Exclusion Bill controversy, where the same arguments for a regency and for altering the succession were supported by the same appeals to the deposition of Edward II and Richard II and the election of Edward III and Henry IV. In the intervening years the historical parallels were alluded to with sufficient frequency to render them commonplace by the time of the revolution. Sir Robert Howard's life of Richard II, first published in 1681, was reissued in 1690 with the addition of a life of Edward II. In his dedication of the double history to William III and in his preface to it Howard makes clear his intention to provide a justifying parallel for the actions of the Convention Parliament.

The royalist reaction was usually to warn against the danger of invoking precedents for breaking the law. As Halifax put it in 1681: 'the frequent mentioning of the fates of Edward II., Richard II., and Henry VI., cannot but alarm his majesty, and restrain him from ever complying with such persons against his brother.'[20] One ingenious Tory pamphleteer of 1679 fabricated a speech supposedly delivered by the Bishop of Carlisle to parliament when they were considering the deposition of Richard II. Something of Shakespeare's character appears to have gone into the speech, but it is chiefly distinguished by a characteristic appeal to examples of non-resistance in the Bible and in Greek and Roman antiquity. Coming a little closer to the immediate matter, the loyal bishop is made to say: 'as for the deposing of King Edward II it is no more to be urged than . . . the murdering of any other good and lawful prince. . . . And yet the kingdom was not then taken from the lawful successor.'[21]

Scott long ago suggested in his edition of the *Somers Tracts* that this Tory invention of the Bishop of Carlisle's speech twenty years afterwards provided Dryden with a hint for his addition to Chaucer's character of the parson. In that imitation Dryden presented the parson's reaction to the deposition of Richard II in terms appropriate to the reaction of non-jurors to the

Williamite succession. The imitation has perhaps received all the scholarly attention it demands, but it is worth pointing out that the contemporary habit of finding precedent for the deposition of James in the deposition of Richard is as relevant to Dryden's lines as the seventeenth-century habit of seeing Chaucer as a Wicliffite who would himself, had he lived in 1690, have cast his parson as a non-juror.[22] The passage from Dryden's *Character* perhaps merits further quotation by reason of its relevance to the discussions of the Convention Parliament and the pamphlets that followed it:

> The Tempter saw him too, with envious Eye;
> And, as on *Job*, demanded leave to try.
> He took the time when *Richard* was depos'd:
> And High and Low, with happy *Harry* clos'd.
> This Prince, tho' great in Arms, the Priest withstood:
> Near tho' he was, yet not the next of Blood.
> Had *Richard* unconstrained, resign'd the Throne:
> A King can give no more than is his own:
> The Title stood entail'd, had *Richard* had a Son.
> Conquest, an odious Name, was laid aside,
> Where all submitted; none the Battle try'd.
> The senseless Plea of Right by Providence,
> Was, by a flatt'ring Priest, invented since:
> And lasts no longer than the present sway;
> But justifies the next who comes in play.
> The People's Right remains; let those who dare
> Dispute their Pow'r, when they the Judges are.
> He join'd not in their Choice; because he knew
> Worse might, and often did from Change ensue.
>
> (ll. 106–24)

That Dryden wished to effect a more complete parallel between James and Richard than history allowed is apparent from his hypothesis of Richard's son. In the triplet containing the hypothesis he is clearly rejecting parliament's view that James II's 'abdication' implied an abdication of his son's right also. In any case, the question of abdication is introduced only theoretically. The sense of 'Had *Richard* unconstrain'd . . .' is obviously 'even if we grant that Richard abdicated, it still did not follow that the next of blood should have been barred; in any case, Richard (and by implication James) did not abdicate; he was deposed.' As Austin Dobbins points out, Dryden dismisses Sherlock's grounds for taking the oath of allegiance to William and Mary. William Sherlock, the Dean of St. Paul's, settled his conscience by the argument for the providential appointment of *de facto* kings which he had found in Overall's *Convocation-Book*.[23] Dryden also rejects the final proposition that the people have the right to choose their king and that William is therefore the lawfully elected ruler, for the raising of the people to the judiciary is as obviously sarcastic as the deification of them in *The Medal*; it is characteristically capped with the standard royalist argument against innovation.

The brief allusion to William III's title by conquest represents a fifth possibility to be set beside the right derived from deposition, abdication, election, and the providential appointment of *de facto* rulers. By his allusion Dryden draws upon one of the major disputes of William's reign. The fact that William landed in England at the head of a military force gave colour to Jacobite claims that he was emulating his conquering namesake. The supporters of the revolutionary settlement took these claims seriously, for nothing is more apparent than the Convention Parliament's honest, if rather muddled attempt to establish the legality of their proceedings. Title by conquest carried unwelcome associations that they felt must be denied, and a number of writers argued that William I himself was not a true conqueror, because he received his title by the unanimous consent of the people. In this context Dryden's couplet implies that William III had followed the precedent of his namesake and that it is specious to argue against title by conquest merely because his invasion had not met with armed resistance.[24]

If the whole passage is considered in terms of its relevance to 1688–89 (and that relevance appears to be its chief point), it is possible to determine from it a coherent attitude toward the Revolution. James II had been forced from his throne by a combination of popular agitation and the conquering invasion of William. The crowning of William was at once a submission to his arms and an assertion of the people's right to elect their ruler. Any attempt to argue divine sanction for such a procedure was both spurious and dangerous, since it afforded an attractive precedent for future usurpers. Whatever the justice of James II's removal, he should in any case have been succeeded by his son.

The *Character of a Good Parson* was written some five years after the lines to Congreve, but the similarity of the later poem to the earlier can be readily demonstrated by once more quoting the passage dealing with the succession to the laureateship:

> Oh that your Brows my Lawrel had sustain'd,
> Well had I been Depos'd, if You had reign'd!
> The Father had descended for the Son;
> For only You are lineal to the Throne.
> Thus when the State one *Edward* did depose;
> A Greater *Edward* in his room arose.
> But now, not I, but Poetry is curs'd;
> For *Tom* the Second reigns like *Tom* the first.

The reference to the two Edwards alone would be sufficient to effect a correspondence between affairs in the kingdom of poetry and the kingdom of England. By applying to his dramatic discussion an historical allusion so frequently used to illustrate contemporary matters of state, Dryden implies a parallel between the disposition of the laureateship and the disposition of the crown. Edward II and Edward III were, in an important sense, types of James II and the young Prince James. By way of history, therefore, Dryden offers himself as literary parallel with the exiled king and Congreve as a similar parallel with the young prince. Moreover, just as the claim of James II's son was dismissed by the Convention Parliament, so Congreve's right has been overlooked by those responsible for appointing the laureate. Their neglect was not unreasonable, for Dryden's offices had fallen vacant in 1689, while Congreve's first publication was the romantic novel, *Incognita*, early in 1692. Between then and the time of Dryden's lines late in 1693 he produced a few poems and two plays. He was in no sense lineal to Dryden's throne when the laureate was deposed after the Revolution. Dryden's implicit attack upon the administration is thus significantly unfair, and is perhaps best explained by a wish to fashion a closer parallel between the poetic and political kingdoms than was provided by the facts. Since Dryden lost his office as a result of James II's dismissal, the parallel becomes especially meaningful. By emphasizing the fact of deposition Dryden is challenging the Convention Parliament's final interpretation of James II's flight as an abdication. In addition, his recollection of the accession of Edward III is a criticism of the overthrow of the hereditary right entailed by the crowning of William and Mary. Only Congreve and by implication the Prince of Wales were 'lineal to the Throne.'

Dryden's wish to give political shape to his literary subject is further revealed by his seemingly gratuitous scorn for Rymer, the '*Tom* the Second' of line 48. The language of the line itself retains the imagery of kingship, but the content is to some extent superfluous to the literary theme. After the Revolution Dryden was succeeded by Thomas Shadwell ('*Tom* the first') in his offices of laureate and historiographer. When Shadwell died in 1692, Nahum Tate became laureate and Thomas Rymer became historiographer. Shadwell was an old enemy from the days of the Jonson dispute and *MacFlecknoe*, while Rymer had offended by his disparagement of the Jacobeans and his covert scorn of Dryden in *A Short View of Tragedy*, published late in 1692 and referred to by Dryden in the dedication of *Examen Poeticum* in the summer of 1693. The passage in the Congreve address is concerned with the laureateship, and the introduction of the historiographer is consequently disturbing. Rymer, it is true, had written in 1678 an unsuccessful tragedy on the subject of King Edgar and his critical eminence might loosely be regarded as constituting a rule over the poets. The disappearance from Dryden's lines of Tate with his recalcitrant first name and the concentration upon two men, the first of whom was dead and the second not even the laureate, emphasize the theme of royal succession by the dynastic note of Tom the first and Tom the second at the same time that it draws attention to the nature of the rule to which poetry is subjected. It appears, in fact, that Dryden has given further political shape to his lines by calling upon the correspondence between William III and his conquering namesake. Against the lineal descent from Edward to Edward is set the actual rule of William III, whose title, like that of the first William, was not hereditary. It may be objected that we have to deal with '*Tom* the Second' not the third, but the political debate itself saw William of Orange as a second William the Conqueror. Once again it must be stressed that Dryden's lines are not about politics, nor is the political implication of equal weight with the overt literary topic. The disposition of the laureateship is given greater significance and a measure of rhetorical shape by placing it within the pattern of contemporary events. The placing entails some minor distortion of literary matters, but Dryden is clearly not concerned to distort them out of all recognition.

We are in fact prepared for the political allusiveness of the analogical centre by the introduction a few lines earlier of matter drawn from the history of the Roman republic. After according Congreve a superiority over his contemporary dramatists, Dryden asserts that the defeated rivals do not envy Congreve's youthful success because his pleasant personality exacts the tribute of love from them (ll. 31–34). Behaviour so unusual recalls to Dryden a time long ago when an old man was moved to envy by the success of a younger:

> *Fabius* might joy in *Scipio*, when he saw
> A Beardless Consul made against the Law,
> And joyn his Suffrage to the Votes of *Rome*;
> Though he with *Hannibal* was overcome.
>
> (ll. 35–38)

These two couplets condense so much detail that it is initially difficult to determine Dryden's meaning. Publius Cornelius Scipio was created consul in 205 B.C. at the age of thirty or thirty-two, after achieving great success against the Carthaginians in Spain. His proposal to lead an expedition against Carthage was attacked by Fabius Maximus, who during his dictatorship and consulships had followed a policy of harassing the army maintained by Hannibal in Italy for fourteen years. Fabius urged that Hannibal be driven from Italy before the war was carried to Africa. Although Fabius himself anticipated the charge of envy that might be levelled against him, it was largely a suspicion that his motives were thus ignoble that procured the necessary support for Scipio's proposal, which was, in the event, completely successful. Hannibal was recalled from Italy and utterly defeated by Scipio in 202 B.C., a year after the death of Fabius.

When Dryden's lines are given their proper context in the second Punic war, four details may cause some surprise. At thirty or thirty-two Scipio was not even 'Beardless' in its usual application to immaturity, nor was he created consul against the law.[25] Fabius was never defeated by Hannibal, although the guerrilla tactics he favoured meant that he never succeeded in driving Hannibal out of Italy. The fourth problem is less explicit, for it derives from the way in which Dryden combines the separate matters of Scipio's consulship and his proposed African expedition. Fabius's opposition was to the second matter, and whatever he felt about Scipio's age and qualifications for the consulship must be deduced from his remarks on youth in the speech against the expedition assigned to him by Livy. Scipio was elected consul by a large popular vote, but the question of whether Africa should be assigned him as a consular province (which would have represented official sanction for his expedition) was not permitted to go before the people. Instead it was settled by the senate, who awarded him Sicily, with permission to invade Africa if he thought it justified. Dryden's combination of the two matters could well derive from the passage in Livy where Scipio is reported to have said that he had been created consul to finish not continue the war, an end he could only achieve by an African expedition, for which he would seek popular sanction if he met with senatorial disapproval.[26]

As an historical illustration of Dryden's literary topic the Scipio allusion provides a few difficulties. We may grant that Dryden is presenting the hypothesis that, had Scipio possessed as attractive a personality as Congreve, Fabius would not have opposed him. In general, Fabius is the epitome of Congreve's 'foil'd Contemporaries' (l. 32), but his age and singularity specifically associate him with Dryden. The immaturity somewhat gratuitously assigned to Scipio is certainly more appropriate to the 'blooming Youth' (l. 31) of the twenty-three-year-old Congreve, but even then the emphasis appears undue. But the chief problem is provided by the mutual enemy, Hannibal, who had, we are told, previously defeated Fabius. Whether we see Fabius as a type of Dryden or of Congreve's older contemporaries in general, it would be difficult to find a satisfactory candidate for Hannibal, unless he is to be seen as an anticipation of the two Toms.

To some extent he is, but it is perhaps because both passages refer to political matters. Fabius carries suggestions of the defeated James II, who is imagined to be ready to step aside in favour of his infant son, even though it was 'against the Law' for the prince to succeed while his father was alive. Rome in this interpretation would represent the large party of Jacobites who pinned their hopes on the eventual accession of the infant prince, feeling as they did that the chances of James II's own restoration were limited. Hannibal, so awkward on a wholly literary level, becomes a type of William III, both of them foreign invaders established in the native land of Fabius or Dryden or James II. James II had been defeated by William III; Fabius had been 'overcome' by Hannibal; but Prince James will prove victorious over William, just as Scipio routed Hannibal and Congreve precociously demonstrated his superiority to his older rivals.

In the couplet which links the Scipio passage with the allusion to the Edwards Dryden transfers his material from republican to Renaissance Rome: 'Thus old *Romano* bow'd to *Raphel*'s Fame; / And Scholar to the Youth he taught, became' (ll. 39–40). Once again we have an opposition between age and youth, and whatever the reason for Dryden's mistaking Raphael's pupil for his master, it is obvious that his version of history finds its place in the sequence of thought and allusion. Congreve, Scipio, and Raphael had in common great achievements in their respective spheres while they were still young men. In addition, Giulio Romano (who was actually nine years younger than Raphael) permits, in Dryden's terms, an easy transition from Fabius. 'Old *Romano*' the painter is clearly suggested by that rugged old Roman(us), Fabius Maximus. There is a progressively closer relationship between the three pairs of youth and age; Fabius the past consul and Scipio the present give way to the master and pupil in Romano and Raphael, who are in turn replaced by the father-son relationship of the two Edwards.

The rapid accumulation of political suggestion in the three historical allusions contrasts with the slower development and more general reference of the opening thirty-four lines. In effect, they establish a political potential similar to that established by the opening of the Howard address, although, unlike the earlier poem, they at least partially realize the potential at the moment of its introduction. Dryden places the progress of seventeenth-century English drama within a general constitutional and political context. The second couplet of the poem establishes a correspondence between the kingdoms of England

and poetry by concentrating upon martial qualities in each realm: 'Strong were our Syres; and as they Fought they Writ, / Conqu'ring with force of Arms, and dint of Wit.' Drama and warfare are but specific manifestations of a general temperament. Similarly, the accession of Charles II had both social and theatrical relevance: not only the dramatists were tamed to manners (l. 9). Between the two ages comes the flood, and it is apparent that it has the rebellious overtones it possessed in the opening analogy of the coronation panegyric and in the Prologue to *The Unhappy Favourite*. The Interregnum, it will be recalled, not only affected political matters, for it also witnessed the closing of the theatres.

The first fifteen lines of the poem work through a persistent biblical imagery that is noticeably absent from the remainder of the poem. The opening announcement that 'the promis'd hour is come at last' has overtones of scriptural reference to divine promises and covenants. In the New Testament the coming of Christ is regarded as prefigured in the promised arrival of Moses to lead the Israelites out of Egypt. For Dryden the promise is fulfilled in the arrival of Congreve 'the best Vitruvius (l. 15), who is to erect a third temple superior to those of the Jacobean and Restoration dramatists. But the first two temples are presented in biblical terms: the second was inferior to the first, just as the temple rebuilt at Jerusalem after the exile was inferior to Solomon's. Against this scriptural note must be set the classical allusions, subdued in the giants, coming to the surface in Janus (but still containing suggestions of Noah), and finally realized in the figure of Vitruvius and his temple. The first nineteen lines are typically Drydenian in their strong forward progress, their accumulation of imagery and allusion, their gradual refinement of a basic opposition, and their final discharge in a climactic triplet with alexandrine. The rhetorical effect is similar to that achieved by the opening of *Religio Laici* with its gradually evolved opposition between faith and reason. The application of the Vitruvius reference thus has particular force. In a sense, all that precedes the final alexandrine is a commentary upon it. Genius, wit, and strength on the one hand, skill, art, and manners on the other, are resolved in the aphoristic utterance of line 19: 'Thus all below is Strength, and all above is Grace.'

The opposition is similar to that of the lines to Howard, but the values are reversed. Strength in the earlier poem associated itself with the acquired virtue of the *utile*; in the later poem it represents innate genius. The sweetness of Howard's verse paralleled the inborn mercy of Charles II; the grace of Congreve's plays is indicative of his tutored skill. But the theological overtones of the overtly literary grace are suggestive of divine dispensation, just as the literary strength of the Jacobeans is described in terms of human warfare. It should not be forgotten that the whole passage is directed toward the sequence of seventeenth-century rule by the reference to Charles and the preceding flood. Just as the giant race of the Jacobeans gives place to the rebellious flood, which is, in political terms, identical with their martial activity, so the roughness and violence of their 'boistrous' wit is endowed at the restoration with the art of Charles II (l. 10), which is within a few lines to become synonymous with grace.

It may be postulated, then, that the political potential of these lines is contained within the literary qualities of grace and strength as they are presented by imagery and allusion. Strength suggests the virtues of *de facto* rule, its coercive force, here represented by martial imagery. Grace suggests the virtues of divine right, which are nugatory without actual power. In terms of the Vitruvian temple, *de facto* power is an essential support to the *de jure* crown of the Corinthian capital (ll. 17–18). The Restoration monarchy leaned too heavily upon the grace of divine right, just as the Restoration drama depended too greatly upon the literary grace of the rules. The neglect by both monarchy and drama of the essential support of strength led to the deposition of Edward and the accession of Tom the Second. What is needed is a new access of strength to restore both monarchy and drama; the grace of art and of divine right can be left to take care of itself.

. In the lines to Howard we are presented in both poetry and politics with a ruler at once *de jure* and *de facto*. In the lines to Congreve we are presented with a *de jure* monarch whom Dryden regards as possessing the virtues necessary to achieve *de facto* rule, virtues whose lack had led to the abrupt termination of the Stuart succession:

Yet this I Prophesy: Thou shalt be seen,
(Tho' with some short Parenthesis between:)
High on the Throne of Wit; and seated there,
Not mine (that's little) but thy Lawrel wear.

(ll. 51–54)

(It may be noted in passing that the syntax of the sentence en-
acts its meaning. The formulation of the prophecy is interrupted
by a syntactic parenthesis asserting that the fulfilment of the
prophecy will be delayed or interrupted by a temporal parenthesis.) Because Congreve is not yet a ruler in fact, Dryden concentrates upon the virtue that will rectify the situation. Because
Charles II and Howard's verse were both *de facto* and *de jure*,
Dryden was able to concentrate upon effecting a balance between the opposed virtues of the two conditions. In each case
it is the immediate political situation which helps direct where
his emphasis will lie. This emphasis is reflected in the different
rhetorical ends of the two poems. The wholly panegyric purpose
of the Howard address permits a consistent parallel, expressed
or implied, between political and poetic qualities. The deliberative end of the Congreve address requires that an initial establishment of the playwright-prince's qualifications for rule
(effected through encomium) be followed by a counsel that he
succeed the laureate-king. The rhetorical purpose would thus
demand the use of different terminology in the *narratio* and
probatio. Because the full topical allusiveness of the Edwardian
succession coincides with the *probatio* or advice, there is a less
exact correspondence with the epideictic *narratio* than was possible in the wholly epideictic address to Howard. This is why
the opening lines have in part at least to realize their political
potential at the moment of introduction.

Immediately after the temple image Dryden offers a brief
passage comparing Congreve with his dramatic contemporaries
and predecessors. Within its eleven lines the strength-grace
criterion of the temporal opposition is given practical application. During this application the political suggestion is in abeyance, suspended while Dryden demonstrates the validity of his
critical evaluation. The specific allusion to actual dramatists
itself strips the lines of political potential. It must be remembered that Congreve as Prince James has no logical rival to the
throne other than the ex-king, who has, perforce, waived his

right to rule. But Congreve as Congreve has very real contemporary rivals to the throne of wit, and he must therefore be shown as superior to them. Similarly, the later objection that Congreve has not mastered the rules and its refutation by reference to the precedent of Shakespeare again involves a consideration of specific qualities in the playwright's work that have no relevance to the case of Prince James (ll. 55–63).

When the focus is upon Congreve's plays, criticism and the throne of wit predominate: Congreve is unresolvably Congreve. When the focus shifts to Congreve the man the lines can carry implications for the political succession. In the first nineteen lines the balance between man and work is maintained by means of martial imagery, the biblical parallel with seventeenth-century rule, and the concentration upon Charles II's general improvement of the age rather than of the dramatists alone. In those lines the qualities of a writer's works are conditioned by the age he lives in. When Dryden turns to eleven lines of specific comparison his concentration is entirely upon the work and there is consequently no political suggestion. As he moves out of this wholly literary section, Dryden marks the change by turning to the admirable personality of Congreve the man (ll. 31–34), and this shift permits the rapidly developed political potential of the Scipio, Raphael, and Edward lines. The justification of his prophecy once more forces Dryden back to a consideration of Congreve's literary abilities, but this is in turn followed by the final charge to protect the fame of the old poet, which once again concentrates upon personality and therefore upon political suggestion:

> Already I am worn with Cares and Age;
> And just abandoning th' Ungrateful Stage:
> Unprofitably kept at Heav'ns expence,
> I live a Rent-charge on his Providence:
> But You, whom ev'ry Muse and Grace adorn,
> Whom I foresee to better Fortune born,
> Be kind to my Remains; and oh defend,
> Against Your Judgment, Your departed Friend!
> Let not the Insulting Foe my Fame pursue;
> But shade those Lawrels which descend to You.
>
> (ll. 66–75)

Just as Dryden is abandoning the stage, so James II is abandoning his kingdom; and it will be recalled that empire and stage were established as virtual synonyms at the beginning of the poem (ll. 6, 9). The injunction to be 'kind to my Remains' is obviously appropriate to the condition of the critic-harried Dryden, but it is also appropriate to the ill-fated James II. Most striking, however, is the providence couplet. A rent-charge is an obligation laid upon an estate to maintain a pensioner, and since the estate is here that of heaven or God it is clearly appropriate to the exiled James II, who could proclaim at St. Germain nothing but his divine right. But Dryden's total dependence upon the will of God for his survival suggests a degree of destitution that would have been an undue exaggeration of his reduced circumstances. Moreover, the divine reference picks up the note of providential care suggested by the promise of the first line and made manifest in the heaven-sent gifts of Congreve (l. 62). It is also possible that the charity exhibited by Dryden's nameless patron toward the two Toms, a charity which they have not deserved (ll. 49–50), is not simply a reference to the Earl of Dorset's forced disposal of office to Shadwell and Rymer. In terms of the political potential that patron could be one with the heavenly protector of the last lines. It was obvious that William's rule had so far enjoyed divine permission, but there was no reason to accept the Sherlockian position attacked in the *Character of a Good Parson* that this permission constituted a divine right.

I have considered the Congreve address in such detail because I take it to be Dryden's most successful use of the kingdom of letters to suggest a specific relevance to the kingdom of England. Its superiority to the other three poems can no doubt be in part attributed to Dryden's greater maturity, to his skilful discrimination among the analogies available to him, and to the greater point and polish of his rhetoric. Then too, as Professor Hoffman justly observes, Dryden is usually more convincing when he is defending than when he is celebrating the virtues of monarchy by divine right.[27] But beyond this, the dependence of literature upon political conditions is more fully felt and realized than in the earlier works, and the exploitation of topical potential in the kingdom of letters is thus more fully justified. With the possible exception of '*Tom* the Second' the poem avoids the merely clever distortion of literary matters to suit a political meaning to which the Castlemaine address largely succumbed.

In the lines to Congreve, as in *MacFlecknoe*, Dryden's royalism and the vocabulary of politics provide a frame of reference within which the significance of literary achievement can be more clearly seen. The task of justifying the use of that political standard is discharged in the poems considered in this chapter by finding and shaping specific correspondences between the two realms. Particularization of this kind imaginatively renews the ancient analogy, just as the fire stanzas of *Annus Mirabilis* create afresh the commonplace association of destructive war and fire by a perception of the parallel between the fire of 1666 and the civil war of the 1640's. In an important sense the originality of these poems is rooted in their topicality. *MacFlecknoe* achieves its originality and the justification of its political vocabulary through the exploitation of mock-heroic elevation for the purpose of ridicule. It is the continuing joke which confirms the aptness of the monarchic analogy, although there can be little doubt that the satiric point of the succession and coronation in dunceland would have been sharpened by the growing talk of the succession to the English throne when the poem was written (probably) in 1678. *MacFlecknoe* is no doubt a highly topical poem; some of its allusions and its specific occasion still await elucidation, while the critical dispute between Dryden and Shadwell which provides so much of the poem's material is an obviously dated issue. But so much of the satire is conveyed through biblical, imperial, and monarchic amplification that the poetic mode of *MacFlecknoe* depends very little, it seems, on the witty exploitation of topical allusion. In this it is as unlike *Absalom and Achitophel* as it is reminiscent of the greater poem's exploitation of a disparity between the nominal tenor and vehicles.

Epilogue

A T the end of the first chapter I suggested that the accumulation of temporal prepositions and conjunctions in the opening lines of *Absalom and Achitophel* works to imply the relevance of later times, when priestcraft had begun and after polygamy had been made a sin. The exact nature of this relevance seems likely to escape critical definition, and most probably because the relevance is not itself exact. We are accustomed to refer to the allegory of *Absalom and Achitophel*, and to assume that allegory involves (as it so rarely does in practice) a strictly consistent parallelism between two or more levels of meaning that enables us to read on one or other of the levels or on both at once. But while we can say that what is predicated of 'pious times'—that polygamy was no sin—is true of David's reign alone, the implied superiority of personality resulting from an acceptance of this condition is true of both David's reign and the later reign from which true piety has been banished by assertive priestcraft. The divine generosity and fertility, the openness and gusto of David's busy promiscuity, fix a standard of warmth whose value is increasingly felt in the poem by contrast with the cold and narrow furtiveness of his opponents. Not only does the lusty conception of Absalom contrast with Achitophel's son, 'Got, while his Soul did hudled Notions try: / And born a shapeless Lump, like Anarchy' (ll. 171–72), but the whole character of Shimei (ll. 583–629) sums up the uncreative aspect of sedition by combining Whiggish republicanism with dissenting restrictiveness, self-denial, and acquisitive frugality. The opening lines thus use history, as we might expect in a seventeenth-century poem, to reveal the unchanging principles and values of human conduct that are present beneath the accidental differences of two reigns. The historical analogy is further important because it permits more readily than would a literal concentration upon the Restoration an insinuated condonement of the private promiscuity that has produced the threat to the public order. What is strictly a defence of David's actions establishes values that are relevant to the similar actions of Charles II without attempting the more difficult task of specifically defending Charles's libertine propensities.

Absalom and Achitophel functions through an extended historical analogy whose tenor is only implicit. The implication is ascertainable through the extensive editing of the biblical episode to provide a more exact correspondence with contemporary events. Editing commences with the isolation of the royal succession as an important factor, for the biblical Absalom, equipped though he is with somewhat enigmatic motives, seems concerned to establish himself as king in David's place rather than as David's heir. Moreover, Dryden provides an extrabiblical explanation of the succession dispute: the failure of the David-Michal union to provide issue, a failure which is of significance for the succession neither in the Bible nor in the strict terms of polygamy with which Dryden's poem opens. The Davidic succession is thus transformed into the Stuart succession by a process similar to that followed in the imitation of Chaucer's *Character of a Good Parson*, where Richard II is provided with a hypothetical son in order that his situation might more closely parallel that of James II. *Absalom and Achitophel*, in fact, adapts to an original historical poem the principles of two kinds of translation: paraphrase, with its emphasis on capturing the spirit rather than the exact letter of the original and its occasional updating of references to assist comprehension; and, more largely, imitation, where the original serves as guide to an extensive rewriting that produces a contemporary equivalent to the situation or principle contained in the original.

It is certainly true that the course of political events during the Restoration increased the relevance of the biblical story for English affairs beyond that possessed by its more general application earlier in the century. But the poem's in fact slight reliance upon this existing relevance, its conversion of possible into probable and actual reference, is apparent from the thorough revision of the biblical data to suit the circumstances of the

Popish Plot and Exclusion crisis. In addition to the mass of detailed revisions there are such large variations as the concentration upon the problem of succession, the emphasis upon different religious persuasions, the elevation of Achitophel into the chief mover of the plot from the role of counsellor to a conspiracy already far advanced by the initiative of Absalom, the provision of loyal Barzillai with a recently dead son, whose elegy reveals him to have been the pattern of filial duty and a worthy subject in pointed contrast with Absalom, the erring son and subject, and the whole resolution by a speech from the throne instead of a battle in which Absalom is killed, after Achitophel has hanged himself in humiliation at Absalom's neglect of his counsel. Both Dryden's poem and the second book of Samuel describe a plot against the king by the king's son encouraged by one of the king's ministers. Dryden's poem differs from the Bible in its diagnosis of the motive for rebellion and in its peaceful resolution. There are such similarities between the two rebellions as Absalom's courting of popular favour and Shimei's cursing of the king. But the similarities clearly derive from the circumstance that Monmouth sought popularity and Slingsby Bethel (Shimei's Restoration counterpart) had spoken approvingly of Charles I's execution. In general, the course of the conspiracy in Dryden's poem differs from its biblical original almost as much as its motivation and resolution. The consequence of this thorough revision is to make clear that the poem's tenor, its major concern, is England during the Exclusion crisis.

In his preface Dryden remarked, 'Were I the Inventour, who am only the Historian, I shoud certainly conclude the Piece, with the Reconcilement of *Absalom* to *David*. And, who knows but this may come to pass?' Professor Hoffman observes of the opening condition that 'this disclaimer, however, is merely part of the thin pretense that the poem is sheer Jewish history based on Second Samuel. It is a gesture of modesty over the designedly evident fact of the invention exhibited in the combination of the two histories.'[1] In fact, Dryden is advancing himself as the historian of the English, not the Jews. Thus much is clear from the phrasing of 'who knows but this may come to pass': everyone already knew that it did not come to pass in the second book of Samuel. Dryden's disclaimer is reminiscent of his earlier assignment of *Annus Mirabilis* to the genre of historical rather than epic poem on the grounds of his being 'ti'd too severely to the Laws of History' to effect a true unity in the poem. The emphasis of *Absalom and Achitophel* is so strongly upon the Exclusion crisis that it is difficult to follow Professor Hoffman's argument, crucial for his general evaluation, that 'by being about two histories at once, *Absalom and Achitophel* is about neither. Jewish history is modified to fit English history, and English history modified to fit Jewish history; as a result, the action of the poem is a *tertium quid*, removed from the specifications of both histories and, in an important sense, not history at all.'[2] Professor Hoffman gives two examples of the modification of Jewish history, and he could obviously have given many more. He gives only one example of the modification of English history: Achitophel's reference to David's harp and the ballads he composes (ll. 439–40), but if this is 'more clearly appropriate' to David, it is, as Professor Kinsley notes, far from inappropriate to a Charles II who owned a guitar and wrote some verses as dull as Achitophel claims David's to be. The only moment in the poem that is significantly more about David's than Charles's reign is the opening description of 'pious times,' and the emphasis here, I have suggested, is required partly by the need to insinuate the rhetorically difficult 'approval' of promiscuity and partly by the fact that the poem is concerned to recall the general relevance before realizing and re-creating the particular relevance within the terms of the poem itself. In much the same way, the Howard address initially concerns itself with poetry alone, but in a way not inimical to its subsequent joint concern with poetry and politics. Apart from the opening, it could be argued that Achitophel's temptation is 'removed from the specifications of both histories.' But in the context of the Exclusion crisis, it represents a reasonable interpretation of what happened and was said that is based upon the known characters and actions of the two men. In just this way, Livy assigned to his historical figures speeches for which there was little evidence, on the ground that the speeches were appropriate and served to point some historical precept.

The justification of the temptation scene suggests one value of the historical analogy. It permits the relative freedom of a conscientious historical novelist who fleshes out the skeletal facts in accordance with a principle of reasonable supposition. The measure of detachment brought by this relative freedom was invaluable to Dryden's attempted view of the three hysterical years that preceded his poem. The events of those years are certainly modified, but they are modified to fit the poem's interpretation of them, not to fit the Jewish history of the second book of Samuel. The poem is journalistic to the extent that it constitutes an editorial assessment of three crowded years that attempts to isolate and interpret the major causes and consequences of public actions. The historical analogy assists this process of isolation and interpretation because it makes the poem at once obviously and indirectly about the Exclusion crisis, at once factual and quasi-fictional, benefiting both from the freedom of an historical novelist and the authority of an exact historian. If the poem is a *tertium quid*, it is because it reconciles fact with interpretation by elaborating fact in accordance with interpretation.

The historical analogy is of further value because, as Professor Hoffman points out, it associates English history with the established moral order of the Bible. To 'prove' that Shaftesbury was an Achitophel, Buckingham a Zimri, Bethel a Shimei, and Monmouth an Absalom helps reveal the full significance of their actions by aligning them with actions of agreed significance. It also helps to generalize the satire in terms of political types without sacrificing the necessary specificity of satire. The satirist's problem is always to make his attack at once generally relevant and demonstrably particular. If it is wholly general, it is vulnerable to dismissal on the grounds that no one is actually like that. If it is wholly particular, it is likely to be shrugged off as true only of the specific objects of the attack. By demonstrating through analogy the consonance of specific men and actions with established types the poem simultaneously comprehends the general and the particular. To this extent *Absalom and Achitophel* can transcend its topicality, but its total achievement can only be appreciated in an awareness of the way its general relevance is rooted in topicality.

For the analogy is also of value because it provides opportunities for the exercise of that wit which is one of the satirist's chief weapons. *Absalom and Achitophel* is only intermittently a funny poem, but its occasional witty indulgence is of obvious importance to the general tone of the work, a tone appropriate to a man of good sense addressing others of good sense, commenting without passion, although with full commitment, upon events in which passion had too evidently escaped the control of reason. It is tedious to explain jokes and difficult to say why a joke is funny, but it does seem that the historical analogy equipped Dryden with a large witty potential because the account of biblical characters and nominally biblical events in terms appropriate to Restoration England could involve an element of incongruity. The biblical names and settings automatically endow the characters with an appropriate gravity which can be exploited either affirmatively, for the purpose of panegyric upon Barzillai or David, or negatively, by puncturing an implied pretension, much as *MacFlecknoe* equips Shadwell with an imperial (and biblical) context in order to amplify his ludicrousness. It is witty enough to say of a Buckingham that 'in the course of one revolving Moon, / [he] Was Chymist, Fidler, States-Man, and Buffoon' (ll. 549–50), but the wit is edged when it is directed at someone called Zimri, partly because the terms of the charge are largely anachronistic and partly because it refuses to take seriously a figure linked with times when everyone, it seems, took themselves and other people wholly seriously. (This is one reason why we should avoid the corrigenda approach to the poem, automatically substituting Restoration names for biblical.) The witty potential of anachronism is perhaps best felt in the isolated couplet where it is exploited to the full: 'Some thought they God's Anointed meant to Slay / By Guns, invented since full many a day' (ll. 130–31). In terms of the vehicle, the biblical setting, the ludicrousness of the supposition is emphasized by its patently anachronistic impossibility. But this ludicrousness is reflected back upon the tenor, where it finds a ready counterpart in the implausibility of the charge by Oates and Tonge that the wretched Pickering and Grove had planned to shoot Charles on several occasions, but had failed on each through such oversights as neglecting to use powder or to check the flint. If the account was true, their plot was farcical. The account was, in fact, too farcical to be true, and it is this suggestion which is pithily realized by the deliberate anachronism. In yet another way, the deliberate biblical gravity of 'their Scribes Record' sets off and sharpens the wit of the following lines:

For, govern'd by the *Moon*, the giddy *Jews*
Tread the same track when she the Prime renews:
And once in twenty Years, their Scribes Record,
By natural Instinct they change their Lord.

(ll. 216–19)

Just as the opening line of the Congreve address, 'Well then; the promis'd hour is come at last,' couples an assertion sounding of biblical prophecy with a conversational aside, so the whole tone of *Absalom and Achitophel* depends for its effect upon the consistently urbane and contemporary description of men and events nominally set in remote times the traditional accounts of which were not conspicuously urbane. The opening apology for promiscuity would not be inappropriate on the tongue of a Restoration libertine. This awareness of an incongruity between the social norms of the two reigns, coupled with an ability to exploit it fully by the polished turns of rhetoric, and without damaging the relevance of the Bible's political and religious standards for Restoration England, constitutes perhaps the most important of the poem's many achievements. In its own day it raised *Absalom and Achitophel* above other attempts to comment in verse upon recent events under the guise of a biblical parallel, and more than anything else it has ensured the poem's continued readability.

The final value of the analogy is that it controls by its ubiquitous relevance the various scenes, characters, and passages of comment. It is the poem's substitute for a clear and consistent narrative line, and represents the solution to the problem posed by the first part of *Annus Mirabilis*. *Absalom and Achitophel* shares with the earlier poem a loose ordering of events and personalities that are examined for topics both eulogistic and dyslogistic. The relevance of separate episodes and characters for each other depends upon thematic similarities between the topics selected for praise or attack and upon the place of the separate deeds and events within a single historical sequence: a war and attempted rebellion. Both are historical poems in the sense that they describe events in order to comment upon them and not in the sense that they give a narrative history of the war or the rebellion, although some of the materials for such a history can be pieced together from their commentary. In *Annus Mirabilis* such connections proved inadequate by themselves, and the individuality of the details was blurred by the sameness of the praise they were accorded. Because there was no overall metaphoric control, each amplifying similitude tended to serve a wholly local point in setting off a particular proposition or description, and the likeness it offered was accordingly superficial and lacking in an imaginative perception of significant identity. In *Absalom and Achitophel* the consistent pursuit of the historical analogy ensures both a constant local excitement and complexity in the language as the poet creates more and more correspondences between the reigns, until they are at once different and the same, and the relevance of all the details to each other because they are expressed in terms of the same analogy. The poem is constantly anticipating and answering the question, 'how does this piece fit the analogy?' Because the question is implicitly prompted throughout, attention is focused upon the particularity of each detail. Because the question is implicitly answered throughout, attention is focused upon the general relevance of each detail. This is the poem's achievement, not its meaning.

It is an achievement which establishes a coherent context within which variety can be maintained by further, subsidiary analogies and by the larger patterns of contrast and similarity. It is these elements, or some of them, which Professor Hoffman takes to constitute 'the symbolic embodiment' of the action, the poem's 'fundamental action' which 'dominates the whole mass of particulars of both histories' by setting the kingdom of David and Charles within the value order of the kingdoms of Adam and of God.[3] But such a view reverses the poem's emphasis by raising subordinate and intermittent analogies above the dominant and persistent historical analogy.

The divinely abundant creativity of David contrasts, I have suggested, with the cold frugality of Shimei. This contrast is characteristically conveyed in the poem by a horticultural analogy which draws simultaneously upon the political values of the Garden of Eden, with the temptation and Fall of Adam and Eve, and the commonplace association of seditious men with weeds that choke the garden of the land. Absalom reveals his royal descent by the paradise that is 'open'd in his face' (l. 30), while Achitophel's ambition is a 'Cockle, that opprest the Noble seed' of judicial virtue (l. 195). Absalom's ambition is also a 'Vitious Weed,' although the prince's error is significantly palliated:

> Desire of Power, on Earth a Vitious Weed,
> Yet, sprung from High, is of Cælestial Seed:
> In God 'tis Glory: And when men Aspire,
> 'Tis but a Spark too much of Heavenly Fire.
>
> (ll. 305–8)

Achitophel points out to Absalom that praise is barren, a 'Gaudy Flower, / Fair only to the sight' (ll. 297–98), and reminds him that David 'to his Brother gives Supreme Command; / To you a Legacy of Barren Land' (ll. 437–38). When the narrator details the grievances of the malcontents, he refers to a group who

> thought Kings an useless heavy Load,
> Who Cost too much, and did too little Good.
> These were for laying Honest *David* by,
> On Principles of pure good Husbandry.
>
> (ll. 505–8)

The general horticultural allusions support and widen the specific references to Eden, which take the form of associating rebellion or ambition with the gathering of fruit from a tree (ll. 202–3, 250–51) and thus with a political fall. The general and specific references together create a context within which, as critics have noticed, a Satanic Achitophel can shed 'his Venome' (l. 229) in a temptation of Absalom that repeats the pattern of Satan's temptations of Eve and Christ. The context of the temptation is further strengthened by echoes from Milton's epics. These echoes (and perhaps, too, the metaphoric use of husbandry) are dependent upon the exploitation of biblical gravity and the biblical setting permitted by the controlling analogy.

Other patterns of contrast and similarity are those between the three sons: David's, Achitophel's, and Barzillai's; and between a settled throne and constitution, expressed in terms of an edifice (ll. 801 ff.), with 'the Pillars of the Laws' (l. 874) and the 'Pillars of the publick Safety' (l. 176), and supported by the reiterated steadfastness and stable virtue of the 'short File' of those loyal to David, and, against all this, the inclination of both

Achitophel and Absalom to shake the pillars (ll. 176, 955–56), of the rebels to bring siege engines 'To batter down the lawful Government' (ll. 917–18), and the instability of seditious men, observable in the conventionally fickle crowd (ll. 45 ff.) and summarized in the whole character of Zimri, 'A man so various, that he seem'd to be / Not one, but all Mankinds Epitome' (ll. 545–46). A further contrast is that between the healthy vigour of David and the healthy beauty of Absalom on the one hand, and on the other the frequent representation of rebellion as a disease of the body politic (ll. 136–41) and the account of Corah's (or Titus Oates's) unlovely person (ll. 646–48). There is finally, as might be expected, a consistent opposition between the zeal and enthusiasm of the crowd and plotters and the sense, reason, and prudence of the king and loyalists, virtues epitomized in the characters of Zadok, Adriel, and Jotham and reinforced by the dominant tone of the poem.

The diffused values associated with these patterns of contrast and similarity and with the subsidiary analogies are chiefly collected in two places: the extended commentary upon the political issues involved in the action (ll. 753–810) and the character of Achitophel (ll. 150–99).

The extended commentary considers the related issues of legitimate succession and indivisible sovereignty in terms that draw upon disease in the body politic, the Fall of Adam, the lunatic instability of rebellion, and the attempted destruction of the constitutional edifice. The commentary thus shares topics and analogies with the action embodied in the controlling analogy, and the interdependence of events and their interpretation is accordingly assured. Inasmuch as the reasonable tone of the passage has led some commentators to feel that Dryden—or the poem—expresses modified approval for a Hobbist theory of covenant between sovereign and people, it is worth emphasizing that any 'approval' is highly conditional. As a reasonable man, the narrator proposes to investigate dispassionately his opponents' claims. It comes as no surprise when he discovers that they involve either faulty logic or conclusions which no one would accept. The syntax of the commentary is characteristically, 'if this is so, then it follows that,' but the implied syntax is subjunctive: '(even) if this were so (and it is not, of course), then it would still follow that.' The final dis-

missal of all theories of popular sovereignty and covenant between king and subjects is evident in the sarcasm of 'Yet, grant
our Lords the People Kings can make' (l. 795).

Achitophel combines within himself the inconstancy of
Zimri and the crowd, the unattractive appearance of Corah,
and the disease of rebellion; the generation of his son inverts
lusty conception of Absalom, and his weed-choked soil parodies
the fertility of David and the paradisiacal features of Absalom.
He shakes the pillars of the land and at least pretends to zeal.
Comprehending all malignant elements in the land, he adds to
them ambition, sagacity, boldness, and an elevated intelligence
that is just short of insanity. These added qualities are what
make him dangerous. They equip him as the adversary of his
king, and render appropriate his representation as the political
counterpart of the arch-adversary of the King of kings.

As an historical poem, although not a narrative history,
Absalom and Achitophel embodies more extensively and successfully than Dryden's other works the prevailing historiography
of his age. The providential view of events as always relevant
to each other informs such varied applications as the conflation
of the great fire and the great rebellion in *Annus Mirabilis*, the
univisionary concluding prophecy of *The Medal*, the updated
imitation of Chaucer's good parson, the adaptation of Lucan's
epigram on Cato in the Castlemaine address, the prose analysis
of the Postscript to *The History of the League*, and the drama of
The Duke of Guise. Dryden was far indeed from being the sole
beneficiary of this historiographic inheritance, for the large
contemporary production of prose parallels was augmented by
such plays as Otway's *Venice Preserv'd*, whose topical relevance
was perhaps as great as that of *The Duke of Guise*, and by verse
ephemera like *Tarquin and Tullia*, *Naboth's Vineyard*, and many
of the pieces included in the collections of *Poems on Affairs of
State* at the end of the century. The existence of this large literature, much of it of little merit, assured a ready audience for a
poem as rooted in historical analogy as *Absalom and Achitophel*.
The enthusiasm with which the age played its favourite intellectual game of drawing up parallel columns of ancient and
modern traitors or loyalists is evidenced by the often wildly
conjectural identifications of *Absalom and Achitophel's* characters
inserted in the margins of early editions.

The stamina of Dryden's poems, the ability of so many of them to meet the different standards of their posterity when the bulk of his contemporaries' work has passed into the oblivion from which he summoned Corah, is referable to no one quality that they possess. The larger patterns of *Absalom and Achitophel* contribute to the poem's integrity, but no more than the constant local felicity of its rhetoric do they constitute the sole enjoyment of later times. We fortunately do not have to choose between appreciation in spite of the poem's topicality and enjoyment because of that topicality. Different ages, like different realms, reveal the same general principles beneath their accidental differences. Dryden's acceptance of the full consequences of this simultaneous sameness and difference was of crucial importance for his characteristic poetic. By transferring to one age or realm the accidents of the other he ensured the full relevance of the general principles and committed himself to an imaginative realization of identity. David's reign *is* Charles's reign; the second book of Samuel is both relevant and, in an important sense, strictly irrelevant to *Absalom and Achitophel*. The process by which identity is embodied in language and in the total image realized by a poem ensures a constant imaginative excitement, as the full implications of an analogy are revealed. Sometimes, there is a further exploitation of a residual difference between two realms, ages, or events, residual after the effective creation of identity. In the fire stanzas of *Annus Mirabilis* the fire repeats or renews the earlier act of rebellion at the same time that it is a consequence of and punishment for the rebellion. In *Absalom and Achitophel* the urbane tone emphasizes and exploits the different social norms of the two reigns at the same time that the analogy establishes their identity. Even if some of the details of the topical reference inevitably escape a modern reader, his appreciation is still conditioned by the original creation of that reference. Awareness of the prior analogy between the depositions of Edward II and James II confirms the probability that the Congreve address creates a meaningful interrelation of literary and political affairs. But the language of the poem enables a careful reader to respond to some at least of the consequences of that interrelation without a knowledge of the prior analogy. This response is but part of the total appreciation, which involves also a response to the rhetoric, to the critical, political, and social theory embodied in the images, and to the larger patterning of the poem: its shaping of praise in terms of an historical survey and its application of that praise in advice on the maintenance of continuity in literary standards.

Whatever its particular emphasis, no critical theory that accepts the integrity of a literary work can operate upon a poem in order to cut away some topical appendix that is unnecessary to the healthy working of the body. Such literary salvage work inevitably recovers but half the treasure. Nothing is more hostile to the special value and the special pleasures of literature than a parochial wish to seize upon all that confirms our own principles and experience and to throw away all that contradicts and all that lies outside. The conditions of other ages forced into prominence values and assumptions that are now, perhaps, subordinate, although few indeed are wholly irrelevant to modern experience. Literature is but one way of apprehending those assumptions in due prominence and thus of prompting a more informed, a more imaginative appreciation of them, subordinate as they now are. Potentially at least, a literary work offers a complete, coherent, and renewable experience. Any reading is concerned first to apprehend that complete experience by reintegrating the dated and the dateless elements that it comprises. All else—the acts of evaluating and determining the relevance of the experience—is ancillary to an apprehension of the experience itself.

If it is true that a major author is so because he makes a special and unrepeatable, or at least unrepeated contribution to the literature of his country, then Dryden's can scarcely be the rhetorical mastery of versification for which alone he was so long praised. This contribution was not only repeated, it was in many respects surpassed by Pope. But without Dryden our literature would be deficient in a poetry that successfully celebrates the public values of peace, security, authority, and political order. Dryden's royalism was more than a definable political position—although it was that too, and it is important that we define it; it conditioned his whole interpretation of experience and provided him with a vocabulary, an order of values, and a wealth of analogies with which to realize, to affirm, to re-create the public significance of the men and events he celebrated or attacked. We have been told so often that Dryden is a master of statement, of the prose virtues of poetry, that we may be in danger of forgetting his appeal to the eye as well as the ear and the reason. Of course he argues, and argues well, but the superimposition of kingdom upon kingdom fills his poems with people and actions. Driden hunts and rules at Chesterton as James II had once hunted and ruled in England. Cromwell lives and dies in Roman grandeur, and the fires of rebellion destroy the streets of London. Howard restores Charles; Charleton crowns him at Stonehenge; and Congreve succeeds his brother. Anne Killigrew rules the muses' empire, and Oldham departs a Roman hero. Shaftesbury sheds Satanic venom, and Tom Shadwell is invested with the regalia of dullness.

Notes

ANALOGIES FOR POETRY

[1] Bernard N. Schilling, *Dryden and the Conservative Myth* (New Haven and London, 1961), p. 254.

[2] W. K. Wimsatt, Jr., *The Verbal Icon* (Lexington, Kentucky, 1954), pp. 149–50.

[3] John A. Winterbottom, 'The Place of Hobbesian Ideas in Dryden's Tragedies,' *JEGP*, LVII (1958), 665–83; see also, Louis Teeter, 'The Dramatic Use of Hobbes's Political Ideas,' *ELH*, III (1936), 140–69.

[4] William S. Clark, 'The Definition of the "Heroic Play" in the Restoration Period,' *RES*, VIII (1932), 437–44.

[5] *Somers Tracts*, ed. Scott, VIII, 87.

[6] Ruth Wallerstein, *Studies in Seventeenth-Century Poetic* (Madison, Wisconsin, 1950), pp. 115–42.

[7] *Essays*, ed. George Watson (1962), II, 68. Unless otherwise stated the place of publication is London.

[8] Roswell G. Ham, 'Dryden as Historiographer-Royal,' *RES*, XI (1935), 284–98.

[9] Ralegh, *The History of the World* (1614), A3r, D2r: italics reversed.

[10] *Essays*, ed. Watson, II, 91–92.

[11] *The History of the Reigns of Edward and Richard II* (1690), p. iii.

[12] Puttenham, *Arte of English Poesie*, ed. G. D. Willcock and A. Walker (Cambridge, 1936), III, xix, pp. 245–46.

RHETORIC FOR POETRY

[1] *Essays*, ed. Watson, I, 98: the 1688 reading of *deriving* for *driving* in 1667 and 1668 is more obviously appropriate to the context.

[2] Jay Arnold Levine, 'The Status of the Verse Epistle before Pope,' *SP*, LIX (1962), 658—84.

[3] 'Turn' was the general word in the seventeenth century for syntactic figures of speech (e.g., pun, antithesis, syllepsis, alliteration, assonance). A turn varies either the thought or the cadence of a proposition by emphasiz-

ing an apparent syntactic parallel or by asserting a parallel where it is not apparent. See the discussion by George Williamson, *The Proper Wit of Poetry* (1961), pp. 117–19.

⁴ My reading of the poem is inevitably similar to that given by Arthur W. Hoffman, *John Dryden's Imagery* (Gainesville, Florida, 1962), pp. 92–98: the poem contains no major interpretative problems. But since Professor Hoffman concentrates on the images and I am more interested in the rhetoric, the partial duplication of analysis seemed justified.

THE KINGDOM OF ENGLAND

¹ Waller, *A Panegyrick to my Lord Protector* (1655), ll. 145–52; *Memoirs of the Life and Actions of Oliver Cromwell*, ed. Francis Peck (1740), pp. 54, 80–81, 112 [text and trans. of the anon. *Panegyrici Cromwello Scripti* (1654)]; 'A Modest Vindication of Oliver Cromwell,' in *Somers Tracts*, VI, 416; Marvell makes implicit use of the analogy in *An Horatian Ode* by allusion to Lucan's *Pharsalia*.

² Bodin, *République*, trans. [as *Commonweale*] Richard Knolles (1606), p. 86; Dryden, *Vindication of the Duke of Guise* (1683), in *Works*, ed. Scott and Saintsbury (Edinburgh, 1882–93), VII, 172.

³ Peck, pp. 54, 80–81; *Somers Tracts*, VI, 416.

⁴ *An Horation Ode*, ll. 85–90, makes this point most clearly.

⁵ *Patriarcha and other Political Works*, ed. Peter Laslett (Oxford, 1949), p. 232.

⁶ *Bishop Overall's Convocation-Book MDCVI* (1690), p. 59; Robert Sanderson, *Lectures on Conscience and Human Law*, trans. Chr. Wordsworth (Lincoln, 1877), pp. 136–37 [*De Obligatione Conscientiae*: delivered at Oxford, 1647; ed. prin. 1660]; for a discussion of this aspect of royalism see J. W. Allen, *English Political Thought 1603–60* (1938), pp. 102–15.

⁷ Filmer, p. 233.

⁸ *Georgics*, III, 345.

⁹ J. W. Allen, pp. 518–19.

¹⁰ Filmer, p. 41.

¹¹ *Leviathan*, ed. Michael Oakeshott (Oxford, 1960), p. 210; see also Sanderson, p. 286.

¹² The main discussion of royal monarchy is on pp. 204 ff.

¹³ *Harleian Miscellany*, ed. Oldys and Park (1808–13), I, 11.

¹⁴ 'The Trew Law of Free Monarchies,' in *Political Works*, introd. Charles H. McIlwain (Cambridge, Mass., 1918), p. 63.

¹⁵ By Beatrice Reynolds, *Proponents of Limited Monarchy in Sixteenth Century France: Francis Hotman and Jean Bodin* (New York, 1931).

¹⁶ J. W. Allen, pp. 449–55.

¹⁷ 'A Plea for Limited Monarchy,' *Harleian Miscellany*, I, 14–18.

¹⁸ Filmer, p. 306.

¹⁹ Filmer, p. 293.

²⁰ According to the scholastic distinction popular in the tracts between

commands that are directive and those that are coercive, coactive, or coercitive. A directive tells you what to do; coercion makes you do it when you refuse.

21 *Cobbett's Parliamentary History* (1808), IV, 16.

22 Cobbett, IV, 42.

23 *Commonweale*, pp. 216, 218.

24 *Essays*, ed. Watson, I, 268–73.

25 *The Subtler Language* (Baltimore, 1959), pp. 53–61.

26 *Commonweale*, pp. 545–68; for an account of other contributors to the climate theory of government see Samuel Kliger, *The Goths in England* (Cambridge, Mass., 1952), pp. 241–52.

27 *The Poetry of John Dryden* (New York, 1920), p. 45.

28 Van Doren, p. 47.

29 Edward N. Hooker, 'The Purpose of Dryden's *Annus Mirabilis*,' *HLQ*, X (1946–47), 49–67; the material for this article is reproduced in the introduction and notes to the poem in the Clark Dryden.

30 Morris Freedman, 'Dryden's Miniature Epic,' *JEGP*, LVII (1958), 211–19; A. B. Chambers, 'Absalom and Achitophel: Christ and Satan,' *MLN*, LXXIV (1959), 592–96; Schilling, op. cit., pp. 195–99, 226; Hoffman, op. cit., pp. 74–84.

31 Bodin, pp. 8, 14–15, 20; see also [Richard Mocket's] *God and the King* (1663), pp. 2, 8–9, 14–15, 33—a tract 'published by his Majesties Royal Proclamation, for the Instruction of all his Majesties Subjects in their Duty and Allegiance' (t.p.).

32 *HMC, Ormonde*, N.S., VI, 236–42 (cited by Kinsley).

33 See Marjorie H. Nicolson, 'Milton and Hobbes,' *SP*, XXIII (1926), 405–33; Louis Teeter, 'The Dramatic Use of Hobbes's Political Ideas,' *ELH*, III (1936), 140–69; Herschel Baker, *The Wars of Truth* (Cambridge, Mass., 1952), index under *rationalism* and *voluntarism*.

34 *Leviathan*, pp. 25–26, 144.

35 In *Paradise Lost* Satan and his followers see God in Scotist terms, emphasizing his power and will. God himself explicitly rejects this attitude and substitutes the intellectualist alternative when he instructs Abdiel to subdue the rebels by force since they reject 'Right reason for thir Law,' VI, 39–43.

36 Calvin, *Institutes*, I, vi.

37 *Institutes*, I, v, 14–15.

38 *Institutes*, III, xviii.

39 Earl R. Wasserman, 'The Meaning of "Poland" in *The Medal*,' *MLN*, LXXIII (1958), 165–67.

40 *Proceedings . . . upon the Bill of Indictment for High Treason against Anthony Earl of Shaftsbury* (1681).

41 This division of the poem is based upon Quintilian's recommendations for a forensic oration in the *Institutio Oratoria*, trans. H. E. Butler (1921), Bks. IV–VI.

THE KINGDOM OF ADAM

[1] Frances A. Yates, 'Queen Elizabeth as Astraea,' *Journal of the Warburg Institute*, X (1947), 27–82.

[2] *History of the World* (1614), I, ix, 3, p. 182.

[3] *The Epilogue Spoken to the King at the Opening the Play-House at Oxford*: this poem, delivered at the time of the Oxford Parliament in March 1681, sees Oxford as a haven of peace, a landfall for the rebellion-tossed ark of the land, ll. 17–22.

[4] Filmer, p. 300.

[5] Arnold Williams, *The Common Expositor* (Chapel Hill, N.C., 1948), pp. 220–24.

[6] Josephine Waters Bennett, 'Britain among the Fortunate Isles,' *SP*, LIII (1956), 114–40.

[7] In the Preface to *The Fables* Dryden puts Chaucer on a level with Homer and Virgil for his handling of subject in *The Knight's Tale*, but scores him low on cadence: *Essays*, ed. Watson, II, 281, 290–91.

[8] George L. Craik, *A Compendious History of English Literature* (1861), II, 103. The Duchess's Plantagenet ancestry is also praised (rather whimsically) in a letter Dryden wrote to her in December 1698 while she was in Ireland (*The Letters of John Dryden*, ed. Charles E. Ward [Durham, N.C., 1942], pp. 107–8. Ward's identification of the recipient with the Duke rather than the Duchess is convincingly corrected by Pierre Legouis, *MLN*, LXVI [1951], 88–92). There are a number of interesting parallels between the letter and the poem.

[9] *Timaeus*, trans. R. G. Bury (1929), 39D, p. 83.

[10] Pierre Duhem, *Le Système du Monde* (Paris, 1954), I, 70–77, 275–76, 284, 287–88, 294–95; A. O. Lovejoy, G. Boas, et al. *Primitivism and Related Ideas in Antiquity* (Baltimore, 1935), pp. 79–84.

[11] *HMC, Ormonde*, N.S., VIII, xxx.

[12] Hoffman, p. 143.

[13] *Secular Masque*, l. 74; see too Dryden's version of *The Knight's Tale*, where the love goddess of the original is converted into a Venus Genetrix replete with Lucretian echoes (*Palamon and Arcite*, III, 129–44).

[14] Matthew Poole, *Synopsis Criticorum* (1669), I, 110.

[15] Giraldus Cambrensis, *Topography of Ireland*, trans. Sir Richard Colt Hoare, rev. and ed. Thomas Wright (1863), pp. 47–48. Dryden's description of Ireland as the 'Holy Isle' (l. 85) is in Camden, *Britain*, trans. Holland (1610), 2nd pag., p. 62.

[16] A fair sample of these pieces is included in *A Collection of State Tracts, publish'd on occasion of the late revolution in 1688 . . .* (1705), II, 564–613, 653–92. The chief points of the debate have been summarized by Arnold E. Miller in *JMH*, XVIII (1946), 306–13.

[17] Professor Hoffman, pp. 139–47, offers an interesting reading of the poem which sees it as simultaneously concerned with the Duchess and with 'what it is like and what it means to write poetry.' Professor Hoffman treats this second concern as part of Dryden's 'argument,' but the hypothetical

enquiry into the nature of inspiration in the opening lines seems to be conducted solely in order to create a rich context of amplification about the figure of the Duchess.

¹⁸ Maren-Sofie Røstvig, *The Happy Man* (Oslo, 1954), I, index under *Golden Age*, has discussed the connection between the retirement theme and the earthly paradise, although without drawing out the constitutional implications of Eden.

¹⁹ *Lectures on Dryden* (Cambridge, 1914), pp. 43–44.

²⁰ *Political Works*, p. 70.

²¹ *Works*, ed. Scott and Saintsbury, V, 321.

²² *Letters*, ed. Ward, p. 120.

²³ For the realization of the integrity of the work in the constitutional possibilities of Eden and the physicians I am indebted to Jay A. Levine, who has recently published his own reading of the poem in *JEGP*.

THE KINGDOM OF LETTERS

¹ See J. B. Trapp, 'The Owl's Ivy and the Poet's Bays,' *Journal of the Warburg Institute*, XXI (1958), 227–55.

² *Essays*, ed. Watson, I, 69.

³ Hoffman, pp. 27–29.

⁴ Hoffman, p. 28.

⁵ *The Subtler Language*, p. 17.

⁶ The connection is made explicitly in *Annus Mirabilis*, l. 5: 'Trade, which like bloud should circularly flow.'

⁷ *Commonweale*, pp. 87, 721–34.

⁸ *Lectures on Conscience and Human Law*, pp. 216–17.

⁹ Filmer, pp. 309–13.

¹⁰ *The Goths in England*, p. 118.

¹¹ *Harleian Miscellany*, I, 16.

¹² *Chorea Gigantum* (1663), p. 48.

¹³ *Chorea Gigantum*, p. 52: italics mine.

¹⁴ *Chorea Gigantum*, pp. 63–64.

¹⁵ There is a useful discussion of these eulogistic 'characters' by Godfrey Davies in *HLQ*, XIX (1955–56), 245–75.

¹⁶ In his *Congratulatory Poem, on the . . . Return of Charles II* (1660), p. 14, Alexander Brome described the Interregnum as a time when malefactors 'did dispence, / And rack the *Laws*, 'gainst equity and sense, / Which way the *Buff* would have them turn.'

¹⁷ *Diary*, ed. Henry B. Wheatley (1893), III, 51.

¹⁸ Preface to the play in *Works*, ed. Scott and Saintsbury, II, 27.

¹⁹ *Cobbett's Parliamentary History*, V, 50.

²⁰ *Somers Tracts*, VIII, 234.

²¹ *Somers Tracts*, VIII, 135.

²² Austin C. Dobbins, 'Dryden's "Character of a Good Parson,"' *SP*, LIII (1956), 51–59.

[23] Charles F. Mullet, 'A Case of Allegiance: William Sherlock and the Revolution of 1688,' *HLQ*, X (1946–47), 83–103.

[24] For a discussion of the analogy between the two Williams see Wasserman, *The Subtler Language*, pp. 144–17.

[25] It is possible that Dryden confused Scipio Africanus Major, who was opposed by Fabius in 205 B.C., with Scipio Africanus Minor, who was created consul in 147 B.C. before he had held the necessary qualifying offices. Dryden seems also to have confused the two Scipios in his *Character of Polybius* (1693): see *Prose Works*, ed. Malone (1800), III, 262 and note.

[26] Livy, trans. Frank G. Moore (1949), Loeb. ed., VIII, 161.

[27] Hoffman, p. 90.

EPILOGUE

[1] Hoffman, p. 73.

[2] Hoffman, p. 73.

[3] Hoffman, p. 80.

Index

Abingdon, Countess of, 111
Absalom, 1, 13, 21, 185, 187, 189, 192–95
Achilles, 150, 155
Achitophel, 1, 13, 21, 28, 185, 187–89, 192–95
Adam and Eve, 73, 87–88, 90–91, 103–4, 106–13, 127–29, 131, 192–94
Adriel, 194
Aeneas, 140–41, 155–56, 164
Albemarle, 1st Duke of, see Monck, George
Alexander the Great, 8–9, 28, 132
Alfred the Great, 147
Allen, J. W., 65, 200
Anne, Queen of England, 1, 169
Apuleius, Lucius, 4
Aquinas, St. Thomas, 94–95
Aristotle, 71, 142–45
Arnold, Matthew, 36, 48
    Dover Beach, 11–13
Arthur, King, 30
Astraea, 104, 106, 118–19, 121

Baker, Herschel, 201
Barzillai, 187, 190, 193
Bennett, Josephine W., 202
Bethel, Slingsby, 187, 189
Blackmore, Sir Richard, 132–34
Boas, G., 202
Bodenham, John, 137
Bodin, Jean, 30, 66–68, 71–74, 109, 145, 147, 200–1, 203
Bracton, Henry de, 64, 66

Bredvold, Louis I, 48
Brome, Alexander, 203
Buckingham, George Villiers, 2nd Duke of, 189–90
Burton, Robert, 4
Bury, R. G., 202
Butler, H. E., 201

Caesar, Augustus, 32, 47
Caesar, Julius, 28, 52–54, 161
Calvin, Jean, 99, 201
Camden, William, 202
Carlisle, Bishop of, 171
Castlemaine, Barbara Villiers, Countess of, 159–61, 163–65
Cato the Younger, 161, 195
Chambers, A. B., 201
Charles I, 25–26, 53–56, 68–71, 83, 98, 107, 138, 152, 155–56, 162, 187
Charles II, 1, 7, 13, 19, 25–26, 31–34, 57, 60, 63–64, 69–71, 74, 76, 81–82, 85, 87, 90, 92, 96, 105–6, 110, 139–42, 144–47, 149–65, 169, 179–82, 186, 188, 190, 192, 196, 198
Charleton, Walter, 141, 144, 146–47, 203
Chaucer, Geoffrey, 37, 114–17, 121, 123–24, 171–72, 186, 195, 202
Clarendon, Edward Hyde, 1st Earl of, 32–33, 70–71
Clark, William S., 199
Cobbett, William, 201, 203
Coke, Sir Edward, 64, 66

Coleridge, S. T., 135
Columbus, Christopher, 143
Congreve, William, 174
Corah, 194–96
Craik, George L., 202
Cromwell, Oliver, 52–64, 83–84, 86, 96–97, 139–40, 145, 155–56, 161–62, 198
Cromwell, Richard, 60, 62

Danby, Thomas Osborne, 1st Earl of, 133
Darius, 8–9, 28
David, 1, 13, 21, 28, 32, 71, 185–86, 188–90, 192–93, 195–96
Davies, Godfrey, 203
Dido, 124, 150, 155–56
Dobbins, Austin C., 172–73, 203
Donne, John, 20–21, 137
Dorset, Charles Sackville, 6th Earl of, 183
Dryden, John:
    Absalom and Achitophel, 1–2, 4–5, 12–14, 17–19, 21, 30, 33, 38–39, 75, 80–81, 88–89, 99, 106, 111, 184–96
    Absalom and Achitophel, Part II, 24
    Alexander's Feast, 8–9, 13, 28
    All for Love, 21–22, 133
    Annus Mirabilis, 20, 33, 74–87, 89, 106, 133, 184, 187, 191–92, 195–96, 203
    Astraea Redux, 26, 32–33, 62–64, 68–69, 71, 81, 105–6, 113–14, 140, 152, 157
    Britannia Rediviva, 81, 113–14, 169
    Character of a Good Parson, 171–74, 183, 186, 195
    Character of Polybius, 29, 204
    Dedication of Examen Poeticum, 175
    Don Sebastian, 21–22
    The Duke of Guise, 29–31, 195
    Eleonora, 111–13
    Epilogue Spoken to the King at Oxford, 202
    Epilogue to The Conquest of Granada, Part II, 136, 139, 166

Essay of Dramatic Poesy, 137, 166
Essay on the Dramatic Poetry of the Last Age, 166
Fables Ancient and Modern, 124
Heroic Stanzas to the Memory of Cromwell, 51–64, 75, 161–62
The Hind and the Panther, 1, 9, 16, 19, 33, 80, 112–13
The History of the League, 16, 29, 136, 195
MacFlecknoe, 40, 137, 175, 184, 190, 198
Marriage à la Mode, 72
The Medal, 7–8, 27, 33, 72–73, 87–103, 106, 108, 111, 113–14, 136, 138, 168, 173, 195
Palamon and Arcite, 114, 202
Preface to The Fables, 202
Prologue at Oxford 1680, 138
Prologue to Albumazar, 137
Prologue to Aureng-Zebe, 166
Prologue to The Duke of Guise, 31
Prologue to The Kind Keeper, 138
Prologue to The Tempest, 166
Prologue to The Unhappy Favourite, 106–7, 112–13, 179
Prologue to The Wild Gallant, 158–60
Prologue to Troilus and Cressida, 166
Religio Laici, 9, 16, 76, 81, 179
Secular Masque, 120, 202
The State of Innocence, 111
Threnodia Augustalis, 60, 113–14
To Dr. Charleton, 133, 141–48, 151, 153, 156, 160, 165, 198
To Driden of Chesterton, 7, 8–9, 19, 23, 124–35, 198
To His Sacred Majesty on his Coronation, 64, 70, 73–74, 105–6, 113–14
To John Hoddesdon, 41–44
To Lady Castlemaine, 141, 148, 158–65, 184, 195
To Mr. Congreve, 42–43, 105, 138, 165–84, 191, 196–98
To Mr. Granville, 138–39, 166
To Mr. Northleigh, 31

Dryden, John *cont.*
  To Mr. Southerne, 166
  To My Lord Chancellor, 32–33, 64, 70–71, 113–14, 140–41
  To Peter Motteux, 166
  To Sir Robert Howard, 32–34, 141, 148–58, 160, 165, 178, 180–81, 188, 198
  To the Duchess of Ormonde, 18, 23, 113–24, 133
  To the Earl of Roscommon, 140
  To the Memory of Anne Killigrew, 198
  To the Memory of Mr. Oldham, 44–48, 198
  Upon the Death of Lord Hastings, 23–27, 77, 81
  Vindication of the Duke of Guise, 200
  Virgil, 133
  The Wild Gallant, 158–59, 161
Duhem, Pierre, 202
Duns Scotus, Johannes, 95

Edward I, 115
Edward II, 32, 170–71, 174–75, 178, 180–82, 196
Edward III, 28, 170–71, 174–75, 178, 181–82
Edward IV, 170–71
Edward, the Black Prince, 30, 115
Eliot, T. S., 36
Elizabeth I, 106
Emily (in *The Knight's Tale*), 114–17, 119, 121
Etherege, Sir George, 167
Euripides, 164
Euryalus, 45
Eve, *see* Adam and Eve

Fabius Maximus, 176–78
Fairfax, Thomas, 3rd Baron, 55
Fair Maid of Kent (Joan, Countess of Kent), 115–19, 121, 123–24
Filmer, Sir Robert, 52, 58, 61–62, 65–66, 68, 109–11, 146–47, 200, 202–3
Flecknoe, Richard, 40

Fletcher, John, 166–67
Fortescue, Sir John, 66
Freedman, Morris, 201

Garth, Sir Samuel, 132, 134
Gaunt, John of, 111, 115
George I, 1
Gilbert, William, 143, 145
Giraldus Cambrensis, 202
Giulio Romano, 178
God, 17, 25, 27, 52, 61, 64, 66–67, 71, 82, 88, 90–92, 94–95, 98, 102, 113, 121, 162–65, 183, 192, 201
Grove, John, 190

Halifax, George Savile, 1st Marquis of, 171
Ham, Roswell G., 199
Hannibal, 29, 132, 176–78
Harmonia, 72
Harvey, William, 143, 145
Henry IV, 171
Henry VI, 171
Hesiod, 104
Hoare, Sir Richard Colt, 202
Hobbes, Thomas, 22, 58, 65–66, 95–97, 107, 109, 145, 194, 200–1
Hoffman, Arthur W., 2, 119, 137–38, 183, 187–89, 192, 200, 202–4
Holland, Philemon, 202
Homer, 114, 116, 124, 202
Hooker, Edward N., 81, 86, 201
Hooker, Richard, 94
Horace, 125
Howard, Sir Robert, 32, 74, 149, 151, 170–71, 199
Howell, William, 29
Hunton, Philip, 68, 147

Ithuriel, 90

Jacob, 7–8, 19
James I, 67, 130, 200, 203

James II, 7, 9, 28–29, 32–33, 60,
    98, 113, 122, 130–31, 139, 165–
    66, 169–70, 172–74, 177–78,
    182–83, 186, 196, 198
Janus, 105–6, 166
Jehu, 97
Johnson, Samuel, 33, 37
Jones, Inigo, 141–42, 144, 147, 156
Jonson, Ben, 137, 166–67, 175
Josephus, 29
Joshua, 60
Jotham, 194
Juvenal, 68

Keats, John, 4
Kinsley, James, 188, 201
Kliger, Samuel, 146, 201, 203
Knolles, Richard, 200

Laslett, Peter, 65, 200
Lee, Nathaniel, 29
Legouis, Pierre, 202
Lenthall, John, 70
L'Estrange, Sir Roger, 68
Levine, Jay A., 199, 203
Livy, 177, 188, 204
Locke, John, 109–10
Louis XIV, 8, 165
Lovejoy, A. O., 202
Lucan, 161, 163–64, 195, 200
Lucretius, 120–121, 202

Maimbourg, Louis, 29
Malone, Edmond, 204
Marcellus, 47
Mars, 72
Marvell, Andrew, 139, 200
Mary II, 168–69, 173, 175
Mary of Modena, 169
McIlwain, Charles H., 200
Meres, Francis, 137
Michael, 91, 109
Michal, 186
Milbourne, Luke, 132–34
Miller, Arnold E., 202
Milton, John, 4, 13, 59, 140
    Paradise Lost, 76, 90–91, 97–98,
    106–9, 111, 201

Mocket, Richard, 201
Monck, George, 1st Duke of Albe-
    marle, 63, 79, 149–51, 156–57
Monmouth, James, Duke of, 1, 187,
    189
Moore, Frank G., 204
Moses, 60, 179
Mullett, Charles F., 204

Naboth's Vineyard, 195
Nicolson, Marjorie H., 201
Nimrod, 108–9
Nisus, 45
Noah, 29, 67, 74, 105–6, 120–21
Northleigh, John, 31

Oakeshott, Michael, 200
Oates, Titus, 190, 194
Ockham, William of, 95
Og, 24
Oldys, William, 200
Ormonde, James Butler, 2nd Duke
    of, 117, 119, 122–23, 202
Otway, Thomas, 195
Overall, John, Bishop of Norwich,
    173, 200
Ovid, 81, 104

Palamon (in The Knight's Tale), 117
Pandora, 25
Park, Thomas, 200
Parker, Henry, 147
Peck, Francis, 200
Pemberton, Sir Francis, 101–2
Penelope, 124
Pepys, Samuel, 159, 203
Petronius, 75
Pickering, Thomas, 190
Plato, 108, 116, 118, 202
A Plea for Limited Monarchy, 146, 200
Poems on Affairs of State, 195
Pompey the Great, 28, 53–54, 161–
    62
Poole, Matthew, 202
Pope, Alexander, 36–37, 39–40,
    137, 197
Prometheus, 41–42
Puttenham, George, 32, 199

Quintilian, 201

Racine, Jean:
  Phèdre, 22
Ralegh, Sir Walter, 29–30, 32, 107–8, 199, 202
Ransom, John Crowe, 38
Raphael, 178, 182
Rebecca, 7
Reynolds, Beatrice, 200
Richard II, 32, 64, 170–72, 186
Richards, I. A., 15
Røstvig, Maren-Sofie, 203
Russell, Edward, Earl of Orford, 166
Rymer, Thomas, 175, 183

Saintsbury, George, 200, 203
Salisbury, Countess of, 115
Salmoneus, 100, 103
Samson, 150, 154
Sanderson, Robert, Bishop of Lincoln, 145–46, 200, 203
Satan, 27, 87–91, 97–98, 100, 103, 193, 198
Saturn, 106, 110
Schilling, Bernard N., 17, 19, 23, 27, 88, 199, 201
Scipio, Publius Cornelius, Africanus Major, 29, 176–78, 182, 204
Scipio Aemilianus, Publius Cornelius, Africanus Minor, 204
Scott, Sir Walter, 171, 199–200, 203
Scotus, *see* Duns Scotus
Semper Iidem: or, a Parallel betwixt the Ancient and Modern Fanatics, 30
Shadwell, Thomas, 40, 175, 183, 190, 198
Shaftesbury, Anthony Ashley Cooper, 1st Earl of, 1, 7, 13, 77, 87–92, 96–103, 113, 189, 198
Shakespeare, William, 36, 111, 166, 168, 171, 182
Sherlock, William, 172–73, 183, 204
Shimei, 185, 187, 189
Sidney, Algernon, 110

Sidney, Sir Philip, 31
Sleidan, John, 29
Solomon, 31, 179
Southerne, Thomas, 167
Spenser, Edmund, 1, 36
Sprat, Thomas, 60
Statius, 149–50, 155–57
Strafford, Thomas Wentworth, 1st Earl of, 93
Stuart, Charles Edward, the Young Pretender, 165–66
Stuart, James Francis Edward, the Old Pretender, 165–66, 169–70, 173–74, 177–78, 181–82
Swift, Jonathan, 1

Tarquin and Tullia, 195
Tate, Nahum, 175
Teeter, Louis, 199, 201
Tennyson, Alfred, 1st Baron, 37
Theseus (in *The Knight's Tale*), 117
Tonge, Israel, 190
Tourville, Comte de, 166
Trapp, J. B., 203
Tyrell, James, 110

Van Doren, Mark, 48, 56–57, 80–81, 201
Venus, 26, 72, 120–21, 123, 202
Verrall, A. W., 129–30, 203
Virgil, 33, 45, 47, 63, 77–79, 104, 114, 116, 118–21, 124, 149–50, 155–56, 200, 202
Vitruvius, 179–80
Von Galen, Bernhard, Bishop of Münster, 75–76

Walker, A., 199
Waller, Edmund, 200
Wallerstein, Ruth, 25, 199
Ward, Charles E., 202, 203
Warwick, Richard Neville, Earl of, 170
Wasserman, Earl R., 72, 101, 141–42, 144–47, 151, 158, 201, 203–4
Watson, George, 199, 201–3
Wheatley, Henry B., 203

Wicliffe, John, 172
Willcock, G. D., 199
William I, 173, 175, 204
William III, 8–9, 28, 117, 119, 122, 131, 133–34, 139, 165, 168–69, 172–73, 175, 178, 183, 204
Williams, Arnold, 202
Williamson, George, 200
Wimsatt, W. K., Jr., 19, 28, 39, 199
Winterbottom, John A., 21–22, 199

Wordsworth, Christopher, 200
Wordsworth, William, 38, 48–49
Wright, Thomas, 202
Wycherley, William, 167

Yates, Frances A., 202

Zadok, 194
Zephon, 90
Zimri, 189–90, 194–95